Making Sense of Social Development

Child Development in Families, Schools and Society 3

The companion volumes in this series are:

Cultural Worlds of Early Childhood
Edited by Martin Woodhead, Dorothy Faulkner and Karen Littleton

Learning Relationships in the Classroom
Edited by Dorothy Faulkner, Karen Littleton and Martin Woodhead

These three readers are the core study material for students taking the course ED840 Child Development in Families, Schools and Society. This course may be taken as part of the Open University MA in Education programme. The course may also be taken as part of the Open University MSc in Psychology.

The Open University MA in Education

The Open University MA in Education is now firmly established as the most popular postgraduate degree for education professionals in Europe, with over 3500 students registering each year. The MA in Education is designed particularly for those with experience of teaching, the advisory service, educational administration or allied fields.

Structure of the MA

The MA is a modular degree and students are therefore free to select from a range of options the programme that best fits in with their interests and professional goals. Study in the Open University's Advanced Diploma and Certificate in Continuing Professional Development programmes may also be counted towards the MA. Successful completion of the MA in Education entitles students to apply for entry into the Open University Doctorate in Education (EdD) programme.

OU supported open learning

The MA in Education programme provides great flexibility. Students study at their own pace, in their own time, anywhere in the European Union. They receive specially prepared study materials, are supported by tutorials, and have opportunities to work with other students.

How to apply

The Professional Development in Education prospectus contains further information and application forms. To request your copy please write to the Course Reservations and Sales Centre, The Open University, PO Box 625, Walton Hall, Milton Keynes MK7 6AA.

Making Sense of Social Development

Edited by Martin Woodhead,
Dorothy Faulkner and
Karen Littleton

London and New York
in association with
The Open University

First published 1999
by Routledge
11 New Fetter Lane, London EC4P 4EE

Simultaneously published in the USA and Canada
by Routledge
29 West 35th Street, New York, NY 10001

Typeset in Garamond by RefineCatch Limited, Bungay, Suffolk
Printed and bound in Great Britain by
Clays Ltd, St. Ives PLC

British Library Cataloguing in Publication Data
A catalogue record for this book is available from the British Library

Library of Congress Cataloging in Publication Data
Woodhead, Martin.
    Making sense of social development / Martin Woodhead,
Dorothy Faulkner & Karen Littleton.
        p.   cm.
Includes bibliographical references and index.
    1. Child development.   I. Faulkner, Dorothy.   II. Littleton,
Karen.   III. Title.
HQ783.L57   1999
305.231 – dc21   98–25642
                        CIP

ISBN 0–415–17374–4

Contents

Figures

Acknowledgements

We would like to thank the authors who contributed their chapters, as well as colleagues within and outside The Open University who gave advice on the contents. Special thanks are due to Helen Boyce (Course Manager), Bronwen Sharp and Christine Golding (Course Secretaries) and Jenny Monk (Copublishing) for their assistance in the production of this book.

The Open University would also like to thank all those who have granted permission to reproduce copyright material in this volume. The publishers have made every effort to contact copyright holders with regard to permission to reproduce articles and will be happy to handle any queries relating to these.

Introduction

This book is about children's social development during the school years, especially their peer relationships, playground behaviour, moral understanding and social competence. We include chapters by sociologists and social anthropologists, as well as by developmental psychologists. In part these chapters build on themes in the first two books in this series, about early childhood and about classroom learning (Woodhead *et al.*, 1998; Faulkner *et al.*, 1998). As before, the chapters in this volume emphasise the importance of relationships and social context, and they recognise the plurality of childhood experiences, both within and between cultural contexts (see especially Chapters 4, 9, 10 and 12). We argue that these features of child development are most satisfactorily encompassed within a socio-cultural perspective. In this volume we also draw attention to the problematic status of cultural understanding about children's social development. Specifically, we ask about the relationship between 'the world of adults' (who care for children, teach them, make decisions for them, carry out research and construct theories about them) and 'the world of children' (who are cared for, taught, organised, studied and theorised about). Important issues are about the image of childhood conveyed by studies of children's social development and about some of the assumptions that underlie research methods (addressed most directly in Chapters 13 and 14).

Conventional research in child development seeks to describe and explain children's emerging psychological competences in the context of family, school and playground. Such knowledge is also frequently applied, in terms of advice given to parents or the design of approaches to teaching. Observing children, questioning them in standardised procedures, and interpreting their responses in terms of prevailing theories of socialisation and social understanding has enabled researchers to construct a picture of children's gradual progress towards mature competence and social adjustment, and to identify the factors that variously facilitate or inhibit that progress. Without disputing the value of much of this research in its own terms, the underlying paradigm is increasingly being recognised as a partial account of childhood, in both the descriptive and evaluative sense of that word. Much research on child development is conceptualised, designed and interpreted in terms of (rarely articulated) cultural preconceptions about the contexts, goals and processes of development; it also reflects power relationships between children and the adults who assume responsibility for their development. This is most clearly evident in accounts of socialisation, in which various approaches to parenting are compared for their effectiveness (e.g. Baumrind, 1971); and in theories of cognitive development in which children are described as initially egocentric, only gradually achieving powers of reasoning that comply with expectations for rational, adult thinking (Piaget, 1950). In both cases, the evaluation of children's role and competence is implicit, but it is an evaluation nonetheless.

By entitling the collection *Making Sense of Social Development* we emphasise the idea that adults are not the only ones with a view on the subject. Children are themselves trying to make sense of their social world (Bruner and Haste, 1987). Childhood researchers should be cautious about treating what children say and do simply as research data – as evidence of their developmental status, reasoning abilities, social adjustment etc. Children have their own perspective on the issues that concern parents, teachers and psychologists, which we would argue has legitimacy in its own right. In their own way, children are also trying to understand about social development, and their own place within it, as they interpret the behaviour, demands and expectations of adults and other children, and as they construct a repertoire of ways of acting and reacting (Dunn, 1988). Accordingly, Schaffer introduces his textbook *Social Development* by explicitly rejecting traditional accounts of socialisation: '. . . it has become clear that, far from being at the mercy of whatever external forces they happen to encounter, children actively select and shape their own environment' (Schaffer, 1996, p. xiv). From this point of view, young people are just as intent on influencing the course of a parent's development as vice versa, although adults don't generally like to see it that way! This image of children actively negotiating their social development is elaborated by many of the chapters in this book. Some of the wider implications are considered in Part IV, especially in terms of beliefs about children's status as competent social actors.

The socio-cultural and political dimension of dominant beliefs and theories about childhood and child development has been articulated most strongly by those who urge a more reflective and self-critical attitude among researchers (e.g. Bradley, 1989; Burman, 1994; Morss, 1996; James and Prout, 1997; James *et al.*, 1998). Re-positioning 'the child' in child development theory is also affected by a broader re-valuation of children's social status and rights, witnessed most tangibly at a global level in the United Nations Convention on the Rights of the Child (1989), and at a local level within The Children Act (England and Wales 1989), along with equivalent legislation in Scotland and Northern Ireland (Davie *et al.*, 1996; Hill and Tisdall, 1997). These trends don't just alter the socialisation processes that child development researchers seek to describe, understand and explain. They also place new obligations on academic work, requiring that social researchers re-examine the way children are conceptualised in their theories, as well as the way they are treated as participants in research (Alderson, 1995; Morrow and Richards, 1996).

So long as psychologists continue to work within a conventional 'developmental' framework, they will be open to the charge that they emphasise relative incompetence, immaturity and dependency in ways that implicitly diminish children's status. The present volume, like the others in the series, is designed to represent children as young citizens who participate in their social development from the very beginning. Within this image, notions of 'competence' are viewed as problematic, informed by cultural beliefs and negotiated by participants in particular social contexts.

The first two parts, 'A world apart?' and 'Conflict and cooperation', examine the significance of children's friendships and peer cultures in their social lives. According to Blatchford (1994), among developmental psychologists and educators there have been two prevailing views on the social worlds children inhabit: the 'romantic' view, and the 'problem' view. One version of the 'romantic' view is that the play and games, jokes, teasing and playground rituals which characterise children's cultures are unique to children. Corsaro (1985) claims that these cultures allow children to create a sense of distance and privacy from adults, and that they provide contexts in which children's own interests and concerns can surface. According to this view, adults have no role to play in these cultures and should not interfere or attempt to impose their own agenda on them. Another 'romantic' interpretation is that the cultures children and adolescents create for themselves represent adult society in a microcosm mirroring the relationships and social institutions of adult societies (Sluckin, 1981). According to this 'anticipatory socialization' view, the peer cultures of childhood and adolescence provide safe contexts in which, through play, games and ritual, children gradually come to terms with the goals, values and behaviours of the larger adult society. Both of these views of peer culture see children's social worlds as relatively benign. It is clear, however, that for many children this social world has a darker, more 'problematic' aspect.

As studies of children's playground behaviour have shown, bullying, teasing, aggression and acrimonious power struggles between rival groups and individuals are also a feature of peer cultures (e.g. Blatchford, 1994; Olweus, 1993). In recent years a major research effort has been devoted to studying both this aspect of children's peer cultures, as well as to studying the characteristics of particular subgroups of children who are either the perpetrators or the victims of these kinds of behaviours. As well as perceiving the adverse effects aggression, bullying and controlling behaviour can have on children at certain times in certain societies, adults (parents, teachers, youth leaders) and authorities have perceived 'youth sub-cultures' as challenging and undermining adult cultures. The apparent 'segregation' between adolescent peer cultures and adults has been a cause for concern (e.g. Coleman, 1987). 'A segregated youth culture, by definition, reduces opportunities for adults to be included in youth networks and vice versa [and] individuals separated by cultures and age would potentially lack a sense of mutual responsibility to support one another' (Youniss, Chapter 1, this volume). Seen in this way, youth cultures are 'worlds apart' from adult cultures and cannot act as anticipatory socialisation contexts which aid young people's transition from adolescence to adulthood.

We would do well to remember, however, that the social constructions adults impose on 'problematic' and antisocial behaviour and attitudes may be very different from the meanings constructed by children and young people. It is also the case that what is deemed 'problematic' behaviour according to one set of socio-cultural criteria, may well be seen as positive and adaptive according to another. The authors of the chapters in Part I critically examine the various perspectives and explanations concerning the nature and developmental functions of children's peer cultures, and the friendships which support them.

In Chapter 1, Youniss addresses a theoretical conundrum. Psychologists who have studied adult networks and support start from the premise that adults are 'self-sustaining individuals, who rely on their own resources for functioning in society'. By contrast, psychologists who study children and young people have shown that 'normal development entails a history of engagement in social construction in which individuals learn about interdependence and mutuality' (Youniss, Chapter 1, this volume). This research shows that children's friendships are based on reciprocity and mutual obligation which fosters the development of the 'relational self' rather than the 'individual self' presumed by adult research! Youniss offers a critical appraisal of contemporary accounts of the nature of adolescents' relationships with their parents, and of the notion that peer cultures are inevitably segregated from adult cultures. He argues that current evidence on children's friendships and adolescent peer culture necessitates a reappraisal of the nature of adult identity and the networks and support systems which sustain it.

Chapter 2 focuses on peer relationships during the years from 7 to 13. Corsaro offers a detailed account of how children address issues relating to self, identity, cooperation, conflict and autonomy from adult control. He argues that participation in the activities and practices of peer cultures performs a vital function which allows children to work through these issues. Acknowledging that most of the evidence has been gathered from studies of white, middle-class children in Western societies, Corsaro shows how research which crosses racial, ethnic and social class groups has begun to challenge prevailing views about the gendered nature of children's peer relationships in middle childhood. He argues that the transition from childhood to adolescence will be facilitated where children have the opportunity to reflect on and evaluate the meanings of their changing worlds with both peers and adults.

Next, Berndt examines the nature and role of friendship and peer cultures in adolescence. The first section of Chapter 3 examines the place of friendships in the social worlds of adolescence, and discusses the formation of friendship groups. The second section focuses on both the positive and the negative qualities of adolescent friendships, and on the nature of intimacy and conflict. Finally, Berndt outlines the processes and outcomes of friends' influence on one another and presents evidence which challenges the popular assumption that peer pressure is a major cause of undesirable behaviour in adolescence.

In the final chapter in Part I, Schneider draws on a rich variety of accounts of children's peer cultures in different parts of the world in order to compare and contrast differences between collectivist and individualist societies. Like other authors in this section, Schneider argues that we should not base our understanding of the processes which contribute to the development of young people's identity and values solely on the study of individualistic, middle-class, American adolescent peer cultures.

Part II, 'Conflict and cooperation', focuses on the social worlds of playgrounds and schools, with detailed accounts of the 'positive' and 'negative' aspects of children's experiences within these settings. In Chapter 5, Blatchford reports on a recent programme of British research which has examined children's play during school breaktimes. This chapter reviews peer relations in the playground, including the role of play, games and friendships. Blatchford draws attention to the dangers of focusing too exclusively on the 'negative' aspects of children's breaktime experiences. An important challenge facing schools is how to achieve a balance between the goal of protecting children and controlling their behaviour, and the goal of respecting their privacy and autonomy, including facilitating their development towards independence.

This question is taken up in Chapter 6. Smith, Bowers, Binney and Cowie review research on the nature and extent of bullying in schools. They describe the relationships of children involved in bully/victim problems, and outline how bullying affects the lives and development of children who are its victims. Next they discuss the characteristics and antecedents of bullying and evaluate alternative explanations for this kind of behaviour. They draw on observational studies to show that the bully's perspective may be contrary to adult understandings. From the bully's point of view, their behaviour can give them prestige and status within their particular peer cultures.

These sensitive issues are followed up in Chapter 7. Cowie addresses the design of school-based interventions to help both bullies and victims break free from the bully/victim cycle. She argues for strategies that recognise peer relationships are at the heart of the solution as well as the problem. For all children, the experience of developing close friendships is an important part of growing up. For children who experience rejection, bullying and harassment, however, the long-term emotional consequences are bleak. So, too, are the prospects for children who base their social relationships on an abuse of power. What is also becoming clear, Cowie argues, is that collusion, either actively as an assistant, or passively as a bystander in bullying incidents, also has negative effects on children. For example, she cites the adverse effects on self-esteem which result from feelings of powerlessness to offer appropriate help to peers in distress. It is on these grounds that Cowie believes young people can themselves play an active part in reducing bullying, to the benefit of bullies, victims and themselves. The chapter outlines a range of peer support systems designed to train young people in techniques which enable them to offer help to children in need. Cowie argues that where schools have implemented these strategies the emotional climate of the school undergoes a marked change. Instead of being based on competition, distrust and rivalry, the ethos becomes more oriented to care and responsibility for the needs and rights of all pupils in the school.

Whereas the first half of the book focuses mainly on children's relationships with each other – as mediated, regulated and interpreted by adults – chapters in the second half are concerned more directly with children's relationship to the adult world. Part III, 'Moral development in context', addresses questions about children's understanding of moral issues in the broader context of the way developmental goals and processes are conceptualised in child development research. Part IV, 'Negotiating competence', is about the way children negotiate their position within family and school as well as about their status within the research process itself.

In Chapter 7, Sharp and Cowie have already discussed the potential for children themselves to play a more active role in school strategies to combat bullying. Teachers' willingness to include children in this way will in part be shaped by beliefs about children's competence, need for protection, capacity for making judgements and acting appropriately etc. In Chapter 8, Short addresses these themes in the context of the curriculum, focusing on the way theories about children's social, moral and political understanding have influenced teachers' willingness to incorporate controversial issues into their teaching. Short first addressed this topic in a chapter written ten years earlier, in which he argued that idealised constructions of 'innocence' combined with 'stage theories' of development prevented primary teachers from recognising the importance of including race, gender and other controversial issues as part of their teaching. In this new chapter, Short revisits the topic, arguing that rejection of cruder expressions of Piagetian theory and the increased interest in applying Vygotskian principles open up a much stronger rationale for teachers to encourage children's social, moral and political understanding. Short reviews extensive evidence that very young children are already aware of issues of race, gender and nationality. Yet he concludes that the prospects are not good for *significant* inclusion of social, moral and political education. While teachers no longer work within such a strong protectionist framework on child development, the introduction of the National Curriculum has effectively marginalised these topics.

In Chapter 9, Burman offers a very different critique of the way developmental theories shape beliefs about children's moral understanding. She argues that these theories originate among Western scholars, premised on dominant, Western, male constructions of morality, but that they are projected on to children in all societies through standardised, highly verbalised, de-contextualised testing encounters. For Burman, the issue is not just about the way development is constructed for children within the Euro-American contexts in which the research originates; it is also about the way the resulting images of childhood are exported within global discourses about childhood. Typically, universalistic constructions of development become a foil for asserting the necessary superiority of rational, individualised views of moral autonomy. Burman argues that applying supposedly universal models globally serves to pathologise childhoods that are seen as failing to match dominant norms. Burman's account draws attention to the case for reconstructing social development in a much more inclusive way, in which goals for development are neither presumed nor prescribed. Instead, they need to be *re*-searched and *re*-negotiated.

In Chapter 10, Haste takes up this challenge by proposing a more pluralistic framework for thinking about children's social and moral understanding. She begins by acknowledging a fundamental division in perspectives on child development, between those who assert the primacy of individual processes of progressive construction, and those who argue for the primacy of social and cultural processes in shaping individual thinking, and indeed, individuality itself (see also Chapters 1 and 4). In attempting a synthesis, Haste builds on Vygotsky's insights into the relationship between individual processes, social processes and cultural processes. She proposes the concept of 'lay social theory' to describe shared cultural knowlege and beliefs about moral and social issues, into which children are initiated through processes of guided participation, and which in due course children reconstruct as their own personal belief system. Reviewing the evidence on cultural variations in concepts of self and morality, as well as studies on gender differences in orientation to moral and social issues, Haste rejects universal models of moral development, arguing that a pluralist perspective permits integration of social and individual processes in a more adequate account of the way children make sense of interpersonal and cultural experiences of self and of morality.

Some of the most powerful cultural beliefs shaping children's lives concern their competence and status to make judgements about important issues, participate in decisions affecting their lives, take responsibility for their own well-being, be treated as autonomous individuals, etc. In Western contexts, these beliefs are neither prescribed, nor consistent; children learn to negotiate a repertoire of 'competences' appropriate to the cultural expectations of relationships and contexts, notably with parents at home, teachers in the classroom and peers in the playground. The chapters in Part IV have been selected to highlight the extent to which childhood is a negotiated status.

Children's participation in personal health care issues is the starting-point for Chapters 11 and 12. In both chapters the authors describe studies of both children's and their parents' perspectives on issues of responsibility and autonomy in decision making. Mayall describes her research in an inner-city primary school, drawing attention to contrasts between school and home in the construction of children's competence. She argues that at home parents related to their children 'as people not projects'. They expected that their relationship would be negotiated from the start, and they valued evidence of their children's independence, as relieving some of the pressures of day-to-day care. While home and school experiences were united by children's awareness of the power imbalances between children and adults, Mayall argues that children's experience of their primary school was marked by much less respect for their individuality, their potential independence and autonomy. Little scope was afforded for children to negotiate their goals, activities and relationships in a context heavily constrained by institutional structures and routines, and the pressures of a prescribed curriculum.

Brannen's chapter also originated in a study of the way young people negotiate health issues in families, but her focus is on 16-year-olds, and her study encompassed a broad range of family perspectives within London communities. Brannen begins by recognising that professional discourses of adolescence are informed by childhoods constructed within psychology and sociology. She argues that these shape public policy and health advice in ways that fail to recognise the diversity of young people's experience, especially in relation to their gender and ethnic background. Brannen distinguishes three broad groupings of adolescent experience. The first group conforms most closely to those described in Mayall's chapter. Young people are expected to become autonomous as they become more capable of self-control and independent decision taking. They are expected to continually renegotiate their position within a relationship of mutual trust and sharing. While parents of the second group also expected young people to become more autonomous, their status was regulated less through relationships and more through social norms and status changes associated with young people's age and their transition into work. Third, Brannen summarises the experiences of a group of adolescents for whom the goal of development was not autonomy at all. This group were expected to remain subject to parental influence and continue to contribute to the family. Brannen's study echoes the accounts of competing cultural values in earlier chapters (especially 4 and 10). They serve as a reminder of the power of beliefs and practices in mediating children's developing competence and sense of personal identity, within and outside the family.

In Chapter 13, James follows up Brannen's comments about the power of psychological and sociological discourses in framing the way we think about children's status and competences. She argues that these issues aren't only negotiated with parents, teachers and others in children's social world, but that researchers are also part of the process. Through the theories they construct and the research methods they adopt, social scientists construct a (generally unarticulated) model of childhood. James elaborates her argument by distinguishing four models or images of 'the child', varying on two dimensions: the extent to which childhood is seen as a 'world apart' from adulthood, and the status accorded to children's expressions of competence. The first model is the 'developing child', constructed by conventional psychological research. The child is closely observed, tested and differentiated in terms of ways of thinking, playing and learning. This child is subordinated to adults in terms of their position on the stage-like journey to mature competence. Second comes the 'tribal child', described especially in ethnographic research and illustrated by some of the studies in Part I. Studying children at play, in the home, the playground and the street, this approach recognises children's separateness from the adult world, but (in the style of anthropology) celebrates their competence in their own cultural terms. The third model is less common. Images of the 'adult child' most often emerge when researchers encounter children living outside the protected space of modern childhoods. James illustrates the 'adult child' through studies of children coping with multiple hospital operations. In these circumstances the children's superior understanding of their situation places an obligation on the researcher to listen to their perspective. Finally, James proposes a model of the 'social child', which accords children status within the research process, as social actors competent within their own abilities and interests, and respectfully researched within adult–child relationships that enable children genuinely to participate in the process (James *et al.*, 1998). One implication here is that we need to recognise children 'not just as objects of concern but also as subjects with concerns' (Prout, 1998).

In the final chapter of this collection, Greene offers an overview of a century of developmental psychology, rehearsing many of the themes of earlier chapters and pointing towards some new directions for the study of social development. Rooted in early ideas about evolution and nourished by visions of a more protected world of childhood, the developmental paradigm has emphasised uniformities of structure and direction as the individual progresses from total dependency towards autonomous maturity. This paradigm has sustained childhood researchers throughout the twentieth century but, Greene argues, it should now be recognised as a straitjacket.

Features of the paradigm include fragmentation and decontextualisation of the child. Yet, as Greene explains, the problem runs deeper than this. It is about the preparation of idealised, standardised childhoods as the laboratory norm. It is only relatively recently that developmentalists have recognised that cultural context is not just the icing on the cake, but part of the structure of the cake (as Richards and Light, 1986, put it). In spite of this, the implication for embracing a more inclusive set of childhood possibilities is still neglected in a world increasingly dominated by globalised childhood discourse (Boyden, 1997). Recognising the cultural status of child development would also benefit attempts to apply the insights of the discipline to practice. Within a natural science model, the recursive relationship of 'Child Development' to its subject is rarely recognised; nor are the unarticulated pedagogies of childhood that underpin its theories in the first place (Singer, 1998).

Finally, Greene addresses one of the central themes of this book, namely the importance of seeking children's perspectives, as active meaning-makers in specific socio-cultural contexts. She sets a challenge, along with other authors in this book, to construct a new, more open-ended paradigm for making sense of social development. This paradigm is about building on a socio-cultural approach, recognising the plurality of childhood possibilities, as well as respecting children as 'persons' and not just as 'potentials' or as 'projects'. It is about self-consciously making sense of social development, in theory, research and practice in ways that recognise young people as active participants, and as the principal stakeholders in the developmental process.

References

Alderson, P. (1995) *Listening to Children*, London, Barnardos.

Baumrind, D. (1971) 'Current patterns of parental authority', *Developmental Psychology Monographs*, 4, 1–101.

Blatchford, P. (1994) 'Research on children's school playground behaviour in the UK: a review', in Blatchford, P. and Sharp, S. (eds), *Breaktime and the School: Understanding and Changing Playground Behaviour*, London, Routledge.

Boyden, J. (1997) 'Childhood and the policy-makers: a comparative perspective on the globalization of childhood', in James, A. and Prout, A. (eds) *Constructing and Reconstructing Childhood*, London, Falmer Press (second edition).

Bradley, B. (1989) *Visions of Infancy: A Critical Introduction to Child Psychology*. Cambridge, Polity Press.

Bruner, J.S. and Haste, H. (eds) (1987) *Making Sense: The Child's Construction of the World*, London, Methuen.

Burman, E. (1994) *Deconstructing Developmental Psychology*, London, Routledge.

Coleman, J.S. (1987) 'Families and schools', *Educational Researcher*, 16, 32–8.

Corsaro, W. (1985) *Friendships and Peer Culture in the Early Years*, Norwood, NJ, Ablex.

Davie, R., Upton, G. and Varma, V. (eds) (1996) *The Voice of the Child*, London, Falmer.

Dunn, J. (1988) *The Beginnings of Social Understanding*, Oxford, Blackwell.

Faulkner, D., Littleton, K. and Woodhead, M. (eds) (1998) *Learning Relationships in the Classroom*, London, Routledge.

Hill, M. and Tisdall, K. (1997) *Children and Society*, London, Longman.

James, A., Jenks, C. and Prout, A. (1998) *Theorizing Childhood*, Cambridge, Polity Press.

James, A. and Prout, A. (eds) (1997) *Constructing and Reconstructing Childhood*, London, Falmer Press (second edition).

Morrow, V. and Richards, M. (1996) 'The ethics of social research with children', *Children and Society*, 10, 90–105.

Morss, J.R. (1996) *Growing Critical: Alternatives to Developmental Psychology*, London, Routledge.

Olweus, D. (1993) *Bullying at School: What We Know and What We Can Do*, Oxford, Blackwell.

Piaget, J. (1950) *The Psychology of Intelligence*, London, Routledge.

Prout, A. (1998) 'Concluding Remarks, Conference on Children and Social Exclusion, Centre for the Social Study of Childhood', Hull University.

Richards, M.P.M and Light, P. (eds) (1986) *Children of Social Worlds*, Cambridge, Polity Press.

Sameroff, A. (1987) 'The social context of development', in Eisenberg, N. (ed.), *Contemporary Topics in Developmental Psychology*, New York, Wiley.

Singer, E. (1998) 'Shared care for children', in Woodhead, M., Faulkner, D. and Littleton, K. (eds), *Cultural Worlds of Early Childhood*, London, Routledge.

Sluckin, A. (1981) *Growing Up in the Playground*, London, Routledge & Kegan Paul.

Woodhead, M., Carr, R. and Light, P. (eds) (1998) *Becoming a Person*, London, Routledge.

Woodhead, M., Faulkner, D. and Littleton, K. (eds) (1998) *Cultural Worlds of Early Childhood*, London, Routledge.

Part I

A world apart?

Chapter 1

Children's friendships and peer culture*

James Youniss

Introduction

The ideas for this chapter begin with a disparity between the literature on children's friendship and peer culture and the literature on adults' social networks and social support. Over the past 15 years, studies of friendship and peer culture have evolved into a fairly coherent view regarding the social construction of the individual, or self, through interpersonal relationships. Children construct themselves in collaboration with peers and friends as well as parents. In the process, they come to realize the necessity of taking account of others' ideas and of reaching consensus with them. Within friendship, children also recognize the normativeness of the principle of reciprocity and understand that personal resources can be shared for mutual benefit. This leads ultimately to a moral sense of interpersonal responsibility and mutual concern (e.g., Corsaro & Eder, 1990; Damon, 1988; Youniss, 1981).

The literature on adult networks and support is grounded in a different set of premises about the individual and interpersonal relationships. Individuals are pictured as independent agents who adapt to reality by using whichever resources they personally have and can elicit from others. This viewpoint seems akin to the old Parsonian version of the adaptive individual in the era of modernity (Parsons & Bales, 1955; Smith, 1980). There is irony to the fact that some of the first studies of networks done by sociologists were generated, in part, to challenge this Parsonian viewpoint (Smith, 1980). Fischer (1982), Wellman (1979), and others attempted to show that contemporary adults living in urban settings in industrialized nations did not view themselves as independent, rational agents whose relationships with others were chiefly strategic. Rather, these persons had and valued close, noninstrumental relationships in which the parties knew and cared for each other, even for the sake of mutuality itself.

---

* This is an edited version of a chapter that appeared in *Social networks and social support in childhood and adolescence*, Berlin: Walter de Gruyter, 1994.

Psychological researchers seemed to have picked up the sociologists' findings on networks and support without taking account of their theoretical
point of departure. They saw the importance of networks as a means of
support but depicted the network members much like figures in Parsonian
modernity. For many theorists, getting into a network and being able to
elicit support were construed as social skills that differ across individuals.
From an individual difference perspective, these skills are similar to traits.
From a social learning stance, skills can be taught to individuals to enhance
their social prowess and personal efficacy. And, this position fits with a prevailing ideology that psychological subjects are, at their root, self-supporting
individuals (Woolfolk & Richardson, 1984).

The goal of the present chapter is to initiate a discussion that will help
bridge these two outlooks. The chapter begins with a sketch of children's and
adolescents' descriptions of friendship. It is shown that the structure of this
relationship introduces children to their responsibility and dependence in
social construction, because friendship is founded on reciprocity. Next, the
chief theoretical concepts that these descriptions imply are identified and
discussed. Focus is given to concepts of interaction, cooperation, and mutual
understanding. Next, studies that have identified basic elements of peer culture are reviewed. It is shown that, for children and adolescents, peer culture
is highly organized by rules that are designed to insure orderly interaction
and to enhance mutual understanding. It is shown also that peer culture need
not isolate adolescents physically from adults or separate them by way of
interactive norms. The last point is elaborated with reviews of findings on
adolescent employment and adolescent altruistic activities in their communities. In conclusion, it is proposed that the data from children and youth
encourage consideration of the developmental and ideological implications
that separate these two areas of study. It is interesting to consider the kind of
adult that could be put into our network and support theories if we paid
serious attention to the psychological individual who developed into an adult
through children's and adolescents' friendships and peer culture.

The roots of reciprocity and mutual understanding

This section of the chapter uses illustrations from our past research on
parent–child and friendship relations. Our initial findings came from stories
6- to 12-year-old children generated when asked to tell us how they would
show kindness or unkindness to a friend (Youniss, 1980; Youniss & Volpe-
Smollar, 1978). The typical story of the youngest children told of one friend
sharing a material item or playing with another friend. The kind friend
mainly shared food or toys, played, or invited another child to play. Older
children told similar stories but qualified them by positing a state of need in
the friend to whom kindness was expressed. For instance, one friend shared
his lunch with another when the latter forgot to bring lunch to school and was

hungry. Or, one friend invited another to her house when the other was lonely and needed to be cheered up.

We initially explored analytic schemes for sorting stories into units of costs and benefits. This approach treated the children as individual actors who were more or less altruistic in sharing resources to help others. It soon became evident that this approach failed to capture the gist of children's intent, which was clear from their accounts of reciprocity. For instance, when asked what they might do after a friend let them ride their bike, younger children said they would let the friend play with their new toy or give the friend some of their potato chips. Such answers depicted a literal form of reciprocity in which one kind action was returned for another. When older children were asked the same question, they answered in a more complex fashion. For instance, one boy said that his friend, who was sick and in the hospital, was not at that time in a position to do anything except to express appreciation. He said, however, that the sick boy would think to himself that were this friend ever sick or in need of some sort, he would return the kindness in an appropriate way.

These stories indicated that children did not think about kindness as a trait of the individual friends; instead they thought of the persons as inter-dependent and ready to offer help when needed. Further, children did not think of the acts as discrete events, but viewed them as links in an on-going series, with each connected to prior acts and having implications for future acts. Letting a friend ride one's bicycle was reciprocal to the friend's having let one read his new book or share candy. It also implies that sharing will continue in the future. Showing sympathy to a sick friend was reciprocal to that friend's previous expressions of sympathy as well as to expected future expressions. Children imagine that they might switch roles between being in need and being able to help. This insight undermines a cost–gain model, because if friends are reciprocally related, the long-run result is mutual gain and interdependence.

This point became even more evident when we asked children about unkind acts. Younger children told stories in which negative reciprocal acts were exchanged literally. When one friend hit another, the other retaliated by hitting back. In older children's stories, the nature of unkindness changed, since they said that unkindness consisted in omission rather than direct nega-tive acts. For instance, one girl told a story in which her friend had missed several days of school due to illness. When she recovered and returned to school, she needed to make up work in order to pass a test. Unkindness occurred when her friend failed to help, even though she understood the friend's need for assistance.

It seems clear that failing to help can be unkind only if children feel they are obliged to help. In any typical classroom there must always be someone in need of help. If every child were expected to respond to the need of every other child, most children would live in a constant state of "unkindness." If, on the other hand, the obligation to help were restricted, then omission would be unkind but within their relationship. In friendship, the obligation to help is incurred through reciprocity, which is the principle on which the relationship is based. Peers who are not in a reciprocal relationship need not feel obliged to help all others in need. But friends do.

These data suggested that children assign specific meanings to actions because they understand the terms of relationships. Visiting a sick friend can be understood as part of a continuing series of actions in which the roles of being in need and being able to help were previously reversed and are potentially reversible in the unstated future. At any moment, circumstances might place one or the other friend in either role. What distinguishes friends from peers in general, therefore, is mutual obligation and interdependence, which develop through reciprocity.

An epistemology grounded in interactions and relationships

Consistent data from several samples of children led us to explore the implications for theories of knowledge. At the time, major theories depicted children as constructing reality by means of individual reflective activity. The general model pictured children as acting on objects, withdrawing to private reflection to form hypotheses, and then acting again to test their schemes. The data from friendship suggested a need to shift from this position to a view in which construction occurred socially as children interacted over time in relationships, jointly reflected on one another's ideas, and subsequently sought mutuality in the understanding of reality. Three major aspects of this view will now be discussed: (a) Interaction is the basic unit in which knowledge is constructed. Individual action is insufficient for ordering social reality; each action invites an action from another person, so both must be taken into account. (b) The distinguishing feature of social construction in friendship is cooperation. Friends do not simply act for individual interest but help one another make cognitive and personal progress. (c) Cooperative co-construction is designed to achieve mutual understanding. Knowledge is not just for oneself but is equally directed toward another person's understanding. Friends do not continually have to define situations for one another, but share common meanings that they carry forward in their relationship.

In seeking a general theory in which to place the above data, we rediscovered Piaget's (1932/1956) analysis of cooperative social construction, which was being rediscovered by others as well (e.g., Chapman, 1986; Damon, 1977: Furth, 1980). Piaget provides a basic epistemology in which individuals jointly seek to order reality through interaction and mutual reflection. He proposes that knowledge begins in and consists in material and mental action. He notes that children's actions engage other persons and induce actions from them. Because children seek order in actions, they must take account of the amendments and revisions that others make with their actions and reactions.

Each part of an interaction potentially provides instructive feedback to other parts, which is analogous to negative feedback in Piaget's classic description of detour. When a child's routine course of action meets a road-block, the child is thwarted and must devise another action that takes account of the blockage. The original routine is altered, and a new scheme that takes account of the blockage needs to be constructed. The social domain provides any number of comparable instances, such as when a child's intended actions are resisted by disparate intentions from other persons. It is obvious that the child's task of rendering order demands that interactions, not just the self's own actions, be the center of attention.

This small but essential addition changes construction from an individual to a social process. This is illustrated nicely by a kindness story from a 12-year-old female who defined a friend as "someone who helps you understand how you feel." She told of a fight with her family and going to a friend to express her confusion. When she told her friend what happened, her friend said she also had fights with her parents about similar issues. On finding this common ground, the two discussed the usefulness of various strategies for dealing with teenager–family conflicts and helped one another understand their feelings.

Cooperation is the chief component that distinguishes co-construction in friendship. It gives co-construction a specific direction it might not otherwise have. One can argue that friendship would not be possible unless children agreed to cooperate. Recall that young children's accounts of kindness and unkindness were marked by the literal use of reciprocity. Such a practice is inadequate for forming or sustaining a friendship because it is destabilizing. If each child is able to replicate the actions of the other, any negative act is apt to lead to retaliation, which would start an infinite regress. Similarly, any statement of an opinion by one friend could lead to a counterstatement, and so forth, which would result ultimately in stalemates as both friends expressed their respective views. Without agreement to cooperate, there is no sure means for breaking the impasse.

While peers practice reciprocity with literal tit-for-tat, friends agree to guide their relationship by the principle of reciprocity. When faced with a potential stalemate, such as in disputes about rules for a game, friends can step back and agree that in order to resolve their differences fairly, both should express their views, but both should also listen to the other's views. Only then can they hope to reach a compromise in a fair manner. The specific procedures that mediate cooperation have to be learned through mutual negotiation of the many challenging moments that come up in any normally variegated relationship (Oswald, 1992). With two active minds seeking to order reality, negotiation is mediated by procedures such as discussion, debate, compromise, argument, and majority rule.

A social system that includes co-construction and cooperation logically leads to a third aspect of mutual understanding. In most standard accounts of cognition, the goal is to explain how children construct valid versions of reality in which concepts match objects. Piaget's (1932/1956) account argues differently that in social and moral domains, validity depends on achievement of mutual understanding through normative procedures. This requires that the two or more cooperating individuals use fair procedures to talk out respective viewpoints so that each listens to the other and each expresses a viewpoint to the other. Validity depends on reaching consensus through procedural norm rather than through asserting truth or invoking external authority.

It is now suggested that studies of children's friendships offer new concepts for approaching the topics of networks and support. Friendships are parts of most social networks. Further, mutual support is inherent to friendship. Friends rely on one another for exchange and feedback in interpreting every-day events. Friends depend on each other for construction of emotional expressions and ideas. Friends believe that the material, emotional, and intel-lectual resources they possess ought to be used for one another's benefit. They feel obliged to share since they comprehend that the roles of being in need and being able to help continually switch between them. Helping, in this relationship, need not be heroic but pertains to making everyday experience comprehensible, valid, and more enjoyable (see Oswald *et al*. 1994).

These concepts also provide a fresh perspective on the self. Although selves are individuals, in friendship, individuals are relational entities because they cannot be separated from the relationship they share. Children's descriptions of kindness left us unable to say who was the chief beneficiary of kind acts. At any moment, the recipient in the guise of a depressed girl or a sick boy could be identified. But, it is equally true that the child who was kind was also a beneficiary, since kind acts are reciprocal to past and future actions. Con-sequently, should the kind child ever need support, her prior act served as insurance for her need at some future time. Thirdly, the relationship also benefited, since each kind act sustained the norm of reciprocity, which, in turn, strengthened the relationship itself. Piaget (1932/1956, p. 360) was on the mark in suggesting that there is no self except within relationships with others.

Peer culture

Corsaro (1985) and Corsaro and Eder (1990) have articulated a helpful approach to the concept of peer culture that sets the social context for the study of children's friendship. Corsaro made participant observations in a nursery school in order to describe the social and psychological organization of children's interactions and relationships (Cook-Gumperz & Corsaro, 1977). From watching children play, quarrel, tell stories, and the like, Corsaro identified five main components of children's culture. Each component will be described in turn, and then the overall relevance of the concept to social support will be discussed.

1   As the school year progressed, children constructed themes that became the focal topics of their everyday play. For example, falling down, getting hurt, and recovering, was a repeated theme that children regularly reenacted. A child need not literally have fallen down for another to invoke the theme. One girl, seeing another sitting alone, might announce that the other was not feeling well and needed care. The other girl might then pick up the theme by agreeing she was indeed ill and in need of help. Such episodes functioned to perpetuate the theme, which, over time, was manifested through several variations. In the process, the themes served as bases for group identification (Kane, 1992).

2   As the school year progressed, children came to agree on the kinds of interaction that were and were not allowable. This made interactions less arbitrary and more amenable to control by rules that the children understood in common. When any child violated the rules, other children could use the authority of shared knowledge to sanction the offender. This form of sanctioning by calling on rules indicates that children comprehend the need for order in their interactions and shows that children believe there is common agreement about rules and the implicit compact to obey them (Kane, 1992).

3   Children's shared knowledge of the meaning for interactions allows them to assign significance to unfolding events rather than having to interpret each discrete act anew (Krappmann, 1992). This is especially evident in symbolic or fantasy play for which a match is lacking between material reality and referred themes. One child might ask another to disobey a command so that a sequence of punishment, atonement, and reconciliation might be invoked. An initial offense was never committed but had to be purposely induced so that a series of routine actions with thematic meaning would go into effect.

4   To some extent, this culture of peers was constructed in order for children to differentiate their culture from that which they shared with adults. Cook-Gumperz and Corsaro (1977) offer illustrations of differences by contrasting children's understandings of questions in child–teacher and child–child interactions. Children realized that often teachers' questions were not actually questions for which teachers lacked and sought information. When teachers held up a yellow card and asked; "Which color is this?," children knew that teachers were not seeking information but were trying to discover which of the children knew what teachers already knew. In distinction, when one child asked another whether she wanted to play the game "queen," the question was a serious invitation, which might be rejected or accepted, to start a specific fantasy engagement.

In Corsaro's study, the themes, rules, and meaning systems of the these two cultures differed so that, at any moment, children knew the culture in which they were participating. It is possible that children want to create distance and privacy and perhaps even want to undermine adult culture. By creating their own cultural system with peers, children establish a culture in which their own interests can be tended apart from the adult culture in which there are other interests operating, such as those specified by the school curriculum. This hypothesis is compatible with our findings regarding distinctions between friendship and parent–child relationships. Friendship is defined by norms of reciprocity, open discussion, and cooperation. The same children whose stories revealed these norms described different norms of obedience and politeness in their relationships with parents. It is suggested that friendship and the peer culture in which it arises may provide children with unique experiences of social life that simply cannot be had in interactions with adults (Knappmann, 1992).

5   Despite their separation, the two cultures are not totally severed, as is shown when aspects of one culture are found to appear in the other. Children import features of one culture into the other, such as when they bring categories of age and intelligence, which are important to adults, into the peer culture. Children are known to use adult-based categories when they attempt to assert individual claims. For example, a child might use age by stating: "I can tell you what to do because I am older," or intelligence by asserting: "I have to be the leader because I know the rules." Obviously, the importing process goes in both directions. A case in point is when children teach adults games by making up the rules as the play progresses. Making rules as you go along is a feature of children's games that contrasts with "adult" games, for which the established rules anticipate most situations that will come up.

Adolescent peer culture

This section extends the discussion of peers to adolescence and assumes that adolescent peer culture continues the peer culture of childhood but modifies it for the purposes and vagaries of adolescence (Corsaro & Eder, 1990). The concept of adolescent peer culture has provoked much concern about segregation between adolescents and adults (Coleman, 1961, 1987). Insofar as there is an adolescent culture of high school, music, clothes, food, sexual habits, and recreation, adolescents may become removed from adults and be less able to adapt to adult society in subsequent years. Coleman (1987) has noted that society consists in norms, values, and daily routines that are shared among adults. Youth who do not share these with adults lack the social capital that would facilitate their entrance into adult society.

A segregated youth culture, by definition, reduces opportunities for adults to be included in youth's networks and vice versa. In a deeper sense, individuals separated by cultures and age would potentially lack a sense of mutual responsibility to support one another. Although either implication is important enough to warrant further consideration, it is now suggested that, while fears about segregation are reasonable, the evidence favors more youth–adult continuity than youth–adult division.

In adolescents' accounts (Smollar & Youniss, 1989; Youniss & Smollar, 1985), friendships are as principled and important as they are in younger children. The basic norms of reciprocity, discussion, and mutual understanding, which were established in preadolescents, were operationally extended into the high school years. What had changed from preadolescence, however, was a new concept of relationship with parents. Whereas younger children viewed parents as figures with unilateral authority, adolescents regarded parents more as individual personalities who were open to sharing authority with their sons and daughters. Adolescents recognized that parents had personal problems and even character weaknesses, but still warranted adolescents' respect because they worked to protect their families, looked out for adolescents' interests, and tried to better their lives.

These results have been interpreted as showing that aspects of peer relationships, in particular, reciprocity and mutual responsibility, become parts of parental relationships during adolescence. Mothers especially are perceived as able to transform their relationships into a more communicative and reciprocal, peer-like form. It is equally notable that while fathers, as a rule, are said to have relatively little contact with adolescents, they are nevertheless respected and seen as caring for the welfare of their families. These data support findings that adolescents need not withdraw from parental relationships in order to develop, but utilize them to construct their emerging sense of individuality (Grotevant & Cooper, 1986). They also fit findings that adolescents seek parental support by way of information and advice in educational as well as emotional–social domains (Meeus, 1992; Wintre et al., 1988). It is important to note that while the focus has been mainly on adolescents in North America, similar conclusions apply to adolescents in contemporary Germany (Hofer et al., 1990; Hurrelmann, 1989).

Another line of evidence comes from studies that have looked at the details of relationships inside adolescent peer culture. Studies of friendships and of crowds have shown that values and behaviors that social scientists posit as normative in adult society are found as normative within peer culture. For instance, loyalty and trust are principles that function among adolescent crowd members who support and protect one another (Eder, 1985). This does not preclude these same adolescents from gossiping about one another or from excluding others from their crowds (Eder, 1985). It should be noted, however, that gossip, jealousy, and exclusion are also parts of adult society. In this regard, teenage crowds have both the principles and behavioral shortcomings that are found in adult society.

Another relevant finding comes from adolescents' descriptions of the main behaviors by which members of their crowds were known within schools (Youniss *et al.*, 1993). For instance, students in popular crowds stressed their skillful sociality, desire to have fun, and also their respect for other students. Students in the brain crowd emphasized their high grades, intelligence, or lack of popularity. Results show that there is more decided differentiation among peers within adolescent than younger age groups. At the same time, differentiation is accompanied by tolerance and respect for differences, even among adolescents who do not want to join other crowds but accept their existence and see positive value in them. These data add to the demonstration that adolescent peer culture contains some of the same qualities that are desired and considered normative for adult society.

A third line of evidence establishes more direct links between youth and adult culture. It is a well-known fact that 50 percent or more of US high school students are engaged in part-time employment while they attend high school (W. T. Grant Foundation, 1988). Although this fact has usually been looked at in terms of whether youth are obtaining proper training for adult work, it can be viewed from another angle that bears on the present topic. The sort of work youth usually do is organized according to modem principles of production and service. In these positions, youth must perform according to clear rules that include coming to work on time, working a full shift, dressing properly, being clean, acting toward customers in a polite manner, and interacting with other workers in a cordial way. Viewed thusly, the fact of youth employment can be understood as a means for youth acquire skills through being engaged in adult norms of social interaction in the workplace. The specific skills that are required of this work may be quite distant from those that would allow self-subsistence in adulthood. But the interactive procedures that are required entail the basic norms that apply to adult, productive work.

A lesser-known fact is that working as well nonworking youth participate in adult society in another way. Numerous charity organizations have chapters in local communities and depend on volunteer services of youth. Youth's services include collecting money, coaching, tutoring, cleaning, telephoning, and the like. These actions not only bring youth in contact with adults but are sponsored by normative institutions that symbolically represent specific adult values. For instance, organizations such as the Red Cross and United Way symbolize the value of responsibility of one citizen to another in the community. Further, work for these organizations requires that youth follow prescribed routines and norms. For instance, as hospital aides, volunteers must dress in a stylized manner and treat patients and staff with a prescribed demeanor.

In a recent national survey of youth (Hodgkinson & Weitzman, 1990), it was found that approximately 50 percent of high school students said they had done volunteer, not for pay, work within the past year in local communities. We checked this finding by asking three available samples of students if they had volunteered, what they had done, and which organizations had sponsored their activities (Youniss, 1993). We found that slightly more than one-half claimed to have volunteered over the past year; this percentage corresponds with the national survey just cited. The activities were, as in the national survey, prosaic and nonheroic in nature. Adolescents baby-sat, visited elderly people in homes for the aged, coached elementary school youngsters, tutored their peers, assisted in hospitals, and collected money for charities.

We found that the sponsoring organizations were typically churches, schools, charity organizations, and local institutions that supplied services to citizens in need. And we found that the activities that were reported put teenagers in direct and meaningful contact with individuals from all age levels in their communities. The range included infants, preschoolers, elementary school age, high school, young adult parents, middle-aged neighbors, and the elderly. While adolescents belong to and are committed to a peer culture, they are not removed from adult society in terms of normative or responsible actions that demonstrate responsibility, commitment, and concern.

Conclusion

Two conclusions can be drawn from the foregoing discussion: First, there is a clear developmental pattern from childhood through adolescence showing that individual selves are established within a multitiered social system. Children are embedded in a peer culture that includes specialized relationships with friends. They learn how to interact to achieve mutual understanding; and in friendship, in particular, they learn how to enact the principles of reciprocity and open communication. Children are also engaged in relationships with parents and other adults such as teachers. Although the structure of these relationships differs from that of friendship, the peer and adult worlds are connected at the practical level of interactive procedures that are required for negotiating interests and desires.

A similar picture applies to adolescents who operate within a peer culture, maintain friendships, and remain close to their parents as they jointly transform the terms of that relationship. In addition, many adolescents participate in adult society through part-time employment, not-for-pay voluntary work, or both. As youth approach their 20s, they have accumulated a history of belonging to social systems and relationships that they actively construct and through which, in turn, they are constructed as individuals.

It follows from these data that normal development entails a history of engagement in social construction in which individuals learn about interdependence and mutuality. From scene-setting in early childhood play through negotiating conflict with parents in adolescence, individuals have learned the mechanics of exchanging material, intellectual, and emotional resources. These procedures provide ample opportunity to experience both sides of exchange so that they are accustomed to receiving and giving support in matters that count for daily existence. Whichever new ecologies adulthood might demand, development has prepared individuals well for responsible participation in close relationships and in societal functioning.

The second conclusion is theoretical in nature and refers to a general psychological model implicit in the network and support literatures. Individuals are treated as discrete actors who vary in their skills for social engagement. These skills create opportunities for becoming members of networks and for being able to elicit support when wanted or needed. This model fits well with the stilted Parsonian image of self-sustaining individuals who rely on their own resources for functioning in society. Such individuals operate on the general ethos of rationality that rewards merit and judges others according to objective criteria.

Available developmental evidence warrants a serious discussion of the adequacy of this model. If an ideology of individualism is assumed, one can undoubtedly find expressions of it in contemporary life. Purposeful distancing from others, competition, detachment from emotional engagement, and the like are not rare events. On the other hand, companionship, cooperation, and commitment to others are not rare either. It is this latter side of contemporary adulthood that seems to have been minimized in psychological theory. It is suggested here that this side be recognized as a complementary part that is needed for a full account of contemporary psychological life. When it is minimized, persons must be infused with specialized skills that allow isolated individuals to perform altruistic acts that would otherwise not be possible. Sociologists, political scientists, and business analysts have come to criticize the stilted version of modernity as an ideology that does not adequately capture observable reality. Whether one observes political negotiation or manufacturing processes, it is clear that where there are persons, there are also relationships, mutuality, and social systems.

Psychologists are aware of this to the degree that they recognize the importance of networks and support. But they tend to approach them using the unit of the discrete, ego-centered individual who independently adapts to macrosocial structure by acting for individual purposes. Psychologists should at least start to debate the limits of this model and the ideology from which it arises. In discussing alternatives, psychologists would be joining other disciplines that are already exploring this issue. They would also be taking seriously the developmental data that show that children and youth understand their own individuality in terms of interpersonal relationships that are structured according to inherent principles of reciprocity, cooperation, and mutual responsibility for one another's welfare.

References

Brown, B. B. (1990). Peer groups and peer cultures. In S. S. Feldman & G. R. Elliott (Eds.), *At the threshold: The developing adolescent.* Cambridge, MA: Harvard University Press.

Chapman, M. (1986). The structure of exchange: Piaget's sociological theory. *Human Development, 29,* 181–194.

Coleman, J. S. (1961). *The adolescent society.* New York: Free Press.

Coleman, J. S. (1987). Families and schools. *Educational Researcher, 16,* 32–38.

Cook-Gumperz, J., & Corsaro, W. A. (1977). Social ecological constraints on children's communication strategies. *Sociology, 11,* 411–434.

Corsaro, W. A. (1985). *Friendship and peer culture in the early years.* Norwood, NJ: Ablex.

Corsaro, W. A., & Eder, D. (1990). Children's peer cultures. *Annual Review of Sociology, 16,* 197–220.

Damon, W. (1977). *The social world of the child.* San Francisco: Jossey-Bass.

Damon, W. (1988). *The moral child.* New York: Free Press.

Eder, D. (1985). The cycle of popularity: Interpersonal relations among female adolescents. *Sociology of Education, 58,* 154–165.

Fischer, C. S. (1982). *To dwell among friends: Personal networks in town and city.* Chicago, IL: University of Chicago Press.

Furth, H. G. (1980). *The world of grown-ups: Children's conceptions of society.* New York: Elsevier.

Grotevant, H., & Cooper, C. S. (1986). Individuation in family relationships. *Human Development, 29,* 82–100.

Hodgkinson, V. A., & Weitzman, M. S. (1990). *Volunteering and giving among American teenagers 14 to 17 years of age.* Washington, DC: Private Sector.

Hofer, M., Pikowsky, B., & Fleischmann, T. (1990, May). *The differential use of arguments in mother–daughter conflicts.* Paper presented at the 3rd International Conference on dialogue analysis, Bologna, Italy.

Hurrelmann, K. (1989). The social world of adolescents: A sociological perspective. In K. Hurrelmann & U. Engel (Eds.), *The social world of adolescents: International perspectives* (pp. 3–24). Berlin: de Gruyter.

Kane, S. R. (1992). *Peer culture and pretend play in a preschool classroom.* Unpublished doctoral dissertation. The Catholic University of America, Washington, DC.

Krappmann, L. (1992). On the social embedding of learning processes in the class-room. In F. Oser, T. Dick, & J. L. Patry (Eds.), *Effective and responsible teaching* (pp. 173–186). San Francisco: Jossey-Bass.

Meeus, W. (1992). Parental and peer support in adolescence. In K. Hurrelmann & U. Engel (Eds.), *The social world of adolescents: International perspectives* (pp. 167–185). New York: de Gruyter.

Oswald, H. (1992). Negotiation of norms and sanctions among children. In P. Adler & A. Adler (Eds.), *Sociological studies of child development* (pp. 93–108). Greenwich, CT: JAI Press.

Oswald, H., Krappman, L., Uhlendorff, H., & Weiss, K. (1994) Social relationships and support among peers during middle childhood, in F. Nestmann & K. Hurrelmann (Eds.) *Social Networks and Social Support in Childhood and Adolescence,* Berlin, de Gruyter.

Parsons, T., & Bales, R. F. (1955). *Family socialization and interaction process*. Glencoe, IL: Free Press.

Piaget, J. (1956). *The moral judgment of the child*. New York: Free Press. (Original work published 1932).

Selman, R. S., & Schultz, L. H. (1990). *Making a friend in youth*. Chicago, IL: University of Chicago Press.

Smith, C. J. (1980). Social networks as metaphors, models. and methods. *Human Geography*, 4, 500–524.

Smollar, J., & Youniss, J. (1989). Transformations of adolescents' relations with parents. *International Journal of Behavioral Development*, 12, 71–84.

Weilman, B. (1979). The community question: Intimate networks of East Yorkers. *American Journal of Sociology*, 184, 1201–1231.

Wintre, M. G., Hicks, R., McVey, G., & Fox, J. (1988). Age and sex differences in choice of consultant for various types of problems. *Child Development*, 59, 1046–1055.

Woolfolk, R. L., & Richardson, F. C. (1984). Behavior therapy and ideology of modernity. *American Psychologist*, 39, 777–786.

W. T. Grant Foundation (1988). *The forgotten half: Pathways to success for America's youth and young families*. Washington, DC: Commission on Youth and America's Future.

Youniss, J., & Volpe-Smollar, J. A. (1978). A relational analysis of children's friendships. In W. Damon (Ed.), *New directions for child development. Social cognition*. San Francisco: Josey-Bass.

Youniss, J. (1980). *Parents and peers in social development*. Chicago, IL: University of Chicago Press.

Youniss, J. (1981). An analysis of moral development through a theory of social construction. *Merrill-Palmer Quarterly*, 27, 384–403.

Youniss, J., & Smollar, J. (1985). *Adolescent relations with mothers, fathers, and friends*. Chicago, IL: University of Chicago Press.

Youniss, J. (1992). Parent and peer relations in the emergence of cultural competence. In H. McGurk (Ed.), *Childhood social development: Contemporary perspectives* (pp. 131–147). Hove, England: Erlbaum.

Youniss, J. (1992, February). *Integrating culture and religion into developmental psychology*. Paper given at Brigham Young University, Provo, Utah.

Youniss, J., & Damon, W. (1992). Social construction in Piaget's theory. In H. Beilin & P. B. Pufall (Eds.) *Piaget's theory: Prospects and possibilities* (pp. 267–286). Hillsdale, NJ: Erlbaum.

Youniss, J., McLellan, J. A., & Strouse, D. L. (1993). "We're popular, but we're not snobs": Adolescents describe their crowds. In R. Montemayor, G. R. Adams, & T. P. Gullotta (Eds.) *Advances in adolescent development. Vol. 5: Personal relationships during adolescence*. Newbury Park, CA: Sage.

Chapter 2

Preadolescent peer cultures*

William A. Corsaro

When does childhood end? That is a hard question to answer. Defining the boundaries of childhood (and deciding on the range and limits of our consideration of the sociology of childhood) is a difficult task. Childhood is a social construction that is clearly related to, but not determined by, physical maturation, cultural beliefs about age, and institutional age grading.

For purposes of this chapter, childhood will include preadolescence, which is generally defined as the period from seven to thirteen years of age. [. . .]

We identify two basic themes in children's peer cultures: (1) *communal sharing*, the strong desire for sharing and social participation, and (2) *control*, children's persistent attempts to actively gain control over their lives. In this chapter we will discuss how these themes are produced and extended in the peer cultrues of preadolescent children. We will be especially concerned with how the extensions of these patterns are related to children's development to unique social selves or identities as they make the transition from childhood to preadolescent peer cultures.

Peer cultures in preadolescence

Most of our knowledge of the peer cultures of preadolescent children is the result of research in Western societies. However, we know from the research which has looked at other societies that children's groups are much less age-segregated in non-Western societies. Children who are seven to ten years of age in these societies spend much of their lives in mixed-age groups caring for and playing with younger siblings and other younger children in their local communities. These preadolescents have much less time for peer play in general, as they take on a range of tasks to help support their families. Furthermore, as we will see below, research across racial, ethnic, and social class groups in the United States challenges some of the well-documented

* This is an edited version of a chapter that appeared in *The sociology of childhood*, Thousand Oaks, CA: Pine Forge Press, 1997.

patterns in the peer cultures of white, middle- and upper-class children. Therefore, we must be careful to keep these differences in mind as we explore the basic themes of sharing and control in the peer cultures of preadolescent children.

Friendship processes in preadolescent peer cultures

Preschool children immensely enjoy simply being and doing things together. They often signal recognition of their ability to carry out joint actions with verbal references to friendship such as "We're friends, right?" (Corsaro, 1985; Parker & Gottman, 1989). However, generating shared meaning and coordinating play are often difficult tasks for young children. Thus, pre-schoolers spend a great deal of time creating and protecting the shared play and peer routines that provide them with a sense of excitement and emotional security.

Things are different for preadolescents. Children seven to ten years of age easily generate and sustain peer activities. However, they now collectively produce a set of stratified groups, and issues of acceptance, popularity, and group solidarity become very important. We will explore the importance and complexity of this increasing differentiation in peer relations by examining social participation and friendship processes, the nature and structure of dif-ferentiated friendship groups, and friendship, differentiation, and gender in preadolescence.

Social participation and friendships

In preadolescence the primarily nonverbal play routines of early childhood (for example, approach-avoidance and other play routines) are gradually replaced by verbal activities that involve planning and reflective evaluation. For example, Rizzo reports that first-grade children appeared to have an internalized concept of friendship that serves multiple functions in peer rela-tions. Specifically, in his year-long ethnography of first graders, Rizzo found that the children "attempted to determine the existence of friendship by comparing the internal concept with specific features of interactions with frequent playmates, to act in accordance with this concept when with friends, and to object when their friends failed to live up to their expectations" (1989, p. 105). In short, the children had the beginnings of a reflective awareness of what a friend should be, and they realized that they did not have to wait until they found themselves playing with a peer to have a friend. They could try to control who their friends would be!

Many times, however, the children found that their friendship bids (asking to be one's friend or being nice to someone) were often not accepted, and were at times actively rejected. Having a better awareness of what being a friend involves did not ensure that they could develop close friendships. In fact, in

Rizzo's study the most enduring friendships were the result of what could best be termed "local circumstances" of play and peer relations. Children became involved in types of play they enjoyed and, like the preschoolers we discussed earlier, they verbally marked and agreed that they were friends. However, unlike the younger children, the first graders would maintain these patterns of shared play with certain children over time and come to mark the relationship as special – by considering themselves to be best friends.

Best friends, then, often tried both to protect their friendships from the possible intrusions of others and to expand their friendship group. It is not surprising that these two processes came into conflict in a variety of ways. First, even though best friends wanted to expand their groups beyond their two-person dyad, they were very sensitive to the possible disruption of the fragile, dyadic best friend relationship. Therefore, they often displayed jealousy when their best friend played with others without them, and they quarreled with their best friend about the general nature of his or her play with others.

Rizzo and others see these disputes and conflicts as serving many positive functions, which I will address in the next section. Here I want to discuss another process in peer relations that develops shortly after best friendships are formed: the increasing differentiation of friendship groups.

Social differentiation and friendships

Preadolescent children's alliances are often linked to change of positions in friendship groups, providing the children with opportunities to test a series of social identities. Children's social identities "are thus oriented towards alliances with other children in activities that also separate the children" (Evaldsson, 1993, p. 258). For example, in Rizzo's study best friends often tried to expand their group by constructing "clubs," with membership offered to other kids they liked. The children would sometimes give names to these clubs, but the clubs seldom had any real purpose except to provide a way of expanding the friendship group. Some children were not offered membership, and others were rejected, resulting in the beginning of the development of stratified groups.

In Rizzo's study these groups were rather loosely bound and often broke down and then reformed. In Anna-Carita Evaldsson's study of the play of Swedish seven- to ten-year-olds in after-school centers, the children formed more stable friendship groups that were centered around different activities in the two centers. In one center the children highly valued possession of things, skills in acquiring these possessions, and competence in disputes and discussions about these valued objects. In this center the children frequently engaged in physical games, especially marbles, but competence in debating who was good at these games, in disputing issues of fair play, and in discussing who had the best possessions (marbles) was valued as much as competence in actually playing marbles. In the second center the children's identities and friendship processes were more relational and emotional. Instead of centering around physical activities, skills, and talk about such, the children in the second center were more concerned with appearance, romances, and involvements in secret activities. These values were displayed "in intimate alliances, where comparisons, guessing, teasing and joint laughter support social differentiation" (Evaldsson, 1993, p. 259).

We will return to Evaldsson's study to look more closely at the nature of these play activities and games in the next section, because they nicely illustrate how children address ambiguities, concerns, fears, and conflicts in peer culture. What is of particular interest here, however, is that gender was not a central factor in the differentiation of friendship groups at the two centers she studied. This finding is quite different from the findings of studies of friendship processes among American white, middle- and upper-class preadolescents.

Social differentiation, friendships, and gender

Many studies have documented increasing gender differentiation in children's peer interactions beginning at around five or six years of age and reaching a peak in the early elementary school years (Adler, Kless, & Adler, 1992; Berentzen, 1984; Gottman, 1986; Oswald, Krappman, Chowdhuri, & von Salisch, 1987; Thorne, 1993). Although there is extensive sex segregation in peer relations in this period, it is rarely complete; most studies show consistent mixed sex grouping and cross-sex interaction (usually on the order of 10 to 20 percent) even in the preadolescent period (Thorne, 1993). What is more important for our understanding of peer cultures is not simply the gender segregation that surely occurs in the preadolescent period, but the nature of interactive patterns and interpersonal processes within the segregated groups. Here there is a growing debate about whether or not girls and boys have different peer cultures.

Thorne argues that a familiar story line runs through the literature on children and gender. "The story opens," notes Thorne, "by emphasizing patterns of mutual avoidance between boys and girls and then asserts that this daily separation results in, and is perpetuated by, deep and dichotomous gender differences" (1993, p. 89). These differences are seen as both affecting and best affected by the structure and nature of activities in gender segregated groups. For example, several studies have found that boys interact in larger groups (Lever, 1976), engage in more aggressive and competitive play (Adler, Kless, & Adler, 1992; Best, 1983), and frequently organize their activities and relations around organized sports (Adler, Kless, & Adler, 1992; Eder & Parker, 1987; Fine, 1987; Lever, 1978; Thorne, 1993; Thorne & Luria, 1986).

In a recent article, Adler, Kless, & Adler (1992) discuss how the nature of these different activities contributes to popularity within the peer cultures of preadolescent boys and girls. They defined popular children as those who "are liked by the greatest number of their peers, who are the most influential in setting group opinions, and who have the greatest impact on determining the boundaries of membership in the most exclusive social group" (1992, p. 172).

Adler, Kless, and Adler found that "boys and girls constructed idealized images of masculinity and femininity on which they modeled their behavior" (1992, p. 169). These images were reflected in a set of *focal concerns* which affected popularity in boys' and girls' cultures. Focal concerns are a specific set of values, interests, and problems central to the peer culture. Boys' focal concerns revolved around a cult of masculinity or being tough, around physical contests, autonomy and self-reliance, and around a culture of coolness or detachment. Girls' focal concerns, in contrast, centered around the valuing of compliance and conformity, a culture of romantic love, an ideology of domesticity that favored intimacy and emotional expression, and an orientation to ascriptive norms related to appearance and material possessions. These findings are generally in line with claims by the psychologist Carol Gilligan (1982). Gilligan argues that girls have a *"different voice"* in that they value relationships and caring, as opposed to boys' concerns with individual rights and abstract notions of justice. Girls are so concerned with maintaining personal relationships that they strive to avoid conflict and negotiate problems indirectly for fear of seeming uncooperative.

Gilligan's work has led to the general acceptance of the "two cultures" view of children's gender socialization, differences in men's and women's styles of talk, and the nature of social relationships across gender groups more generally (Barnes & Vangelisti, 1995; Gilligan, 1982; Hare-Mustin & Maracek, 1988; Maltz & Borker, 1982; Tannen, 1990). However, we should not be too quick to accept this view of children's gender relations. It has recently been called into question for several reasons.

First, most studies have been of white, middle- and upper-class American children. African-American and Latino boys and girls are much less separated in their play than white, middle-class children. Also, the nature of peer activities, concerns, and values of African-American and Latina girls are much different from white, middle- and upper-class American girls (Goodwin, 1990; Schofield, 1982; Thorne, 1993). Goodwin, for example, found that African-American and Latina girls engage in highly complex physical games and play in which competition and verbal conflict are recurrent and highly valued (1990; in press). The important point here is not simply that studies upon which the two cultures view is based have limited generalizability. Rather, the issue is that findings and interpretations in line with the separate culture view implies that there is something about the *very nature of being male or female* which leads to these differing values and social relations by gender. The implication is, therefore, that the pattern should be universal. There is little support for such a claim.

It is important to note that the issue runs deeper than possible class and cultural differences in gender relations among children. There is also the problem of interpreting data *only* in line with the two cultures view, which stresses very clear cut, almost dichotomous, sexual differences and perspectives. In many of the studies exceptions to the general pattern are pushed aside and seldom pursued. Rarely, if ever, is there a search for negative cases. How might things be done differently? How might we go about identifying and interpreting exceptions to the separate cultures view? Thorne has argued for the importance of grounding observations in a wider range of social contexts (focusing on the less visible and peripheral as well as on the most conspicuous and dominant groups and settings). We need to study both the core groups of the leaders and the more peripheral groups of less popular children. Goodwin has championed the intensive microanalysis of naturally occurring events – how children actually go about playing games like jump rope and discussing friendships and gossiping in their everyday lives. Goodwin's point is especially well-taken. Even with the recent increase in ethnographic studies of peer relations, three is still a common reliance on reports of children's activities rather than on direct study of the activities themselves.

Autonomy and identity in preadolescent peer cultures

Everyday activities in peer culture, enable preadolescents to negotiate and explore a wide range of norms regarding friendship processes, personal appearance, self-presentation, heterosexual relations, personal aspirations, and relations with adult authority figures. By participating in organized and informal games, verbal play routines, and collaborative storytelling, preadolescents explore developing norms and expectations about themselves and their place in peer and adult culture without the risk of direct confrontation and embarrassment. Let's explore these activities, looking at how they relate to friendship relations, conflicts and disputes, and the challenging of adult control and authority.

Verbal routines, games, and heterosexual relations

Like preschool children, preadolescents often engage in play routines that involve communal sharing. However, preadolescents with increased language and cognitive skills have more control over when and how such routines might occur. Thus, in addition to more loosely structured play routines, preadolescents often participate in formal games both spontaneously and in organized settings. Children of this age also talk about their play and games in a reflective way, and they can appreciate the subtle and symbolic aspects of play routines both during and after their enactments. Finally, preadolescent children often address concerns about appearance, self-presentation, and heterosexual relations within play routines and games. In this sense they use the "as-if" or pretend frame of play and games as a secure base for addressing sensitive and potentially embarrassing concerns, desires, and ambiguities.

Routines, verbal play, and humor

Preadolescent children often mark allegiance to friendship bonds through participation in sharing routines. These routines are similar to the general celebration of simply playing together among preschool children. Here, though, the very nature of participation in the routines forces children to think about their relation to one another and their place as individuals in a group.

Consider the Israeli sharing routine "Xibùdim," documented by the anthropologist Tamar Katriel (1987). Katriel conducted naturalistic observations of the sharing routine and also interviewed twenty preadolescents (ages nine to twelve) and ten younger children (ages five to seven). Xibùdim usually occurred on the way home from school:

> A group of five children approaches the falafel [snack or treat] stand. One exclaims "I'm buying." Another counters, "Bexibùdim! Bexibùdim!" in a melodious chant. He gets a falafel portion, holds it in his hands, and all take a bite in turn, with a gay clamor. After the third one has eaten, the buyer mutters, "Hey, beraxmanut" (with pity) and offers it to the last child. He then eats his falafel, walking along with his friends.
>
> (Katriel, 1987, p. 309)

As we can see, this routine has a definite structure: (1) the *opening* or announcement of an intention to buy a treat by a particular child; (2) the *acknowledgment* by other children, usually involving the exclamation "Bexibùdim! Bexibùdim!" uttered in a melodious chant; (3) the *purchase* of the treat by the proposer; (4) the *offering* and sharing of the treat, with each accompanying child taking a small bite; and (5) the optional recycling of a second round of sharing. The routine involves delicate negotiation in that, as Katriel has noted, the bite size has to be regulated so that everybody gets a share and about half the treat is left for the owner. (This is illustrated by the owner's request for pity before offering the last bite.) According to Katriel, the sharing of treats in xibùdim "can be viewed as a ritualized gesture that functions to express and regulate social relationships within the peer group" (1987, p. 307). A key element here is the concept of the individual's respect for others in her or his group of friends; xibùdim is derived from the verb lexabed, whose literal meaning is "to respect." In an interview, an eleven-year-old girl explained her insistence on getting a bit of her friend's treat in this way: "It's not that I will die if I don't get a bite of the popsicle, that I will die a day earlier or something, but it is simply . . . respect, as the word says." (1987, p. 307). This statement, along

with the main features of the routine, support Katriel's insightful interpretation of the routine as a "symbolic sacrifice in which one's self-interest and
primordial greed are controlled and subordinated to an idea of sociality
shaped by particular cultural values, such as equality and generalized reciprocity" (1987, p. 318). Finally, on a more concrete level, sharing routines
such as *xibùdim* are fun! Their production "serves to reassert the very existence
of children's peer group culture" as a "celebration of childhood" (Katriel,
1987, p. 318).

Routines like *xibùdim* also are interesting because they simultaneously
assert individual rights and creativity and collective solidarity. Many other
activities in preadolescents' peer cultures possess this characteristic, especially
those related to verbal games and humor. For example, preadolescents produce and embellish a wide range of *children's lore* – games, jokes, chants,
rhymes, riddles, songs, and other verbal routines that are created and trans-
mitted by children over time and across societies. Such lore has been well
documented by child folklorists (Gomme, 1964; McDowell, 1979; Opie &
Opie, 1959, 1969). These activities are rich with laughter, which serves as a
communicative marker. It both signals that the activity at hand is not serious
and "also signifies support; others with you" (Frønes, 1995, p. 223).

The humor and verbal play rituals of preadolescents are often more complex, reflective, and portable than those of preschoolers. Merely saying the
words "pee-pee" or "poo-poo" can generate laughter anywhere or anytime
among preschoolers. However, this joke provides little opportunity for
reflective awareness or embellishment, and its expression in play and games
often disrupts the activity at hand. Preadolescent children collect jokes and
riddles and practice and embellish their presentations, often embedding the
joking and laughter in other peer activities. They try out jokes on older
siblings and parents and discover that this audience also can be the source of
new additions to their developing repertoires. These jokes and riddles often
have a two-step, set-up-and-punch-line structure, which demands a certain
level of cognitive decentering (the punch line or solution must be inferred
from the set up) and language skills (questions must be asked, words phrased
or voiced in a certain way, and so on). [. . .]

Games, secrets, self, and interpersonal relations

Preadolescent children like to play games. They play a variety of games in a
wide range of informal and formal settings. Although there has been a great
deal of work documenting such games and how children's participation influences their cognitive, emotional, and social development, studies of children
actually playing games are rare. Several recent studies have addressed this
neglect.

Perhaps some of the best work on *children's games as situated activities* is that
of Goodwin (1985, 1990) and Evaldsson (1993). By situated activities these

researchers mean games that are produced in real settings with real children who often have long interactional histories. Research that is based on verbal reports of children's participation in games or that relies on analysis of the form and structure of games abstracted from the actual performances miss this "situated" aspect. Such research is bloodless, so to speak. It surely tells us something about how children spend their time and about the developmental implications of participating in games with various physical, cognitive, language, and emotional demands. But if one really wants to capture the rich social world of children's lives and peer cultures it is necessary to enter their play, to be willing to get your pants dirty and shoes muddy.

This is just what Goodwin and Evaldsson have done. Goodwin has studied the play and games of African-American and Latino children in the United States for many years. She has observed, audiovisually recorded, and analyzed these children participating in a wide range of play and games (dramatic role play, team sports, jump rope, hopscotch, racing, pitching pennies, and more) in their neighborhoods and in nearby playgrounds. Goodwin has found that the children's play and games are marked by complex verbal negotiations, disputes, and conflicts through which the children display and develop social identities and organize their peer cultures. We will return to look at Goodwin's work in detail in the next section, where we consider the importance of conflict and disputes in children's peer culture. Here we want to look more carefully at Evaldsson's recent study of children's participation in games in Swedish after-school programs.

Evaldsson studied two different programs for six- to ten-year-old children over an eight-month period. She found that the children repeated games day after day. The children in the Panda center preferred to play and trade marbles, while the children at the Bumblebee center often engaged in jump rope. Marbles is a highly complex game. Piaget (1932) analyzed in some depth the game's contributions to children's negotiation strategies and their moral development. Evaldsson, on the other hand, focused on how children relied on repeated performances of the game to create a locally shared peer culture and to display and evaluate selves and identities in that culture.

Marbles involves skills in playing the game – that is, aiming and shooting marbles at a hole or at another player's marbles, quickly anticipating the flow of play, and shouting various restrictions regarding shooting. Evaluating the value of marbles from a competition and trading standpoint is also important. Although the children in the study played marbles in dyads, there was always an audience of nonplayers who observed and often participated in arranging matches, evaluating the play, and negotiating marble trading. Evaldsson found that boys primarily played the games, with girls more actively involved in evaluating the play and trading.

The games and trades had natural histories in that they occurred over the school term, and during this period of time the children came to assess each other in terms of these various skills. In her documentation of the history of marble play as a complex series of situated activities, Evaldsson found that the children's selves were intimately related to status, which was linked to the possession and negotiated value of marbles as things. In other words, as the children increased and decreased their status in relation to their possession of the valued objects, they used talk to negotiate the value of the objects (Evaldsson, 1993, p. 133). The whole process was made even more complex by shifting alliances of children in judgments and negotiations during both the playing and trading of marbles. Thus we see the developing notion of identity or self embedded in the collectively produced peer culture.

Jump rope, like marbles, is rule-governed and participants are expected to have a particular orientation to one another during play (Evaldsson, 1993; Goodwin, 1985). Although there is a good bit of variation, the general pattern in jump rope is for two children to hold opposite ends of a rope and turn it for a third child who jumps when the rope hits the ground. The child who jumps is normally entitled to continue until she misses. When this occurs the jumper exchanges places with one of the turners, who now has the opportunity to jump. Legitimate misses are the fault of the jumper and not the turner. Therefore, misses are sometimes negotiated to assign fault, and these negotiations can become very heated and complex. Jump rope is competitive because successful jumpers earn high status and often obtain the valued position of "first jumper" in initial rounds of play. However, a most interesting fact of jump rope is that *children must cooperate to compete*. There is a built-in motivation to turn the rope fairly for jumpers because if one turns too fast or not in synchrony with the beat, there is a chance that when the jumper next becomes a turner she or he will do the same for the previous offender (Evaldsson, 1993; Goodwin, 1985).

We can clearly see from the above description that jump rope is much more complex than some previous studies, like those of Lever (1978), suggest. Lever argued that girls' games like jump rope or hopscotch are eventless turn-taking games with much less complex structures than boys' competitive sports games. Such a misperception is the result of not observing, recording, and carefully analyzing the play of the games themselves. However, the complexity and significance of the games is even more apparent when their production and place in peer culture is examined over long periods of time.

Let's consider a typical game of jump rope in Evaldsson's study. She found that in the Bumblebee after-school center, both boys and girls engaged in jump rope activities on a regular basis. The most frequent game was "Cradle of Love." This variant of jump rope can be played a number of ways, but the most common variety at the Bumblebee was this one: A jumper jumps as turners and members of an audience call out the letters of the alphabet. If the jumper misses on a particular letter, others call out the name of another child or of some media character, who then becomes the potential (or pretend) love interest of the jumper. For example, if Amy misses at the letter "P," someone may call out "Paul!" Then Amy jumps to the rhyme, "Paul do you love me.

Tell me truly aye or nay." Then the speed of turning is increased and the rhyme continues: "Yes–No Yes–No Yes–No," with the romantic link confirmed or denied according to when a miss occurs. If a jumper succeeds in moving through the entire alphabet, she can propose the name of the love interest without the constraint of the initial letter. However, in this case other children quickly offer up potential names for the jumper to evaluate.

We can see that repetitions of this game among boys and girls who spend a lot of time together take on characteristics that have as much to do with their developing relationships toward the opposite sex as they do with their competitive skill in jumping. [. . .]

In addition to participating in organized games, preadolescent children also create their own cultural artifacts to organize and share their activities. For example, children at this age often separate themselves from others through the sharing of secrets. Sharing secrets involves activities ranging from verbal whispering to the writing and passing of notes, the establishment of secret clubs, and the production of complex texts and artifacts. The whispering talk and control of space marks the fact that members of a secret club are part of an exclusive group.

The children in Evaldsson's study produced a number of artifacts related to secrets in their peer culture. These included "love lists" and "fortune tellers." Both boys and girls constructed love lists upon which they wrote the names of best friends in order of preference. These lists were then shared with selected friends and often became the topic of discussions, teasing, and sometimes disputes. Children created fortune tellers by folding a sheet of paper into four parts, then folding the corners into the center, and finally folding the paper into four parts again. The folded paper was then arranged to fit two fingers from each hand for opening and closing (Evaldsson, 1993, p. 196. See Figure 2.1).

After constructing the fortune teller, children painted the different parts various colors and wrote messages in the corners that were concealed by the folds. They often talked together as they decided what messages to write. They then played with the fortune tellers in dyads, with other children observing. In play the owner of the fortune teller asks the other player to choose a number and then counts it out, opening and closing the folds. Then the owner asks for a color and upon hearing the response folds back the corner of that color and reads the message aloud. Most messages either teased or insulted the recipient, saying for example that he or she looked like a monkey or was in love with a particular child. The children were fascinated with the magic quality of fortune tellers and greatly appreciated that these artifacts were of their own creation. The creation of and play with fortune tellers is not restricted to Sweden, of course, as they also have been documented among American children (Knapp and Knapp, 1976). Many readers may have constructed them in their youth. They are similar, of course, to toys like the Magic Eight Ball and decoder rings.

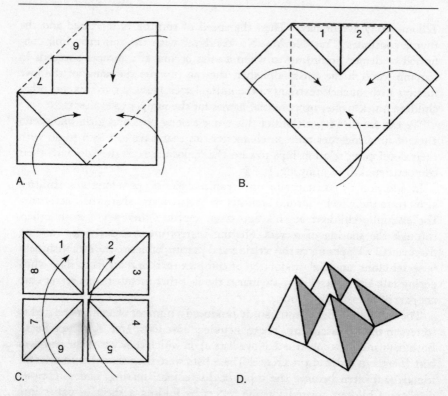

Figure 2.1 Making a "fortune teller"
Source: Evaldsson, 1993, p. 197. Used with author's permission.

An important point about both love lists and fortune tellers is that they are durable creations of peer culture. They only conceal private information and secrets but make them last longer and allow for their transformation outside the situation of actual use. This transformation often generates a traceable history of their use, which can make them subjects of teasing, debates, and conflicts among peers.

Disputes, conflict, friendships, and gender

Many activities that bring preadolescent children together and build friendships are often the source of disputes and conflicts. Rizzo, for example, found that as first graders developed best friendships they set higher expectations for their friends' behaviors. These expectations often led to disagreements and arguments. In fact, it is a common lament of many kindergarten, first, and second grade teachers that so-called "best friends" seem to be fighting all the time! We have to be careful, however, not to accept the adult perspective regarding conflict among young children too readily – most especially the middle-class American adult perspective. Middle-class American adults are often uncomfortable with disputes and conflicts among children. There is wide variation in the nature and evaluation of conflict and argumentation across cultures and across subcultural groups within American society. Furthermore, recent research documents the positive aspects of conflict and disputes in children's everyday lives. Let's look at some of this research. We will first examine verbal conflicts and disputes in peer relations, and then behavioral routines involving cross-gender conflict.

Verbal disputes and conflict in peer relations

What are some of the causes of conflict and disputes among preadolescents? How are conflicts important in their daily activities and peer cultures? The chief cause may be the increased differentiation in friendship groups in pre-adolescence. However, conflict, especially arguments and teasing, also can bring children together and help organize their activities. In this sense cooperation and competition are not mutually exclusive and often coexist within the same activities (Goodwin, 1990, p. 84). Recent research on peer conflict among elementary school children shows how disputes are a basic means for constructing social order, cultivating, testing, and maintaining friendships, and developing and displaying social identity (Davies, 1982; Fine, 1987; Goodwin, 1990; Katriel, 1985; Maynard, 1985; Rizzo, 1992).

Goodwin's work on preadolescent children's play and games in neighborhood settings clearly demonstrates the important role of conflict in the organization of peer activities. For example, Goodwin found that the African-American children she studied organized their talk to *build and highlight opposition*. Boys engaged in arguments and ritual insults as way of dramatizing their play and to construct and display character. Conflicts and disputes seldom reached clear resolution as disagreements between individual children often expanded into group debates. In short, conflict was enjoyed, even relished, and the children actually cooperated to embellish and extend rounds of arguments and insults. Furthermore, the children never complained to adults about peer teasing and insults, rarely excluded peers from play, and did not produce rigid status hierarchies.

Let's take a closer look at Goodwin's work on conflict among preadolescent African-American and Latina girls to capture the tenor of her work. The research is especially important because the everyday lives of these children are seldom carefully studied, but are often misunderstood in American social science.

An especially impressive example of research on children's dispute routines in Goodwin's (1980, 1990) analysis of gossip disputes among black female preadolescents. Unlike the direct competitive disputes of males (Goodwin, 1990; Labov, 1972), black females frequently engage in gossip disputes during which absent parties are evaluated. The airing of such grievances frequently culminates into he-said-she-said confrontations. A *he-said-she-said confrontation* can be defined as a type of gossip routine that is brought about when one party to a dispute gossips about the other party in his or her absence. The he-said-she-said confrontation comes about when the absent party challenges his or her antagonist at a later point in time. Consider the following example.

> In the midst of play, Annette confronts Benita saying: "And Arthur said that you said that I was showing off just because I had that blouse on."
>
> (Goodwin, 1990, p.195)

Annette is speaking to Benita in the *present* about what Arthur told her in the *recent past* that Benita said about Annette in the *more remote past*. This complex temporal structure is crucial to he-said-she-said exchanges because the accusation locates the statement made by the defendant about the speaker as having been made in the speaker's absence. Such "talking behind one's back" is considered a serious offense in the peer culture. In her analysis Goodwin specifies the complex linguistic structures that the children use in such confrontations to order a field of events, to negotiate identities, and to construct social order. The gossip routine is important because it is inappropriate to insult, command, or accuse others openly in the girls' peer culture.

Goodwin's analysis is noteworthy for two other reasons. First, it demonstrates that conflict routinely occurs in the girls' peer interactions even though it may take a more indirect form than that of the boys. These findings dispute the work of Gilligan and others we discussed earlier, which maintains that girls are concerned with maintaining relationships and thus avoid confrontations. Second, the complexity of these speech activities clearly refutes claims that working- and lower-class African-American children rely on a dialect that is "nonlogical" (Bereiter and Engleman, 1966). Researchers who have made such claims have not bothered to study the children's language as it is produced in natural settings.

Goodwin has also recently carried out comparative studies of disputes and conflicts in preadolescent girls' playing of hopscotch. On the surface hopscotch seems to be a simple turn-taking game, demanding a fair amount of physical coordination. [. . .] Hopscotch can also involve a great deal of negotiation about the rules. In the hopscotch play of the African-American and Latina girls that Goodwin studied, nonjumpers intensely scrutinized the body movements of jumpers and were quick to call out infractions and enforce the rules. Consider the following example.

Lucianda takes her turn, jumping twice in square two and possibly putting her foot on the line of square one. Joy sees the violation and yells, "You out."

Lucianda shakes her head no, "No I'm not!"

"You hit the line," counters Joy. And now Crystal comes over in support of

Joy and says, "Yes you did. You hit the line. You hit the line" as she points to the line.

Lucianda leans towards Crystal. "I ain't hit no line!"

"Yes you did," shouts Alisha, who has now come over to the group. Crystal supports Alisha, smiling and shaking her head as she points to the spot of the violation, "You did. You s—"

"No I didn't," interrupts Lucianda.

"Yes you did," counters Alisha again.

"Didn't she go like this?" Crystal asks the others. And then looking at Lucianda she says, "You did like this" as she steps on the line in an imitation of Lucianda's jump. "You did like that."

Joy now walks up to the grid and rubs her foot across the line, "Yeah, you hit that line." Then she taps the line twice with her foot and says "Right there, honey!"

Finally, another nonjumper, Vanessa, comes over and says to Lucianda, "You out now!" (adapted from Goodwin, in press, pp. 18–19).

In this example we see that the girls negotiate and enforce the rules with a great deal of teasing and dramatic flare. In fact, in many cases the stylized disputes and arguments over misses or what were labeled "as attempts to cheat" became more important than the actual play of hopscotch. Rather than simply following the rules or ignoring them, the girls work and play with them, often purposely highlighting opposition (Goodwin, in press, p. 22).

Things were quite different in the hopscotch play of the middle-class white girls Goodwin observed. Instead of closely observing and evaluating the play, the children paid less attention to misses and mitigated their responses to them.

Linsey, Liz, Kendrick and Kathleen are playing. Linsey throws her stone and hits a line. Linsey then begins jumping. "Oh! Good job Linsey! You got it all the way on the 7," says Liz.

Kendrick clearly sees that Linsey has hit a line with her foot. She shakes her head, "That's – I think that's sort of on the line though." "Uh," says Liz to Linsey, "your foot's in the wrong spot."

"Sorry," says Kendrick, "that was a good try."

Later Linsey is jumping again and she makes it through several squares. "You did it!" shouts Cathleen. "Yes!" repeats Linsey. She then hits a line as she nears the end of her turn.

"Whoa," says Cathleen softly. Kendrick then laughing a bit says encouragingly, "You accidently jumped on that. But that's okay." (Adapted from Goodwin, in press, p. 21.)

Some feminist scholars see the mitigated nature of children's speech of this type as positive, arguing that it demonstrates concern for affiliation and promotes relational solidarity (Barnes & Vangelisti, 1995). Goodwin, however, notes that group solidarity can be achieved in a variety of ways. Furthermore, she points to a "lack of accountability for one's action" in the mitigated language style of the middle-class white girls in the above example. She argues that interpersonal conflict is often the heart of social life. In fact, conflicts seldom disrupted play in her data; rather, they added spice and flair. In this view, conflict and cooperation are not opposites but overlapping processes that are embedded in the larger ethos of playfulness. Disputes, teasing, and conflict can add a creative tension that increases its enjoyment (Goodwin, in press, p. 24). We can make one final point on the relation between conflict and cooperation in children's play: when children who have spent most of their time in different sociocultural groups come together for play, they often misinterpret each other's styles. Middle-class white girls, for example, often find the teasing, oppositional style of Latina and African-American girls to be threatening, bossy, and mean, while African-American and Latina girls see the mitigated and polite style of middle-class white girls as patronizing (Corsaro & Rosier, 1992; Schofield, 1982). These findings show the value of research on differences in interpersonal interaction and play styles across sociocultural groups. The identification of sources of misinterpretations can be a first step in improving cross-cultural relations.

Borderwork in cross-gender relations

The relation between teasing, conflict, and tension in peer relations is probably nowhere more apparent than in cross-gender relations among preadolescents. Girls and boys are often apart at this age, but for certain activities they do work and play together with little obvious attention paid to gender. For example, a number of researchers have found that children often play in mixed gender groups in neighborhoods, most especially if the play groups are also mixed in age (Ellis, Rogoff, & Cromer, 1981; Goodwin, 1990; Thorne, 1993; and Whiting & Edwards, 1988). Others have found consistent cross-gender interaction in schools, but primarily in settings that are not controlled by peer groups such as in classrooms and in extra-curricular activities (Lockheed, 1985; Thorne, 1993). However, it is in peer-dominated and highly public settings in schools – like cafeterias and playgrounds – that gender separation is most complete. In fact, many activities and routines of preadolescent children's peer cultures in these settings seem to be all about gender. In these activities and routines, girls and boys try to make sense of and deal with ambiguities and concerns related to gender differences and relations. Many of these activities involve conflict, disputes, and teasing. Thorne has captures the complexity of such activities with her discussion and analysis of borderwork.

Borderwork refers to activities that mark and strengthen boundaries between groups. When gender boundaries are activated, "other social definitions get squeezed out by heightened awareness of gender as a dichotomy and of 'the girls' and 'the boys' as opposite and even antagonistic sides"

(Thorne, 1993, p. 66). In her work in elementary schools Thorne identified several types of borderwork. The first type is *contests* between groups of girls and boys. Among the groups Thorne studied, contests were initiated by both children and teachers. Sometimes teachers pitted boys and girls against each other in math and spelling competitions. On one occasion a teacher named the two teams "Beastly Boys" and "Gossipy Girls," thereby supporting such contests and gender stereotypes (Thorne, 1993, p. 67). Boys and girls would at times play cooperatively in sports games on the playground, but these games were often transformed into competitive boy–girl competitions full of taunts, teasing, and insults usually aimed at the girls.

Another type of borderwork, *chasing*, is also competitive, but this activity is more symbolic in its affirmation of boundaries between girls and boys. Cross-gender chasing is very similar in structure to the approach-avoidance routines of preschool children. In fact, I observed several instances of cross-gender approach-avoidance play in my work with preschoolers. Among pre-adolescents chasing routines usually begin when a child from one gender group taunts the members of the other group. These taunts lead to chases that are often accompanied by threats that are seldom carried out. For example, boys may taunt and tease girls, leading the girls to run after the boys and threaten to catch and kiss them. These routines are generally referred to as "chase-and-kiss," "kiss–chase," and "kissers and chasers' (Parrott, 1979; Richert, 1990; Sluckin, 1981; Thorne, 1993). In her work, Thorne found that the chases had a long history, with children talking about them for days afterward with friends and even parents (1993, p. 69). Children talk about cross-gender chases because this type of borderwork gives rise to lots of tension. Children are experimenting with their growing concerns and desires regarding the opposite sex. In fact, like approach-avoidance play among pre-schoolers, chasing routines include the children's marking and acceptance of safety or free zones where children find relief from mounting tensions of the chase. Among the preadolescents, however, safety zones are more than geo-graphical spaces to which children flee to escape threatening agents. For preadolescents, the areas serve as both physical and psychological havens where the children reflect on and talk about the meaning of their experiences. In this way, the preadolescents have more direct control over the meaning of the play and collectively create shared histories of the events.

Thorne found that episodes of chasing sometimes entwined with *rituals of pollution* in playground activities. Rituals of pollution are play routines or rituals in which specific individuals or groups are treated as contaminated (as in "having cooties"). Pollution games have been observed in many parts of the world (Opie & Opie, 1969; Samuelson, 1980). Thorne found that variants of "cootie games" were very much a part of cross-gender conflict and teasing in that while "girls and boys may transfer cooties to one another, and girls may give cooties to girls, boys do not generally give cooties to boys" (1993, p. 74). Thus, girls are central to pollution games that contribute to boys' power and control over them. In fact, boys sometimes treat objects associated with girls as polluting and threatening to their status in all boy groups.

Like pollution games, the final type of borderwork, *invasions*, has much to do with power and dominance of boys over girls. Thorne found a pattern, which has been observed repeatedly in similar studies of preadolescent children's activities on playgrounds. The boys in Thorne's study would, individually or in groups, deliberately disrupt the activities of groups of girls (Thorne, 1993, p. 76; also see Grant, 1984; Oswald, Krappman, Chowdhuri, & von Salisch, 1987). Boys ran under girls' jump ropes, kicked their markers from hopscotch grids, and taunted and teased the girls in attempts to disrupt their play. Although boys much more frequently invaded girls' space, there were some interesting exceptions to this pattern. First, while some boys specialized in disruptive behavior, the majority of the boys were not drawn to the activity. Thorne suggests that the frequent disrupters may have acted like bullies in their behaviors with peers more generally. Second, Thorne described a small number of fifth- and sixth-grade girls who organized themselves into what she called troupes and roamed the playground in search of action. These girls would often chase boys. The leaders of these troupes were often tall, well-developed girls who somewhat intimidated the boys.

These exceptions are important because they draw our attention to the complexity of interpreting the importance of borderwork. Borderwork, like the jump rope activities among the Swedish preadolescents in Evaldsson's study, is play, but in the play children address issues that are of serious concern. In this way the key feature of these types of play is ambiguity and tension. However, this tension is what makes the activities so appealing to children.

Thorne rightly points out that a good deal of borderwork tips the balance of power to boys, because they are frequently the aggressors, control more space, and seem not to suffer from any negative implications that might be associated with engaging in such rituals. Furthermore, borderwork often supports gender stereotypes and exaggerates gender differences. As a result, girls are clearly more apt to be adversely affected by the negative elements of borderwork than boys. However, Thorne argues that borderwork does create a space where preadolescent girls and boys can come together to experiment and to reflect on how to relate to one another. The trick is how to encourage changes in or set limits to some types of borderwork to preserve that space and the delicate play frame while evening the balance of power, which more often than not now tilts in the boys' direction.

Challenging adult authority and norms

Preadolescents, like preschoolers, see adults as having ultimate power over their everyday lives. Possessed of increased autonomy on the one hand and a lack of adult status on the other, preadolescents continually find themselves at odds with adults. Their challenges to adult authority are at once more subtle and more direct than those of preschoolers, and these challenges are shared and evaluated more reflectively in their peer cultures.

Consider some findings from an innovative study of the corridor behavior of elementary school children by Don Ratcliff (1994). Ratcliff found that the children most frequently moved about hallways in phalanxes. He defined a *phalanx* as two or more people side by side, usually facing the same direction and moving at least temporarily toward some presumed destination. Members of phalanxes normally engage in communication as they move.

The general rule in the elementary school was for children to move as quietly as possible in the halls in files. As a result, moving in phalanxes in hallways was valued in the peer culture, because it gave children control of their interactive space, enabled them to talk and be with friends, and allowed them to challenge the authority of teachers all at the same time. Ratcliff found that "kids like phalanxes." Some children noted that they felt happy, cool, bad, excited, and "as good as anybody else when they were in the phalanx" (1994). In interviews with teachers, Ratcliff found that some teachers saw phalanxes as disruptive but seldom enforced the rule against them. One teacher admitted talking to other teachers in hallway phalanxes and therefore, saw it as hypocritical to forbid them. The children were probably well aware of the teachers' double bind in this situation, and this may have made the behavior even more meaningful and enjoyable for them.

Most preadolescents enjoy getting the upper hand with teachers and parents. They often mock adult rules and imitate and exaggerate adults' communicative styles in rule enforcement. For example, Parker (1991) talks about middle school basketball players who complained about their coaches' strict adherence to practice drills. During a practice drill the players were expected to practice only fundamental basketball moves. As they gathered before practice, the boys would violate this philosophy by dribbling through their legs, throwing passes behind their backs, and taking thirty-foot jump shots. Preadolescents also enjoy creating dramas in which they recall past events involving teachers and parents disciplining them for misbehavior. In these narratives, children often act out the roles of adult authority figures, taking care to precisely capture and mock their voices, expressions, and gestures (Elder, 1988; Fine, 1987; Davies, 1982). Often, certain children become widely known and popular in peer culture for their ability to impersonate, mock, and make fun of adults.

Unlike preschoolers, who sometimes balk at adult authority and rules but eventually give in, preadolescents are much more likely to stand their ground against adult rules. Preadolescents are especially sensitive to what they see as adult hypocrisy and injustice and band together to demand their rights. [. . .] For some preadolescents the challenging of adult authority goes beyond talking back, arguing, or pointing out injustices. In fact, actively defying adult authority, challenging adult rules, and receiving disciplinary action often comes to be valued among preadolescents. Thus, earning a reputation as a troublemaker can result in higher status in the peer group (Adler, Kless, & Adler, 1992). Although challenging adult authority and being in trouble was more highly valued among males, Adler, Kless, and Adler also found that girls who participated in taboo activities or who belonged to a wild or fast crowd were highly popular in their peer culture (1992, p. 179).

Summary

In this chapter we examined the peer cultures of preadolescent children and defined preadolescence as the period from seven to thirteen years of age. Given the lack of research on preadolescent culture in non-Western societies, and because children in these societies often take on adult responsibilities in preadolescence, our discussion focused primarily on Western societies. We were, however, careful to consider racial, ethnic, and social class differences in our review.

We first considered the relation between friendship, social differentiation, and gender. Preadolescents, compared to preschool children, have developed more stable concepts of friendship, and they strive to make their interactions with peers fit their developing conceptions of how best friends should behave with one another. One result of these attempts to link cognitive concepts and behavior is increasing social differentiation in the peer culture. As pre-adolescents forge social alliances and secure friendship relations with peers they also separate themselves from others. These processes of separation are most apparent in gender differentiation in peer interaction, which reaches its peak in preadolescence. Many theorists argue that gender differentiation affects and is affected by deep, dichotomous, and universal gender differences (that is, by the very nature of being male or female). According to this view women have a different voice in that they value relationships and caring for others, while men are concerned about individual rights and notions of justice. These differences have been found among preadolescents, where studies show that girls' concerns center around the valuing of compliance and conformity, romantic love, and an ideology of domesticity, while boys' concerns revolve around a cult of masculinity, around physical contests, autonomy, and self-reliance. Other theorists challenge this separate culture view of peer relations. They argue that the examination of naturally occurring peer interaction in a wide range of social settings and groups reveals a good deal of gender mixing in preadolescent peer relations. Further, these studies of children's situated activities (activities produced in diverse settings by children who have long interactional histories) document a greater complexity in gender relations in preadolescence, which challenges the separate culture view.

Studies of situated activities also provide important information on preadolescent children's lore (games, jokes, riddles, songs, and verbal and behavioral routines) and how children in the process of engaging in these activities address issues related to self, identity, and autonomy from adult control. Our discussion of situated activities focused most specifically on children's games, verbal dispute routines, and cross-gender play and rituals. Evaldsson and Goodwin's studies of the actual play of jump rope and hopscotch within children's peer cultures over time revealed that these games were much more complex than earlier studies, which focused only on the rules and structures of the games, had claimed. Evaldsson found that the preadolescents not only developed certain physical, communicative, and cognitive skills in playing jump rope, but that they also used the game as an arena for addressing personal concerns, feelings, and uncertainties regarding gender relations. Goodwin's research demonstrated the importance of cultural variation in the play of games. She found that African-American and Latina girls took the rules of hopscotch very seriously, engaged in highly complex and dramatic debates about rule enforcement, and teased each other regarding poor performances. This style of play contrasted with that of the middle-class white girls, who often overlooked rule violations and mitigated their responses to their peers' miscues. These findings, along with those from Goodwin's documentation of the complex linguistic structure and importance of conflict rituals like the he-said-she-said dispute routine, show how conflict and cooperation are often overlapping processes that are embedded in the larger ethos of playfulness. Goodwin's work also demonstrates the importance of comparative work for documenting differences in preadolescent peer cultures across sociocultural groups.

How conflict can sometimes contribute to the social organization of preadolescent peer relations and can generate creative tension in preadolescent peer relations also was evident in Thorne's work on borderwork. Borderwork refers to activities that mark and strengthen boundaries between groups. In her study of cross-gender relations among preadolescents, Thorne identified three types of borderwork (contests, chases, and invasions) that heightened the awareness of gender and gender differences. Contests were initiated by children and teachers that transformed classroom lessons and peer games into competitions of boys against girls. Chases, like contests, were competitive, but they were more symbolic in their affirmation of boundaries between boys and girls. In chases boys often taunt and tease girls in line with the aggressive nature of boys' peer culture, while the girls threaten the boys with kissing or affection, resulting in "chase-and-kiss" games. Chases are often intertwined with rituals of pollution, where specific groups are treated as contaminated (as in "having cooties"). It is girls who are normally seen as contaminated in cross-gender chases, and in this way the borderwork often contributes to boys' power over girls. The final type of borderwork, invasions, also has much to do with power and dominance of boys over girls. Thorne found that some boys invade girls' space and purposely disrupt their play and taunt and tease them. Despite some exceptions, Thorne concluded that girls are clearly more apt to be adversely affected by the negative elements of borderwork than boys. She argued that there were creative elements in borderwork and suggested that adults might be able to encourage changes and limits to some types of borderwork, which preserve the creative elements while evening the balance of power between girls and boys.

Overall, preadolescence is a time when children struggle to gain stable identities, and their peer cultures provide both a sense of autonomy from adults and an arena for dealing with uncertainties of an increasingly complex world. The many positive features of their peer cultures (for example, verbal routines, games, and enduring friendships) allow preadolescents to hold on to their childhoods a little longer, while simultaneously preparing themselves for the transition to adolescence. A crucial factor in preadolescent peer culture is children's ability to reflect on and evaluate the meaning of their changing worlds in talk with each other and with adults. In this sense, preadolescents become aware of themselves as individual actors in the collective production of their peer cultures. They also come to recognize how their peer cultures affect and are affected by the more general adult world.

References

Adler, P. A., Kless, S., & Adler, P. (1992). Socialization to gender roles: Popularity among elementary school boys and girls. *Sociology of Education*, 65, 169–187.

Barnes, M. & Vangelisti, A. (1995). Speaking in a double-voice: Role making as influence in preschoolers' fantasy play situations. *Research on Language and Social Interaction*, 28, 351–389.

Bereiter, C. & Engleman, S. (1966). *Teaching disadvantaged children in the preschool*. Englewood Cliffs, NJ: Prentice-Hall.

Berentzen, S. (1984). Children constructing their social world. University of Bergen: Bergen Studies in Social Anthropology, No. 36.

Best, R. (1983). *We've all got scars*. Bloomington, IN: Indiana University Press.

Corsaro, W. (1985). *Friendship and peer culture in the early years*. Norwood, NJ: Ablex.

Corsaro, W. & Rosier, K. (1992). Documenting productive-reproductive processes in children's lives: Transition narratives of a Black family living in poverty. In W. Corsaro & P. Miller (Eds.). *Interpretive approaches to children's socialization*, (p. 69–93). New Directions for Child Development, No. 58, San Francisco: Jossey-Bass.

Davies, B. (1982). *Life in the classroom and playground: The accounts of primary school children*. Boston: Routledge and Kegan Paul.

Eder, D. (1995). *School talk: Gender and adolescent culture*. New Brunswick, NJ: Rutgers University Press.

Eder, D. & Parker, S. (1987). The cultural production and reproduction of gender: The effects of extra-curricular activities on peer group culture. *Sociology of Education*, 60, 200–213.

Ellis, S., Rogoff, B., & Cromer, C. (1981). Age segregation in children's social interaction. *Developmental Psychology*, 17, 399–407.

Evaldsson, A. (1993). *Play, disputes and social order: Everyday life in two Swedish after-school centers*. Linköping, Sweden: Linköping University.

Fine, G. A. (1987). *With the boys: Little league baseball and preadolescent culture*. Chicago: University of Chicago Press.

Gilligan, C. (1982). *In a different voice: Psychological theory and women's development.* Cambridge, MA: Harvard University Press.

Gomme, A. (1964). *The traditional games of England, Scotland, and Ireland.* Vol. 2. New York: Dover.

Goodwin, M. (1985). The serious side of jump rope: Conversational practices and social organization in the frame of play. *Folklore,* 98, 315–30.

Goodwin, M. (1990). *He-said-she-said: Talk as social organization among black children.* Bloomington: Indiana University Press.

Goodwin, M. (In press). Games of stance: Conflict and footing in hopscotch. In S. Hoyle & C. Adger (Eds.), *Language practices of older children.* New York: Oxford University Press.

Gottman, J. (1986). The world of coordinated play: Same- and cross-sex friendships in young children. In J. Gottman & J. Parker (Eds.), *Conversations among friends: Speculations on affective development.* New York: Cambridge University Press.

Grant, I. (1984). Gender roles and statuses in school children's peer interactions. *Western Sociological Review,* 14, 58–76.

Hare-Mustin, R. & Maracek, J. (1988). The meaning of difference: Gender theory, post-modernism, and psychology. *American Psychologist,* 43, 455–464.

Katriel, T. (1985). Brogez: ritual and strategy in Israeli children's conflicts. *Language in Society,* 16, 467–90.

Katriel, T. (1987). *"Bexibùdim!"*: Ritualized sharing among Israeli children. *Language in Society,* 16: 305–20.

Knapp, M. & Knapp, H. (1976). *One potato, two potato: The secret education of American children.* New York: Norton.

Labov, W. (1972). *Language in the inner city: Studies in Black English vernacular.* Philadelphia: Pennsylvania University Press.

Lever, J. (1978). Sex differences in the complexity of children's play and games. *American Sociological Review,* 43, 471–483.

Lockheed, M. (1985). Some determinants and consequences of sex segregation in the classroom. In L. Wilkinson & C. Marrett (Eds.), *Gender influences in classroom interaction* (pp. 167–184). New York: Academic Press.

Maltz, D. & Borker, R. (1982). A cultural approach to male–female miscommunication. In J. Gumperz (Ed.), *Communication, language, and social identity* (pp. 196–216). New York: Cambridge University Press.

Maynard, D. (1985). On the functions of social conflict among children. *American Sociological Review,* 50, 207–223.

McDowell, J. (1979). *Children's riddling.* Bloomington, IN: Indiana University Press.

Opie, I. & Opie, P. (1969). *Children's games in street and playground.* Oxford, England: Clarendon Press.

Oswald, H., Krappman, L., Chowdhuri, I., & von Salisch, M. (1987). Gaps and bridges: Interactions between girls and boys in elementary school. In P. A. Adler & P. Adler (Eds.), *Sociological Studies of Child Development,* vol. 2 (pp. 205–223). Greenwich, CT: JAI Press.

Parker, S. (1991). *Early adolescent male cultures: The importance of organized and informal sport.* Ph.D. Dissertation, Indiana University, Bloomington, IN.

Parker, J. & Gottman, J. (1989). Social and emotional development in a relational context: friendship interaction from early childhood. In T. Brendt & G. Ladd (Eds.), *Peer relationships in child development,* (pp. 95–112). New York: Wiley.

Parrott, S. (1979). Games children play: Ethnography of a second-grade recess. In J. Spradley & D. McCurdy (Eds.), *The cultural experience*, (pp. 206–19). Chicago: Science Research Associates.

Ratcliff, D. (1994). *An elementary school hallway: Scoial formations and meanings outside the classroom*. Ph.D. Dissertation, University of Georgia, Athens, GA.

Rizzo, T. (1989). *Friendship development among children in school*. Norwood, NJ: Ablex.

Samuelson, S. (1980). The cooties complex. *Western Folklore*, 39, 198–210.

Schofield, J. (1982). *Black and white in school*. New York: Praeger.

Sluckin, A. (1981). *Growing up in the playground*. London: Routledge and Kegan Paul.

Tannen, D. (1990). *You just don't understand: Women and men in conversation*. New York: Morrow.

Thorne, B. (1993). *Gender play: Girls and boys in school*. New Brunswick, NJ: Rutgers University Press.

Thorne, B. & Luria, Z. (1986). Sexuality and gender in children's daily worlds. *Social Problems*, 33, 176–190.

Whiting, B. & Edwards, C. P. (1988). *Children of different worlds: The formation of social behavior*. Cambridge, MA: Harvard University Press.

Chapter 3

Friendships in adolescence*

Thomas J. Berndt

[. . .]

The adolescent agenda and the functions of friendship

Each developmental period has its own agenda, that is, its own list of tasks that a person must accomplish. On the adolescent agenda are four items that partly explain the functions of friendships during this period. First, adolescents gradually move out of the family circle and become more independent (Csikszentmihalyi & Larson, 1984). They do not want to become solitary individuals, however. They enjoy having companions who like the same activities. Friends partly replace parents and siblings as companions for adolescents. Stated differently, companionship is an important function of adolescents' friendships.

Second, as adolescents become more independent of their families, they need to find a place for themselves in a new and complex social world (Berndt & Perry, 1990). This new world is largely populated with *peers* – other adolescents who are the same or similar in age. Thus a second function of friendships is to give adolescents a sense of belonging in the social world and allies in navigating through that world. For example, friends can provide support for each other by giving each other help and advice. Intimate conversations with friends can also increase adolescents' self-esteem and self-confidence.

Third, adolescents begin to form their own *identity* – a set of ideas about who they are and what they can do with their lives (Erikson, 1963). Interactions with friends can play a major role in identity formation: On the one hand, support from friends can help adolescents form a positive identity; on the other hand, friends can challenge an adolescent's emerging identity. Adolescents often compare their performance in school, sports, or other activities to that of their friends. These comparisons can lead to rivalry and

---

* This is an edited version of a chapter that appeared in *A lifetime of relationships*, Pacific Grove, CA: Brooks/Cole, 1996.

competition. The intensity of this rivalry and competition can affect adolescents' self-concepts and their social behavior.

Fourth, adolescents need to learn not only about themselves but also about the larger society. Adolescents gradually develop ideas and opinions about other people, social organizations, and legal and political systems (Keating, 1990; Torney-Purta, 1990). Their ideas and opinions are shaped by discussions with friends. Their behavior is also influenced by their friends' behavior. Influences of these types define yet another function of friendships in adolescents' lives. [. . .]

4) The first section of this chapter focuses on the place of friendships in the peer social world. We will discuss not only friendships between pairs of adolescents but also how these pairs link to form groups of friends. The second section focuses on both the positive and the negative qualities of friendships. Special emphasis is given to *intimacy* – a feeling of closeness and understanding that makes adolescents willing to reveal personal information to friends; but, as mentioned earlier, friends may also engage in competition and rivalry that leads to conflicts. The third section focuses on the processes and outcomes of friends' influence on each other. A central issue in this section is the popular belief – more a myth than a reality – that peer pressure often contributes to undesirable behavior by adolescents.

The place of friendships in the world of peers

Adolescents interact with peers during classes at school, when playing sports and other games, and even when working at after-school jobs. They feel most comfortable in these various settings when they have formed close relationships with a few peers whom they view as best friends. You can begin to understand the peer social world by learning how many best friends adolescents typically have, how these friendships form, and how stable they are.

Best friends: one, some, or many?

In Mark Twain's novels, Huck Finn was Tom Sawyer's best friend. In an Old Testament story, Jonathan was David's best friend. These and other examples from literature portray each adolescent as having one best friend and suggest that these pairs of friends travel through their social world together.

In real life, however, when adolescents are asked to name their best friends, they often name several peers (Savin-Williams & Berndt, 1990). The number that they name varies depending on what, exactly, they are asked, but most adolescents asked a general question will name four or five best friends (Hartup, 1993a). Sex differences in the number of best-friend nominations are seldom significant – boys and girls name about the same number.

Not all the best friendships named by adolescents are equally close.

Adolescents usually interact significantly more often with one best friend than with their other best friends (Berndt & Keefe, 1993). They also distinguish between their group of best friends and other peers whom they consider just friends (Hallinan & Williams, 1987). In other words, adolescents limit the number of peers they label as best friends, but they normally have a few best friends rather than only one.

Why do most adolescents have more than one best friend? This question can be answered in several ways. One answer is that an adolescent's very closest friend usually has other friends. When the adolescent and the closest friend get together with the other friends, a friendship group emerges (Brown, 1990; Hirsch & Renders, 1986). Often, all adolescents in the group will consider one another best friends.

Another answer focuses on the benefits of having a few best friends. An adolescent with only one best friend will not have a companion for activities if the best friend has a doctor's appointment or a big assignment to finish. Moreover, suppose that the adolescent and his or her friend have a serious argument and stop speaking to each other for a while. If they have no other friends, they will not have a companion for activities until they settle their argument. Adolescents who have a few best friends are not as likely to be socially isolated in these circumstances (Davies, 1982). In short, a friendship group fulfills one major function of friendship better than does a single best friend.

A third answer to the question states the same points more abstractly. Pairs of friends are the smallest units in the social structure of the peer world, which also includes larger and more complex units. Pairs link into groups as friendships form between adolescents and their friends' friends. Groups of best friends are then linked by weaker ties to other groups, giving the entire structure cohesiveness and stability. Such a structure provides a place for each adolescent and gives each adolescent a sense of belonging.

Making friends: the role of similarity

The division of the peer social world into friendship groups is far from random. Most often, adolescents become friends with peers similar to themselves. Friendships usually form between adolescents who are similar in age, sex, race or ethnicity, and social class (Kandel, 1978; Savin-Williams & Berndt, 1990). Friends' similarity in these characteristics partly reflects the structure of their social world. Friendships can form only between adolescents who have opportunities for social interaction. School and neighborhoods are often segregated by age, race or ethnicity, and social class, so adolescents can most easily interact with peers like themselves on those characteristics.

Of course, schools and neighborhoods are not usually segregated by sex, so the predominance of same-sex friendships has other causes. As mentioned earlier, adolescents prefer friends with whom they can enjoy activities, and girls and boys differ in their activity preferences. For example, boys enjoy sports more than girls do, and girls enjoy talking on the phone more than boys do (Zarbatany, Hartmann, & Rankin, 1990). In addition, boys' style of interaction is rougher and less polite than that of girls, which lessens girls' eagerness to spend time with boys (Maccoby, 1988). Opposite-sex friendships become more common near the end of adolescence, during the senior high years (Epstein, 1983). However, these friendships are seldom like the same-sex friendships of younger adolescents. Instead, opposite-sex friendships often seem to represent a stage in the development of romantic relationships.

Activity preferences also affect choices of same-sex friends. For example, adolescents who are in a youth organization such as the Boy Scouts often become friends with other adolescents in that organization, and adolescents who belong to athletic teams often become friends with other players on their team. The possible bases for friends' similarity in activities are as diverse as the activities of adolescents themselves.

One particularly important basis for forming friendships is similarity in academic achievement (Epstein, 1983). Friends' similarity in achievement has multiple sources. Students similar in achievement often have the same classes, so they have more opportunities for social interaction. They also tend to be similar in their preferences for activities. They are likely to agree, for example, on whether to spend a weekend doing a school project or hanging out at the mall. Therefore, they are likely to be more dependable companions for each other. A third source of friends' similarity in achievement is adolescents' concern with equality. In an early book on moral development, Piaget (1932/1965) argued that peer relationships are based on equality. Peers have no authority over each other, so they are assumed to respect each other as equals. Friends, in particular, think of themselves as equal in all important respects. including academic achievement. One junior high girl described a best friend by saying, "She's in the middle-level math class and I am too, so I know that she's not smarter than I am and I'm not smarter than she is." To this girl – and to many other adolescents – equality in academic achievement is a sign of equality between peers and is a requirement for friendship.

The emphasis on equality between friends adds further structure to the peer social world. An adolescent's position in the social world partly depends on the activity preferences, athletic ability, and academic achievement of his or her friends. In other words, adolescents' reputations are affected by the groups to which they belong (Brown, 1990). Moreover, their reputation affects the formation of their own identity. Having a definite position in the social world also eases the task of making friends with similar adolescents. On the other hand, belonging to a specific group can limit an adolescent's ability to make friends with adolescents in different groups.

Some adolescents deliberately set out to make friends with peers who are different from themselves. These adolescents recognize the structure of the peer social world and want to change their own place in that structure. Some try to make friends with the most popular peers in the school and become part of their group (Hirsch & Renders, 1986). But not all adolescents seeking to change their position in the structure are social climbers or status seekers. Some avoid the popular group, because they consider it snobbish, and make friends with peers who care less about the outward signs of social success (Eder, 1985).

Even adolescents who are not so calculating usually prefer that their friends be well liked by other adolescents rather than disliked. They also prefer that their friends do well at school rather than be low achievers (Cauce, 1986). Thus when adolescents make friends they strike a balance between seeking friends similar to themselves and seeking friends whom they perceive as different from themselves in desirable ways. How they strike this balance is critical to their social lives, because it determines their position in the social world. It is also critical to their self-concept and, therefore, to their personality development.

Friendship stability

Most friendships among adolescents last not for a few days or weeks, but for months or even years (Savin-Williams & Berndt, 1990). This high degree of stability is characteristic of both boys' and girls' friendships. Apparently, the same conditions that affect the formation of friendships also increase their stability.

For example, opportunities for social interactions with peers tend to remain stable. Adolescent friends typically have a similar schedule of classes, ride the same school bus, or live in the same neighborhood for a year or more. In addition, their preferences for activities and their levels of academic achievement are fairly stable across months or years. Thus the same conditions that initially bring friends together often keep them together. These conditions give friends many opportunities for interaction with each other and fewer opportunities for interactions with other peers. Stated more generally, once adolescents have a place in the peer social world, they tend to keep that place. One part of keeping a place is keeping the same group of friends.

Some writers have suggested that adolescents benefit if they lack stable friendships and, instead, change their friends regularly (see Savin-Williams & Berndt, 1990). These writers assume that adolescents can get "stuck" with a group of friends, even as their own characteristics change. Under these circumstances, the argument goes, adolescents who stick with their old friends will miss opportunities to become friends with people whose interests more closely match their own.

There is some truth to this argument. Adolescents need to be able to make new friends as they meet new people and choose new activities. Frequent changes in friends, however, are typical not of socially successful adolescents but of adolescents who have social and psychological problems (Hartup, 1983, 1993a). Adolescents with less stable friendships are generally less well liked by their peers, are viewed less positively by teachers, and more often suffer from emotional disorders. These adolescents do not get along well with their friends and so cannot find a secure place for themselves in the peer world. The instability of their friendships is not a sign of their psychological growth; on the contrary, it reflects their inability to find a friendship group that they consider acceptable and that welcomes them.

Developmental changes in the peer social world

Children generally name more best friends than adolescents name, and adolescents name more than adults name. One reason is that children differentiate little between types of relationships – young children sometimes say that all their classmates are their best friends. As children grow older, they begin to contrast friendships that are especially important with those that are less important. As children move into adolescence, they distinguish even more sharply between best friendships and other friendships.

Adolescents begin to reserve the label of *best friend* for the few peers with whom they have a particularly close relationship (Berndt & Hoyle, 1985).

The differentiation among social relationships continues into adulthood. Adults typically make very fine distinctions among social relationships (Duck, 1991; Matthews, 1986). To exaggerate a bit, adults place the people they know into categories like best friend (singular), close friends, good friends, "just" friends, coworkers, neighbors, acquaintances, and strangers. Consequently, many adults assume that adolescents can *really* have only one best friend. When adults make this assumption, they are using a definition of best friendship that holds for them but not for most adolescents. As adolescents move toward adulthood, however, their definitions of friendship become more adultlike.

Similarity is important for friendship formation not only in adolescence, but also in childhood and adulthood. Changes occur, however, in the type of similarity that most affects friendship formation. During early adolescence, friends are most similar in objective characteristics such as where they go to school. During middle and late adolescence, similarity in psychological characteristics is more strongly related to the formation of friendships (Duck, 1975).

Friendships may also be affected by developmental changes in the social structure of the larger peer group. Friendship groups with well-defined identities first emerge in early adolescence (Crockett, Losoff, & Petersen, 1984). During those years, the social structure of the world of peers may be most rigid. In late adolescence, near the end of high school, the social structure seems to become more flexible (Brown, 1990). Adolescents change their groups more freely and form friendships with peers in very different groups. Perhaps old boundaries between groups seem unimportant because high school seniors realize that graduation will bring an end to a social world that has defined their lives for years. Unfortunately, too little is known about this phase of adolescence to make this hypothesis more than a guess.

Finally, best friendships seem about as stable during adolescence as they were during the elementary school years (Berndt & Hoyle, 1985). However, it is impossible to draw definite conclusions until changes in adolescents' friendships are studied more carefully.

Qualities of friendship: support and conflicts

The qualities of adolescents' friendships may have stronger effects on their psychological development than the number of friendships they have or the stability of these friendships. When adolescents describe their friendships, they mention many positive qualities (Berndt, 1986; Youniss & Smollar, 1985). For example, they say that friends help them when they have problems and make them feel better when they are upset. In more general terms, friends provide support for one another. Adolescents also mention negative qualities of friendship, however. For example, they say that their friends sometimes annoy them and boss them around. These behaviors are often the source of conflicts between friends. Both positive and negative qualities, or support and conflict, are important for a complete description of friendships. We will consider positive qualities first because they have received more emphasis in major theories.

Intimate friendships as supportive relationships

As mentioned earlier, one function of friendships is to support adolescents as they adjust to the many changes in their lives. Most theorists agree that the central element of a supportive friendship is its intimacy (Berndt, 1989; East & Rook, 1992; Sullivan, 1953; Youniss, 1980). During intimate conversations, best friends provide practical advice and emotional support for each other. Friends' support enhances adolescents' self-esteem and improves their ability to cope with stressful events. Intimate conversations in which a friend shares personal information also give adolescents a better understanding of other people and a broadened perspective on the world.

The benefits of intimate conversations are suggested by an eighth-grade girl's comments about her friendship with Sally, another eighth-grader:

> Sally is my best friend because she never tells my secrets. She understands what I'm going through, because she has the same problems that I do. Her parents are divorced and my parents were divorced, and now they're back together but they're not married. She understands what I mean when I talk about that.

The comments about Sally illustrate some facets of an intimate friendship.

Most important, intimacy involves self-disclosure. Adolescents can tell their best friends all their secrets and problems. Intimacy also involves trust. Adolescents can tell secrets to friends without worrying that the friend will tell others. In addition, intimacy involves understanding and emotional support. Adolescents know that their best friends can appreciate how they feel and give them good advice about how to solve their problems. This girl's comments also suggest that her conversations with Sally have helped her cope with her parents' divorce and its aftermath.

Intimacy first becomes an important feature of friendships in adolescence (Douvan & Adelson, 1966; Savin-Williams & Berndt, 1990). When adolescents are asked to complete questionnaires designed to measure the quality of their friendships they typically rate their friendships higher on the items measuring intimacy than do children (e.g. Berndt & Keefe, 1993). In addition, when adolescents describe their friendships in response to open-ended questions, they mention intimate conversations with friends more often than children do. [. . .]

The emergence of intimate friendships during adolescence has also been documented in other cultures. Adolescents in the former Soviet Union, Ijo adolescents in Nigeria, and adolescents from the Inuit tribe in the Canadian Arctic all described intimate conversations as central to their friendships (Condon, 1987; Hollos & Leis, 1989; Kon, 1981).

During adolescence girls have more intimate friendships than boys do, both in the United States and in other cultures (Berndt, in press; Youniss & Smollar, 1985). Several kinds of evidence have shown this sex difference: When adolescents describe their ideas about friendship, girls refer to intimacy more often than boys do; when describing their own friendships, girls give higher ratings for intimacy than boys do. In addition, more boys than girls say they would not share intimate information with friends because they think the friends might tease or laugh at them. You should *not* conclude from these findings that adolescent girls have intimate friendships and adolescent boys lack them. Rather, you should assume that the level of intimacy in friendships is higher, on the average, for girls than for boys.

Both the functions of intimate friendships and the benefits of intimate conversations are easier to appreciate when you know the usual topics of these conversations (Hollos & Leis, 1989; Gottman & Mettetal, 1986; Raffaeli & Duckett, 1989; Rawlins & Holl, 1987). Many of these conversations can be described as gossip. Adolescents talk with friends about the appearance, activities, and personalities of their peers. They talk about the peers they like, the peers they dislike, and the reasons for their feelings. These conversations are valuable in helping adolescents understand their social world and judge the standards for behavior in that world. Gossip about peers is more common in girls' conversations than in boys' conversations. Boys, by contrast, spend more time than girls talking about sports. Boys and girls also talk about their experiences at school and their leisure activities. These conversations help adolescents make decisions about how to spend their time both in work and in play.

Some conversations between friends, like those of the eighth-grade girl with her friend Sally, are about family relationships. Others are about sexuality, and others are about life plans or other decisions. These conversations are less frequent than gossip or most of the other topics mentioned earlier. However, their frequency is probably not a good indication of their importance. Frequent or not, such conversations may be critical to adolescents for understanding the peer social world, forming an identity, and shaping beliefs about the larger society.

Other features of supportive friendships

Intimacy is not the only important feature of a supportive friendship. Another feature is prosocial behavior. Prosocial behavior includes helping, sharing, and comforting another. Also part of a good friendship is self-esteem support. Friends bolster adolescents' self-esteem by praising them for their accomplishments or encouraging them when they feel bad about something. These features may be especially important to adolescents as they form an identity and develop a distinct self-concept.

One feature of a supportive friendship is loyalty (Berndt, 1986). Stated informally, adolescents expect their friends to act like friends when they are around other people. Loyal friends stick up for you in a fight with other kids, don't talk about you behind your back, and don't leave you for somebody else. Remember that adolescents live in a complex social world composed of loosely connected friendship groups. Adolescents need friends who will stand by them when they have quarrels with peers from another group. They don't want their friends to abandon them and join other groups.

The features of supportive friendships explain why these friendships are so valuable to adolescents. Adolescents' development must be enhanced by having friends who talk with them about their joys and sorrows, who help them when they are in need, who encourage them, and who are loyal. Adolescents whose friendships have these supportive features also have better psychological health than those whose friendships lack them (Berndt & Savin-Williams, 1993; Cauce, 1986; Kurdek & Sinclair, 1988). Adolescents who have supportive friendships have higher self-esteem and suffer less often from loneliness, anxiety, and emotional problems. When interacting with other people, these adolescents are more generous and helpful than other adolescents. They also have more positive attitudes toward school and higher levels of academic achievement. The relation of supportive friendships to psychological health has been found for both white and African-American adolescents in the United States and for adolescents in several other countries.

Although the evidence from research is impressive, it leaves one question open: Do supportive friendships actually improve psychological health, or do psychologically healthy adolescents form more supportive friendships? Perhaps adolescents with emotional problems and low self-esteem are so self-absorbed or so timid that they have difficulty developing supportive friendships. By tracking changes in friendships and psychological health over time, researchers have obtained a tentative answer to this question (Berndt, 1989; House, Umberson, & Landis, 1988). Adolescents' psychological health does affect their ability to form supportive friendships. But having supportive friendships also affects psychological health. That is, the direction of effects goes both ways – support from friends has an impact on adolescents' psychological adjustment and vice versa.

Developmental changes in friends' support

You know already that intimacy emerges as an important feature of friendship in early adolescence. Many years ago Sullivan (1953) suggested that intimate friendships first appear in the preadolescent years, the years just before puberty. Later research has not confirmed this hypothesis. Although children can rate their friendships on intimacy items in friendship questionnaires, they rarely make comments that suggest they have an intimate friendship. For example, children rarely say that they share secrets with friends or that they talk about their worries and fears with friends. By contrast, sixth- and seventh-graders often mention their ability to share intimate information with friends and their friends' understanding of them.

After intimacy emerges as a feature of friendships, its level does not change consistently with age. Some evidence suggests that intimacy in friendships increases during adolescence (Blyth & Traeger, 1988), but other evidence suggests that it does not (Furman & Buhrmester, 1992). Evidence on any changes in friends' prosocial behavior and loyalty is equally mixed (Berndt & Perry, 1990). During adulthood, intimacy continues to be the most central feature of close friendships (Clark & Reis, 1988; Matthews, 1986). Prosocial behavior, self-esteem support, and loyalty are other features of supportive friendships among adults. We can conclude, therefore, that adolescence is the period in which friendships first develop all the features of supportive social relationships (Berndt, 1989).

Conflicts in friendship

Of course, friendships are not always supportive. Friends have arguments with each other and sometimes even fight with each other. Despite their many similarities, friends often have different ideas, opinions, and preferences. These differences can lead to disagreements and then to conflicts. Under some conditions, conflicts may be more frequent between friends than between other peers because friends feel more free to state their views openly. In other words, friends are less concerned with behaving in a polite way (Hartup, 1993b).

The special nature of friendship can also contribute to interactions between friends that can sometimes have negative overtones. Remember that Piaget (1932/1965) assumed that equality and mutual respect are the hallmarks of peer relationships. Friends, in particular, are expected to view one another as equals. Yet Piaget was mistaken when he assumed that all peer relationships, and all friendships, are based on equality. As noted earlier, the motive for equality is opposed by strong motives to prove one's own competence through competition with others. Because friends often compare their performance, competition with close friends can be especially intense, although not always negative (Duck & Wood, 1995). This intensity is illustrated by the following comments of an eighth-grade boy about his friend Matt:

> We both play the drums, but I'm the lead drummer. We had a parade and I had a solo part on the drums. Matt wanted to do my solo halfway through the parade but I told him no. We're rivals on that, and on other things. In sports, Matt says he's better than I am, but how good he does in schoolwork doesn't count to him – he admits defeat at schoolwork.

This boy and his friend Matt compete in many areas. They constantly compete in playing the drum and in sports. Apparently, they once competed in academics, but this competition ended when Matt conceded that he isn't as good a student as his friend is. Friends may compete on other things too. One friend may claim to be more popular than the other. One friend may come from a wealthier family or have more expensive and stylish clothes than the other does.

Abraham Tesser (1984), a social psychologist, has suggested that competition and the conflicts that it provokes are common in all close relationships. Competition exists because people in close relationships often engage in social comparison: They compare their own performance in important domains with the performance of their relationship partner. If their performance is inferior to that of the partner, they are upset. In response, they may compete more intensely as they try to equal their partner. Or they may reduce the closeness of their relationship with their partner or even end the relationship.

Competition between friends is less intense when the friends have a strong motive to avoid interpersonal conflicts. In studies done a few years ago, Mexican-American children were found to be less competitive and more cooperative with their friends than were Anglo-American children (Kagan & Madsen, 1972). Competition is often discouraged in small, closely knit human groups, such as the Mexican-American population, because serious conflicts could threaten the survival of the entire group.

One anthropologist observed groups of adolescents among the Inuit people in the Canadian Arctic (Condon, 1987). He found that even during athletics these adolescents restrained their competition, trying to assure that neither team lost badly. Three years after doing these observations, the anthropologist returned to observe Inuit adolescents again. During the intervening time, the Inuit had started receiving television programs, and the adolescents had become avid fans of televised sports. When Condon observed adolescents' athletic contests this time, he found that they showed much more competitive behavior than they had before. Apparently, the adolescents' exposure to the competitiveness of the mainstream culture through televised sports had made them more willing to compete with their friends.

Of course, not all competition with friends is undesirable; but when competition is intense and leads to enduring conflicts and negative feelings, its effects are likely to be negative. Adolescents who have frequent conflicts with friends also have frequent conflicts with teachers and classmates because of their annoying and disruptive behavior. In addition, adolescents who have frequent conflicts with friends at the beginning of a school year often exhibit an increase in disruptive behavior at school during the year (Berndt & Keefe, 1993). Apparently, negative interactions with friends spill over and contribute to a generally negative interaction style.

Conflicts between friends can be reduced by focusing on their origins. Conflicts that arise from intense competition and rivalry can be discouraged by giving adolescents a different way of thinking about social comparison. In particular, adolescents can be invited to think about themselves and their friends as having complementary strengths and weaknesses (Tesser, 1984). An adolescent may be better than her or his friend at playing the drum, but the friend may be better at playing basketball. On balance, then, they are equal. Their self-esteem does not depend on proving themselves equal to each other in every arena. In other words, adolescents can be encouraged to think positively about themselves even while recognizing that they are not superior to their peers in all arenas.

Differences of opinion are another source of conflicts between friends. Rather than trying to eliminate all conflicts – an impossible task – adults can train adolescents in the skills needed to resolve conflicts successfully (Laursen, in press). For starters, adolescents need to control their anger during conflicts. They also need to rely on negotiation, rather than coercion, as a strategy for resolving conflicts. Finally, they need to view conflicts not as battles that they must win but as potentially positive events that could increase their understanding of one another. That is, conflicts can be viewed as opportunities to learn about the differences in people's attitudes and ideas. Learning about these differences will give adolescents a more accurate picture of social reality. Thus training in conflict-resolution skills could lead to both harmony between friends and better understanding of other people and society.

Developmental changes in friends' conflicts

Because most theories of friendships have focused on their positive or supportive features, developments in conflicts with friends have received little attention. Berndt & Keefe's (1993) friendship questionnaire, however, does include items on quarrels with friends. It also includes items on competition and rivalry between friends. The two types of items, taken together, assess people's perceptions of the negative features of their friendships.

Judging from children's and adolescents' reports, the frequency of negative interactions with friends changes little with age. Adolescents report about as many negative interactions with friends as children do (Berndt & Perry, 1986). Apparently, the greater social maturity of adolescents does not indicate a greater ability to avoid conflicts with friends. But avoiding the conflicts may not be terribly important, because adolescents also say that these conflicts rarely weaken their friendships and may even strengthen them (Laursen & Collins, in press).

Under certain conditions, conflicts with friends do decrease between childhood and adolescence. For one study (Berndt, Hawkins, & Hoyle, 1986), fourth- and eighth-graders were paired in the fall of the school year with a classmate who was a close friend. The pairs of students then worked on a task that gave them opportunities to share with each other and to earn rewards for their performance. They usually did less well and received fewer rewards when they shared more with the friend. Under these conditions the students had two basic choices: They could compete and try to get the most rewards for themselves, or they could share with the friend and perhaps get fewer rewards than the friend did. In the spring, the students did the same task again with the same partners. By then some students were still close friends with their partners, and some were no longer close friends. How these pairs behaved on the task varied greatly with their age. Fourth-graders who were still close friends shared with each other less than did fourth-graders who were no longer close friends. Fourth-graders who were paired with close friends were so concerned about getting fewer rewards than the friends that they competed rather than sharing. Eighth-graders, on the other hand, shared more and competed less when they were still close friends with their partners than when they were no longer close friends. The pairs of friends said that their goal in the game was to achieve equality in rewards by sharing. The pairs who were no longer friends treated the task as a contest that they could win by competing. The eighth-graders' generosity toward close friends and desire for equality suggest that they placed sensitivity to a friend's feelings above competition (Youniss, 1980).

So, does competition with friends disappear as children move into adolescence? Of course not. The comments from the eighth-grade boy about his rivalry with Matt are anecdotal evidence that adolescents' friendships are not always cooperative, harmonious relationships. Under certain conditions, friends' competition may be more restrained in adolescence than in child-hood, but competition and rivalry are significant features of many adolescent friendships. Remember that adolescents must begin to form their own identity. As they do so, they often want to test themselves in competition with friends.

Myths of peer pressure and the reality of friends' influence

The qualities of adolescents' friendships have been virtually ignored by some writers (e.g., Bronfenbrenner, 1970; Steinberg & Silverberg, 1986). Instead, these writers have emphasized the presumed influence of friends' pressure. In both popular and scholarly writings, the prevailing opinion about such "peer pressure" is entirely negative.

More than three decades ago, Coleman (1961) wrote, "Our society has within its midst a set of small teen-age societies, which focus teen-age inter-ests and attitudes on things far removed from adult responsibilities and which develop standards that lead away from those goals established by the larger society" (p. 9). A few years later, Bronfenbrenner (1970) wrote, "Where the peer group is to a large extent autonomous – as it often is in the United States – it can exert influence in opposition to values held by the adult society" (p. 189). Popular writers echoed this refrain then, and they continue to do so. They argue that peer pressure is a big problem, leading to sexual behavior, delinquency, and drug and alcohol abuse (Ansley & McCleary, 1992).

This view of friends' influence is so misleading that it might be called a myth. The usual assertions about peer pressure are inaccurate in their assump-tions about both the direction and the strength of friends' influence. The following narrative by an eighth-grade girl suggests a starting point for drawing a more accurate picture of friends' influence.

> Right now the group that Michelle hangs around with is one that I used to hang around with. They smoke pot but I don't and Michelle doesn't either. The people in the group are nice, but I don't want to get into doing drugs. I'm starting to be friends with other people who are more popular and are not into drugs. Some people call them the Squares but they're not really that way – they like to have fun. But Michelle's starting to hang around with Janice and her group. They smoke a lot of pot and they get in a lot of trouble.

On a quick reading, this anecdote might seem like a perfect illustration of the negative influence of peer pressure – the speaker suggests that her friend Michelle is going to start using drugs because she is becoming friends with a group of drug users. Yet when examined more closely, the comments suggest a more complex picture of friends' influence. A careful analysis of research data also suggests different conclusions about how friends influence each other.

Processes and outcomes of friends' influence

Rather than always being negative, the outcome of friends' influence is variable. One researcher in England spent years observing adolescents' interactions with their classmates at school (Ball, 1981). He observed some classrooms in which friends had a negative influence on one another's behavior and achievement. In these classrooms, friends encouraged one another to disrupt the class and not to study for tests. Friends also reinforced one another's negative attitudes toward school. In other classrooms, however, friends had a positive influence on one another's behavior and achievement. They discouraged disruptive behavior that reduced the teachers' ability to conduct class. They encouraged academic achievement by telling one another to study for tests and giving social approval to students who received high grades.

The critical difference between the two groups of classrooms was the initial level of achievement of the students. Friends had a negative influence in classrooms where most students were low in achievement. Friends had a positive influence in classrooms where most students were high in achievement. Students with high levels of achievement also had positive attitudes toward school. When most students were high in achievement, the few students with negative attitudes did not form a cohesive friendship group; instead they made friends with pro-school classmates and were positively influenced by their friends.

Some adolescents in the United States have friends who are more interested in using drugs or acting tough than in doing well in school (Brown, Clasen, & Eicher, 1986). Other adolescents have friends like the Squares mentioned by the eighth-grader quoted earlier. These students do not use drugs or make trouble in school. Still other adolescents – the "brains" – have friends who value high academic achievement (Brown, Mounts, Lamborn, & Steinberg, 1993). The differences between these groups illustrate that friends' influence is not always negative. For many adolescents the influence of friends is entirely positive. The outcomes of friends' influence depend largely on the attitudes and behaviors of a particular adolescent's friends.

For most adolescents the direction of friends' influence is probably more positive than negative. Most adolescents report that their friends encourage them to study for tests and try for high grades rather than to neglect their school work (Brown et al., 1986). Most adolescents report that their friends discourage cigarette smoking and drinking of alcoholic beverages more than they encourage them (Keefe, 1994; Urberg, Shyu, & Liang, 1990). The behavior of these adolescents might be improved if they were *more* influenced by their friends, rather than less.

Ideas about peer pressure also convey the wrong image of the sources and the processes of peer influence. Some writings about peer pressure suggest the image of a gang of toughs telling a young adolescent, "You be at the fight with the Jets tonight, or else!" This image may sell movie tickets, but it does not describe the usual source of influence on adolescents. Even in gangs most decisions are made by consensus. The group discusses various activities in a casual way until everyone agrees on what to do (Suttles, 1971). In less-organized groups decision-making is even more informal. Adolescents not only are influenced by their friends; they also influence their friends, as they discuss their ideas, attitudes, and possible activities (Downs, 1987). Mutual influence during group discussions better characterizes how friendship groups operate than the image of one adolescent conforming to a group majority.

The processes of influence during group discussions are varied (Berndt & Savin-Williams, 1993). Friends sometimes offer rewards to others – for example, saying, "Let's go to the movies. I'll pay for the gas." One common reward is companionship; a friend might say, "Let's go the mall first, and then I'll play tennis like you want to." In other cases, friends use reasoning to persuade each other – for example, a friend might say, "You'd better study for your test because you'll get grounded if you flunk." In addition, friends use mild forms of punishment to change behavior. Teasing is the most common form. Suppose that an adolescent wears a new shirt to school, and one of his friends jokingly says, "Say, I didn't know they *made* shirts like that anymore! Did you get that from your Dad?" After this bit of teasing, there's a good chance the boy won't wear that shirt to school again!

Contrary to popular opinion, friends rarely use stronger forms of pressure when trying to change friends' behavior. They avoid the use of coercive pressure for at least two reasons. First, friendship is a voluntary relationship that can be ended by either partner. If a friend puts unwanted pressure on an adolescent, the adolescent can choose to end the friendship and not to interact with the other person anymore. Second, many adolescents believe that coercive pressure is incompatible with the mutual respect that is expected in a good friendship (Berndt, Miller, & Park, 1989). Adolescents often say that they are not influenced by their friends because they and their friends don't *try* to influence each other. For example, one adolescent said, "My friend has his ideas and I have mine, and we don't try to change each other's ideas."

Sometimes adolescents directly resist pressure from friends and act independently. Remember what the eighth-grade girl said about Michelle and her group of friends? She said that she had decided not to hang around with that group of friends anymore because she did not want to get into drugs. She made this decision even though her best friend Michelle remained close to the group. In other words, the girl decided that she would rather change her friends than change her behavior and start using drugs.

Adolescents are more independent than stereotypes imply. In one survey (Sebald, 1986) adolescents were asked if they considered their parents opinions or their friends' opinions more important in making decisions such as how often to date and whether to go to college. About 30 percent of the adolescents wrote in answers like, "I'd figure it out myself," although that option was not printed on the questionnaire. These adolescents were, in a small way, making a declaration of their independence.

These statements about adolescents' independence do *not* mean that friends have little influence on adolescents' behavior. Many studies confirm that friends influence adolescents' use of drugs like tobacco, alcohol, and marijuana (Chassin, Presson, Montello, Sherman, & McGrew, 1986; Urberg, Cheng, & Shyu, 1991), as well as their sexual behavior and many other behaviors (Berndt & Savin-Williams, 1993). Friends also influence adolescents' attitudes toward school, their achievement in school, and their college plans (Epstein, 1983). In short, friends have a significant influence not only on relatively trivial matters such as what clothes adolescents buy and what music they listen to, but also on attitudes and behaviors that affect adolescents' physical and mental health and their future lives.

Individual differences in friends' influence

Some adolescents are more susceptible to friends' influence than other adolescents. Girls seem to be more influenced by their closest friends than boys are (Billy & Udry, 1985; Davies & Kandel, 1981). As we discussed earlier, girls typically have more intimate relationships with their best friends than boys do. A highly intimate friendship is likely to be more influential than a less intimate one. However, when researchers have examined the influence of the several friends who comprise a friendship group, they have seldom found gender differences (e.g., Graham, Marks, & Hansen, 1991). It seems, then, that girls are not generally more susceptible to friends' influence but that they have a special relationship with their closest friend which gives that friend unusual influence.

Personality traits also affect an adolescent's susceptibility to friends' influence. Adolescents who lack self-confidence or have low self-esteem are most willing to follow friends rather than to assert their independence (Savin-Williams & Berndt, 1990). Conversely, adolescents who are high in self-esteem, intelligent, popular, and athletic are likely to have more influence on their friends than vice versa. Adolescents with these characteristics are likely to be the leaders rather than the followers in their friendship groups.

Finally, the influence of friends is affected by adolescents' relationships with parents (Dishion, 1990; Steinberg & Silverberg, 1986). Adolescents with permissive parents, parents who are unwilling or unable to monitor their adolescent's behavior, are especially responsive to negative influences of friends. Responsiveness to friends' influence is also high among adolescents with rejecting parents. Such parents rarely praise or show a positive interest in their adolescents. These adolescents, in turn, look to the friendship group as a source of security and self-worth. They care a great deal about maintaining good relationships with friends and so are easily persuaded by them.

Developmental changes in friends' influence

As adolescents move out of the family and into the world of peers, you might expect their susceptibility to friends' influence to increase. Most research data show that friends do have more influence on adolescents than on young children, but friends' influence varies during adolescence (Berndt, 1979; Chassin et al., 1986; Urberg et al., 1991). Friends have the most influence in middle adolescence, or around age 15, for several reasons. Between early and middle adolescence, friends' interactions increase in frequency, and friendship groups become more cohesive. Therefore, friends become more influential. Between middle and late adolescence, romantic relationships become more important. Also, adolescents' capacity for truly independent decision-making increases (Berndt, 1979; Steinberg & Silverberg, 1986). These changes reduce the influence of same-sex friends.

Although the changes in friends' influence with age are noticeable, they are modest in size. Children, adolescents, and adults are influenced by all the people with whom they have formed close relationships, and, throughout life, those people include best friends. People use many techniques to influence one another, and all these techniques are used by adolescents and their friends. You should recognize that most writings about peer pressure exaggerate the influence of friends, but you should not err in the opposite direction. In rejecting the myth of peer pressure, remember the reality that friends can and often do have a powerful influence on the attitudes and behavior of adolescents. [. . .]

References

Berndt, T. J. (1986). Children's comments about their friendships. In M. Perlmutter (Ed.), *Minnesota Symposium on Child Psychology: Vol. 18: Cognitive perspectives on children's social and behavioral development* (pp. 189–212). Hillsdale, NJ: Erlbaum.

Berndt, T. J. (1989). Obtaining support from friends during childhood and adolescence. In D. Belle (Ed.), *Children's social networks and social supports* (pp. 308–331). New York: John Wiley & Sons.

Berndt, T. J., & Perry, T. B. (1986). Children's perceptions of friendships as supportive relationships. *Developmental Psychology*, 22, 640–648.

Coleman, J. S. (1961). *The adolescent society*. New York: Free Press.

Condon, R. G. (1987). *Inuit youth: Growth and change in the Canadian Arctic*. New Brunswick, NJ: Rutgers University Press.

Crockett, L., Losoff, M., & Petersen, A. C. (1984). Perceptions of the peer group and friendship in early adolescence. *Journal of Early Adolescence*, 4, 155–181.

Csikszentmihalyi, M., & Larson, R. (1984). *Being adolescent*. New York: Basic Books.

Davies, B. (1982). *Life in the classroom and playground*. London: Routledge & Kegan Paul.

Davies, M., & Kandel, D. B. (1981). Parental and peer influences on adolescents' educational plans: Some further evidence. *American Journal of Sociology*, 87, 363–387.

Dishion, T. J. (1990). The family ecology of boys' peer relations in middle childhood. *Child Development*, 61, 874–892.

Douvan, E., & Adelson, J. (1966). *The adolescent experience*. New York: Wiley.

Downs, W. R. (1987). A panel study of normative structure, adolescent alcohol use and peer alcohol use. *Journal of Studies on Alcohol*, 48, 167–175.

Duck, S. W. (1975). Personality similarity and friendship choices by adolescents. *European Journal of Social Psychology*, 5, 351–365.

Duck, S. W. (1991). *Understanding relationships*. New York: Guilford.

Duck, S. W., & Wood. J. T. (1995). For better, for worse, for richer, for poorer: The rough and the smooth of relationships. In S. W. Duck & J. T. Wood (Eds.), *Confronting relationship challenges [Understanding relationship processes 5]* (pp. 1–21). Thousand Oaks, CA: Sage.

East, P. L., & Rook, K. S. (1992). Compensatory patterns of support among children's peer relationships: A test using school friends, nonschool friends, and siblings. *Developmental Psychology*, 28, 163–172.

Eder, D. (1985). The cycle of popularity: Interpersonal relations among female adolescents. *Sociology of Education*, 58, 154–165.

Epstein, J. L. (1983). The influence of friends on achievement and affective outcomes. In J. L. Epstein & N. Karweit (Eds.), *Friends in school: Patterns of selection and influence in secondary schools* (p. 177–200). New York: Academic.

Erickson, E. H. (1963). *Childhood and society* (2nd ed.). New York: W. W. Norton.

Furman, W., & Buhrmester, D. (1992). Age and sex differences in perceptions of networks of personal relationships. *Child Development*, 63, 103–115.

Gottman, J. M., & Mettetal, G. (1986). Speculations about social and affective development: Friendship and acquaintanceship through adolescence. In J. M. Gottman & J. G. Parker (Eds.), *Conversations of friends* (pp. 192–237). Cambridge, England: Cambridge University Press.

Graham, J. W., Marks, G., & Hansen, W. B. (1991). Social influence processes affecting adolescent substance use. *Journal of Applied Psychology*, 76, 291–298.

Hallinan, M. T., & Williams, R. A. (1987). The stability of students' interracial friendships. *American Sociological Review*, 52, 653–664.

Hartup, W. W. (1983). Peer relations. In P. H. Mussen (Series Ed.) & E. M. Herherington (vol. Ed.), *Handbook of child psychology: Vol. 4. Socialization, personality, and social development* (pp. 103–196). New York: Wiley.

Hartup, W. W. (1993a). Adolescents and their friends. In B. Laursen (Ed.), *New directions for child development: Close friendships in adolescence* (pp. 3–22). San Francisco: Jossey-Bass.

Hartup, W. W. (1993b). Conflict and friendship relations. In C. U. Shantz & W. W. Hartup (Eds.), *Conflict in child and adolescent development* (pp. 186–215). Cambridge, England: Cambridge University Press.

Hirsch, B. J., & Renders, R. J. (1986). The challenge of adolescent friendships: A study of Lisa and her friends. In S. E. Hobfoll (Ed.), *Stress, social support, and women* (pp. 17–27). Washington, DC: Hemisphere.

Hollos, M., & Leis, P. E. (1989). *Becoming Nigerian in Ijo society*. New Brunswick, NJ: Rutgers University Press.

House, J. S., Umberson, D., & Landis, K. K. (1988). Structures and processes of social support. *Annual Review of Sociology* 14, 293–318.

Kagan, S., & Madsen, M. C. (1972). Rivalry in Anglo-American and Mexican-American children of two ages. *Journal of Personality and Social Psychology*, 24, 214–220.

Kandel, D. B. (1978). Homophily, selection, and socialization in adolescent friendships. *American Journal of Sociology*, 84, 427–436.

Keating, D. P. (1990). Adolescent thinking. In S. S. Feldman & G. Elliott (Eds.), *At the threshold: The developing adolescent* (pp. 54–89). Cambridge, MA: Harvard University Press.

Keefe, K. (1994). Perceptions of normative social pressure and attitudes toward alcohol use: Changes during adolescence. *Journal of Studies on Alcohol*, 55, 46–54.

Kon, I. (1981). Adolescent friendship: Some unanswered questions for future research. In S. W. Duck & R. Gilmour (Eds.), *Personal relationships 2: Developing personal relationships* (pp. 187–203). New York: Academic Press.

Kurdek, L. A., & Sinclair, R. J. (1988). Adjustment of young adolescents in two-parent nuclear, stepfather, and mother-custody families. *Journal of Consulting and Clinical Psychology*, 56, 91–96.

Laursen, B. (in press). Closeness and conflict in adolescent peer relationships: Interdependence among friends and romantic partners. In W. M. Bukowski, A. F. Newcomb, & W. W. Hartup (Eds.), *The company they keep*. Cambridge, England: Cambridge University Press.

Laursen, B., & Collins, W. A. (in press). Interpersonal conflict during adolescence. *Pychological Bulletin*.

Maccoby, E. E. (1988). Gender as a social category. *Developmental Psychology*, 24, 755–765.

Matthews, S. H. (1986). *Friendships through the life course*. Beverly Hills, CA: Sage.

Piaget, J. (1965). *The moral judgment of the child*. New York: Free Press. (Originally published 1932.)

Raffaelli, M., & Duckett, E. (1989). "We were just talking . . .": Conversations in early adolescence. *Journal of Youth and Adolescence*, 18, 567–582.

Savin-Williams, R. C., & Berndt, T. J. (1990). Friendships and peer relations during adolescence. In S. S. Feldman & G. Elliott (Eds.), *At the threshold: The developing adolescent* (p. 277–307). Cambridge, MA: Harvard University Press.

Sebald, H. (1986). Adolescents' shifting orientation toward parents and peers: A curvilinear trend over recent decades. *Journal of Marriage and the Family*, 48, 5–13.

Steinberg, L., & Silverberg, S. B. (1986). The vicissitudes of autonomy in early adolescence. *Child Development*, 57, 841–851.

Sullivan, H. S. (1953). *The interpersonal theory of psychiatry*. New York: Norton.

Suttles, G. D. (1971). *The social order of the slum*. Chicago: University of Chicago Press.

Tesser, A. (1984). Self-evaluation maintenance processes: Implications for relationships and for development. In J. C. Masters & K. Yarkin-Levin (Eds.), *Boundary areas in social and developmental psychology* (p. 271–299). New York: Academic.

Torney-Purta, J. (1990). Youth in relation to social institutions. In S. S. Feldman & G. Elliott (Eds.), *At the threshold: The developing adolescent* (pp. 457–477). Cambridge, MA: Harvard University Press.

Urberg, K. A., Cheng, C.-H., & Shyu, S.-J. (1991). Grade changes in peer influence on adolescent cigarette smoking: A comparison of two measures. *Addictive Behaviors*, 16, 21–28.

Urberg, K. A., Shyu, S.-J., & Liang, J. (1990). Peer influence in adolescent cigarette smoking. *Addictive Behaviors*, 15, 247–255.

Youniss, J. (1980). *Parents and peers in social development*. Chicago: University of Chicago Press.

Youniss, J., & Smollar, J. (1985). *Adolescent relations with mothers, fathers, and friends*. Chicago: University of Chicago Press.

Zarbatany, L., Hartmann, D. P., & Rankin, D. B. (1990). The psychological functions of preadolescent peer activities. *Child Development*, 61, 1067–1080.

Chapter 4

Cultural perspectives on children's social competence*

Barry H. Schneider

[. . .]

Comparisons of social behaviour in different cultures serve many purposes in elucidating the origins of social competence. While one important contribution of cross-cultural research is to trace links between various characteristics of a society and the social behaviour of its members, cross-cultural research is also useful in demonstrating that certain aspects of social behaviour are replicated in virtually all cultures. Indeed, cross-cultural researchers have discovered that there are a relatively small number of 'scripts' for peer interaction which appear to recur in many cultures around the world which have little possibility of mutual contact (Whiting & Edwards, 1988). [. . .]

In all cultures, children display an apparently inherent motivation to become competent and to construct knowledge about themselves and about social interactions (Edwards, 1986). This implies that we should not seek to study only the imprint of culture on the child's social behaviour (i.e. 'how society gets inside the individual' [Corsaro, 1988]), but how such cultural influences impinge upon the child's own inherent propensity to make sense of her world. Reflecting the dramatic impact of the contributions of Piaget and Vygotsky, many scholars have recognized in principle the need for such a constructivist approach. In exhorting developmentalists to move beyond linear models of childhood socialization, Corsaro (1988) advocated increased attention to the role of language and discourse. However, this tacit acceptance of the child's active role has for the most part not been translated into new research strategies. [. . .] Considering the ways cultures vary, however, is one promising way of developing hypotheses about cultural effects of children's social competence.

* This is an edited version of a chapter that appeared in *Children's social competence in context*, Oxford: Pergamon Press, 1993.

Individualism/collectivism

The distinction between collectivistic and individualistic societies has been widely considered the most fundamental dimension of cultural variation (Triandis, 1986). [. . .] In a collectivistic culture, one's identity as a member of a group moves to the forefront. Compared with an individualistic culture, the group's goals achieve greater importance, with individual goals becoming concomitantly less important. Members of a collectivistic society assume greater responsibility for each other's welfare. In many if not most cases, this responsibility includes shared concern for each other's children, and, very often, collective child-rearing arrangements.

The major English-speaking countries, USA, Great Britain, Canada and Australia, are virtually the most individualistic societies known (Hofstede, 1983). Therefore, children in our cultures are surrounded by a belief system which emphasizes a sense of individuality to a far greater degree than almost all Third World cultures or even those of Continental Europe. Their beliefs about others are more likely to be idiosyncratic, rather than common beliefs shared with others. Within a given culture, rural milieux may be more collectivistic than urban centres (Madsen & Shapira, 1970). The many differences between individualistic and collectivistic societies are no doubt profoundly manifest in both the nature of the children's peer relations and the importance they and adults assign to relations with others.

One's group membership is thought to be a more essential part of one's identity in situations where there is extensive contact between groups, as in multicultural societies (McQuire et al., 1978), particularly among minority groups (e.g. Hewstone, Bond & Wan, 1983; Hofman, 1985). As documented later in this chapter, the social adjustment of minority children has been explored in a number of countries, including several where the basic structure of the minority culture differs profoundly from that of the surrounding majority. There are theoretical grounds for predicting two opposite tendencies when a collectivistic minority interacts with a more individualistic majority. One argument would hold that the minority parents cling steadfastly to the orientation of their culture of origin, energetically inculcating its values in order to maintain group identity. However, it has also been proposed that parents actively attempt to transmit to their children the competences necessary for the children to succeed within that culture (Ogbu, 1981). If this is the case, parents who emigrate to a more individualistic society might emphatically alter their parenting styles in order to accommodate their perceptions of the competences needed by their children to adapt.

While individualism/collectivism is commonly seen as the most important dimension in cultural variability, as well as the dimension which seems likely to affect children's social competence to the greatest extent, several of the other dimensions reviewed by Gudykunst and Ting-Toomey suggest important cultural differences in the social rules that must be mastered by the child as part of the process of becoming socially competent. For example, Hall (1976) observed that in certain cultures individuals explicitly communicate information about relationships to each other (as may be the case in the English-speaking countries), whereas in others (for example, China, Japan or Korea) the message is largely inferred from the context. In high-context cultures, the socially competent child must become particularly adept at making inferences based upon knowledge of situations rather than from precise messages received from others at the time of each social transaction, though the ability to understand and interpret social situations has been seen as crucial even in relatively low-context cultures (see, e.g., Argyle, Furnham & Graham, 1981).

Gudykunst and Ting-Toomey (1988) maintained that the dimensions of cultural individualism/collectivism and high/low context together influence the extent to which interpersonal relations are characterized by a need to 'save face' as an individual, or maintain a positive public image of oneself. In individualistic, low-content cultures there may be a greater need to maintain one's own public image whereas in collectivistic, high-context cultures, it may be more important to maintain the mutual face of one's group. However, it can also be argued that it is important in a collectivistic culture to cultivate an individual public image that is not at variance with the group's norms and beliefs. Loss of face is often seen as particularly devastating by adolescents even in the highly individualistic North American culture. In this and many other areas, increased attention must be given to the interaction of developmental differences and cultural differences, as cultural differences may be more evident at certain levels of development.

Tolerance for ambiguity and diversity

Different cultures also have divergent thresholds for ambiguity in relationships and for tolerating diversity in behaviour (Hofstede, 1979). Where there is little tolerance for adversity, there is greater pressure on the child and his/her parents to eliminate social behaviours which depart from the norm. As well, the child learning about peer relations in such an environment may learn to reject potential companions whose social behaviour is atypical. In a cultural context where uncertainty is avoided, a child may come to expect more formal rules for social behaviour and less informal negotiation. Where there is a need to avoid uncertainty, interpersonal relations may be characterized by more frequent displays of emotion and higher levels of stress.

Hofstede (1980, 1984) also established that individuals in certain cultures more easily accept that power is unevenly allocated. In high-power-distance cultures, children may be more likely to value social conformity and to assume authoritarian beliefs. Childrens relationships with adults would be based on unquestioned obedience.

Rules

Argyle (1983, p. 123) defined a social rule as 'a shared belief that certain things should or should not be done' within the confines of a particular setting. All social situations have rules; failure to follow them inevitably leads to some degree of rejection by peers. Within a given culture, rules differ from one setting to another, i.e. there may be fewer rules governing some types of relationships than others. Cultures are known to differ somewhat in terms of the rules which apply to different settings. For example, Japanese adults are expected to restrain the expression of emotion and defer to others far more than their counterparts in Britain (Argyle *et al.*, 1986). There are also rules for relationships among children and between children and adults; these probably vary according to age, culture and setting. However, few data are available regarding cross-cultural differences in rules for children's relationships. [. . .]

Peer relations in collectivistic and individualistic societies

Warm Springs children: divergent rules for speaking in group situations

Philips (1972) studied the use of speech by native Indian and non-native children in rural Oregon, inspired by teachers' remarks that Indian children tend not to speak or participate in class. At the time of the study, the Warm Springs Indian tribe numbered about 1,500. Income from the sale of timber had greatly altered the economic context, which was previously one of abject poverty. An observational procedure was used to compare the use of speech in all-Indian classrooms on the reserve and non-Indian classrooms for pupils of the same age at an Oregon school off the reserve. Classes for two age groups were observed: 6 and 12 years old. Differences between the Indian and non-Indian groups were striking, and depended greatly upon the *participant structure* of the particular activity. Indian children eschewed involvement in activities wherein a child had to speak in the presence of a group, such as lessons directed by the teacher or teacher-appointed student leader. They would almost never volunteer an answer and, if called on, would respond, if at all, as briefly as possible in a soft tone of voice. Their behaviour was markedly different during portions of the day when children were assigned tasks to work on at their desks, with the teacher available for help. While the younger Indian children initiated little contact with the teacher at the beginning of the school year, such contact increased after a 'warm-up' period of several weeks, reaching the same frequency of initiation as in the non-Indian classrooms. In the classrooms for 12-year-olds, pupils initiated contact with the teacher far more frequently than in non-Indian classrooms. When the children were assigned projects to complete in small groups, the Indian children participated eagerly, with sustained attention that far exceeded the level observed in non-Indian classrooms. When an Indian pupil was reprimanded for not following classroom procedures, classmates would begin to defy as well. If one child was rebuked for putting his or her feet on a chair, others would immediately place their feet on the furniture. During outdoor play activities, the Indian youngsters would organize themselves into groups and teams without adult or peer direction, and persist at such activities without incident far longer than in non-Indian schools. If teachers tried to structure the outdoor activity, no child would volunteer to be the leader, and if one were appointed, he/she would hesitate to give instructions to the others until prodded. In contrast, non-Indian children would plead to be appointed to such positions of authority.

Philips identified a number of parallels between the Indian children's social behaviour in school and the structure of the Indian society on the reserve. The youngsters' 'peers' or play companions on the reserve tend to be their siblings and cousins; thus the bond with play companions tends to be stronger than in other cultures, and to endure for extended periods of time. Children learn many skills by an extended process of observation, then demonstration, then trial. By the time they are 10 or 11 years old, they are considered capable of spending afternoons or evenings with their age-mates in groups; specific permission to leave the home or to participate in a particular activity is not required. All social events are community-wide, not organized by individuals and families, with participation by both adults and children. During tribal councils, anyone may speak. There are nominal leaders, but they wield little absolute authority. If one person does contribute more, it would be because he knows more about the subject at hand; this would vary from topic to topic.

In terms of the typologies introduced above, the Warm Springs culture is emphatically collectivistic, with low-power distance in interpersonal relationships. Philips observed that the more experienced, flexible teachers at the reservation school adapted themselves by reducing formal lessons and competition among pupils. Less successful teachers might attempt to confront the culture of their charges head on, ignoring the intense bonds among the children and the style of learning to which they were accustomed. The likely result was poor mastery of content due to inadequate instructional communication, as well as alienation from the school experience.

Philips's study presents a more fine-grained analysis than most others of differences in the interpersonal communication between the more collectivistic atmosphere of North American Indian communities and other settings within North America. Similar findings are reported by other researchers using other tools. Madsen's (1971) marble-pull game, portrayed in Figure 4.1, is an example. This game involves a table on which an eyelet has been

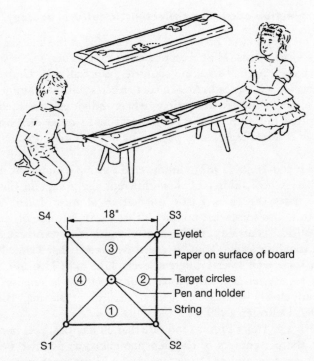

Figure 4.1 Co-operation board
Source: Madsen, A. C. & Shapira, A. (1970). Co-operative behaviour of urban Afro-American, Anglo-American, Mexican-American and Mexican village children. *Developmental Psychology*, 3, 16–20. By permission.

screwed into each end. A marble is held at the centre of the table by a weight, which is held together by a two-part magnet. The object of the game is to have the marble drop into a pocket. The apparatus can be set up by rigging from the eyelet to the weight in the centre in such a way that the marble will drop only if it is pulled in one direction, making co-operation more adaptive. If the string is pulled simultaneously in both directions, the two parts of the magnet separate, and the marble rolls away. While this type of game does permit efficient quantitative comparisons across cultures, removal of play behaviour from its naturalistic context may be problematic. Therefore, this tool is perhaps best used as one of several measures of co-operative or competitive behaviour. [. . .] For example, Miller and Thomas (1972), using Madsen's co-operation board, found that Blackfoot Indian children aged 7–10 years, residents of Canada's largest Indian reserve, worked co-operatively even on a task in which rewards were to be dispensed on an individual basis, whereas the comparison group of Canadian urban children were engaged in competitive behaviour which impeded their success on the task.

Does peer rejection occur in a collectivistic cultural ecology?

Measures of peer reputation have often been regarded as the 'marker variable' of children's social status. Most recent research on children's peer status has been conducted in English-speaking countries, especially the United States. In the absence of widespread cross-cultural replication, one might wonder whether in a more collectivistic society, where individuals are theoretically more committed to group identity, one would find similar dimensions and proportions of children regarded as popular by others, or children rejected by their peers.

Kupersmidt and Trejos (1987) administered a group sociometric interview to 328 primary schoolchildren of three different age groups in Costa Rica. Costa Rica shares the collectivistic orientation of most Latin American countries, but is also somewhat unique in that region because of its 40-year history of political neutrality, non-violent changes of government and lack of a formal standing army. Thus, it could be argued that Costa Rica is a collectivistic society on several different levels. Like most Hispanic cultures, Costa Rican society tends to emphasize family relations as opposed to peer relations, and clearly defined traditional sex roles (Biesanz, Biesanz & Biesanz, 1982; DeRosier, 1989).

Kupersmidt and Trejos's results indicate that on identical peer nomination instruments the percentages of children nominated as popular were quite similar to American samples (11 per cent versus 13 per cent), as was the case for peer rejection (11 per cent versus 15 per cent); similar results were reported by Young and Ferguson for their study of southern Italian adolescent boys, as discussed later in this chapter. However, the specific behaviours associated with peer rejection were slightly different. For example, in Costa Rica, withdrawing from social interaction was associated with peer rejection; this has not been clearly demonstrated in American studies. Therefore, it may be useful for future cross-cultural comparisons to focus on the impact of social withdrawal on rejection by peers. In a collectivistic society, social withdrawal may mean non-participation in the collective experience which is so fundamental to identity formation. In contrast, such non-participation may be seen in a more individualistic culture as an individual's prerogative and, as such, may be much more acceptable to peers. On the other hand, despite the greater commitment to the group, children in more collectivistic cultures seem to have likes and dislikes for specific individuals which appear as marked as those of youngsters in less collectivistic cultures.

DeRosier (1989) studied Costa Rican children's perceptions of their network of close relationships. She administered the Network of Relationships Inventory (Furman & Buhrmester, 1985) to 148 Costa Rican primary school pupils from predominantly working- and middle-class homes. Comparative American data were readily available in Furman and Buhrmester's original article. The Costa Rican children assigned more positive rating than

American children of the same age to most persons in their networks (i.e. parents, siblings, grandparents, best friends and teachers), and indicated that these relationships were less conflictual. DeRosier speculates that these positive attitudes towards others are connected with the prosocial, co-operative nature of surrounding culture.

The Costa Rican children reported that, of the individuals in their social networks, mothers and siblings provided the highest levels of companionship, a function which American children attribute to their best friends. In both countries, teachers were reported to provide the lowest levels of companionship. The relationship with the best friends was described as the least affectionate of all, a position assigned by American children to their teachers. In contrast with American youngsters, the Costa Ricans reported that relationships with their best friends were characterized by higher degrees of conflict and lower levels of affection; they were also less satisfied with their relationships with their best friends. Thus, cultural ecology may impact upon the relative importance of peer relations and the relative functions of supportive individuals. DeRosier's study is of particular importance because, in contrast with most others mentioned in this chapter, it deals with closer, more intimate relationships rather than peer relations in larger groups.

The result of these Costa Rican studies are fully consistent with extensive other data documenting the collectivistic nature of Latin American society and children's culture in comparison with the Anglo-Saxon North American society with which it frequently interacts. Space precludes extensive consideration of all relevant studies, but it is reasonable to conclude that the collectivistic orientation of Latin American children has been demonstrated at a wide range of ages using a wide spectrum of measures. These have included Madsen's co-operation board (Madsen, 1971), as well as semi-structured interview used by Hart, Lucca-Irizarry and Damon (1986) to illustrate the extent to which Puerto Rican children and adolescents focus on the social qualities of the self in defining themselves as individuals. [. . .]

Correlates of peer acceptance by Hopi Indian and Afro-American children

Some additional insight into the specific behaviours associated with peer acceptance in different cultures is provided by Weisfeld, Weisfeld and Callaghan (1984), who compared peer reputation patterns among Hopi Indian children in north-eastern Arizona and Afro-American children in Chicago. The Hopi live in desert areas. This matrilineal subculture is known for its non-violence and collectivistic orientation. Community decisions are taken by a tribal council whose procedures are very democratic. Aggression among children is totally unacceptable to parents, and leads to punishment. The Afro-American children studied were predominantly of middle socioeconomic status. Urban centres in the United States are known for high incidence of violence.

There were dramatic differences in the social play of the two samples. The Afro-American boys played competitive football and softball; the girls played jump rope (skipping). In comparison, the Hopi boys changed the rules for the game of basketball, so that the object of the game was for the group (rather than the individual team) to score as many points as possible. (In other accounts, Hopi children have been found to play basketball without keeping score [Thompson, 1950].) The observers' records indicated that fights occurred in the Chicago playground about once per hour, whereas there was only one incident of shoving in several hours of play in the Hopi playground, and this was stopped by other children. (Unfortunately the report contains little detail of the observation procedure, definition of 'fight', etc.) In contrast, sociometric ratings of the two groups were very similar, with athletic ability associated with popularity in both cultures. These data, together with other findings discussed throughout this chapter, suggest that observational data may be more sensitive to cultural differences than peer reputation measures. Status among peers is more based on relative position along a particular dimension. Even in a non-violent culture, one child is likely to be more aggressive than another. That child may be rejected by peers because of his aggression, though he may be much less aggressive than age-mates in most other cultures.

Hupa Indian and Anglo-American preschoolers in California

Bachtold (1984) conducted another study of co-operative behaviours among American Indian populations. The Hupa Indians live in a remote valley in California, whose isolation limited the penetration of the majority culture until World War II. After the war, traditional ways of earning a living were largely replaced by a wage economy. Like those of most other American Indian tribes, Hupa values emphasize co-operation rather than non-co-operation. Bachtold's comparison group was Anglo-American preschoolers in the Davis region, where the population is composed of two main groups, the descendants of early settlers, whose religious orientation she described as Calvinist, and university students and faculty associated with the University of California at Davis. Hupa patterns of child rearing are permeated by the parents' needs to instil respect for the group and its rules, far more than the more individualistic Anglo-American socialization practices. Observations of the twenty-six 2–4-year-olds in the study were recorded on videotape for analysis. While there were many similarities in the play behaviours of the two groups, the Hupa preschoolers were significantly more sociable and intimate with each other, whereas the Davis children were significantly more authoritarian and aggressive.

Preschoolers' relations with the 'neighbours' in America and Italy

Corsaro (1985, 1988) used a combination of observational techniques to study the peer culture of nursery schools in the United States and Italy. His observations are of particular value because they were conducted over extended periods of time (10 months in the USA, 6 months in Italy) in each case, and combined passive observation, videotaped recording and participant observer techniques. The American study was conducted at the laboratory preschool at a university, whilst the Italian study was conducted in a nursery school in a northern Italian urban centre.

Corsaro defined peer culture as 'a stable set of activities or routines, arti-facts, values and concerns that children produce and share' (1988, p. 3). His cross-cultural comparisons have focused on selected routines or rituals which re-occur frequently in the children's play. Examples of such routines include insult and teasing sequences, mimicry and mockery of adult-imposed rules and approach-avoidance of an attractive but threatening stimulus. The data reveal that a great many of these play sequences are similar in both countries. For example, coming close to, then fleeing, a pretend 'monster' is a common routine within the peer culture of both Italian and American preschoolers. Should these routines be observed in yet other cultures, one might infer that they are a universal feature of social development.

However, there were some differences in routines between Italy and the United States which may have potential theoretical importance. Corsaro (1988) detailed differences in territoriality routines, for example. These occur when a group of youngsters playing together delineate an area of the play-room as belonging to them. Groups of both Italian and American children displayed this tendency to protect their interactive space in this manner. In some cases, Italian children were similar to their American counterparts in their displays of hostility when their 'territory' was invaded. However, in some of the examples, Italian children were much less defensive and, in fact, sometimes even accommodating when an 'outsider' attempted to gain entry to a group's playspace. They might explain the play to the newcomer, or impose conditions on his or her entry. Corsaro remarked that this mirrors the greater concern in Italian city life with 'relations in public', brief meetings and greetings with casual acquaintances, neighbours, etc. In both countries, the territoriality ritual may be understood as part of the children's efforts at understanding interpersonal relations and their preparation for later roles in their communities. The fact that the differences between Italian and American play patterns may not be as dissimilar as, say, between an Oriental and an American culture is not surprising given the fact that the adult societies which surround are not as dissimilar. However, the very high degree of individualism known to characterize American peer culture may be reflected in these subtle differences even when compared with Italy, which is still considered relatively high in individualism in relation to non-Western societies (Hofstede, 1983, 1984).

An explicitly collectivistic subculture: the Israeli kibbutz

The psychosocial adjustment of children growing up on Israeli kibbutzim has been subjected to exhaustive investigation. The kibbutz is unique in a number of respects. The ideology is emphatically collectivistic, but there is continual and active contact with the less collectivistic surrounding Israeli society. Those who join kibbutzim freely elect to share belongings and work responsibilities with other members. They or their offspring are free to leave the community, which does regularly occur. The fact that kibbutzniks join a collectivistic subculture by choice makes the kibbutz probably the best setting for research on the effects of collectivistic ideology.

Kibbutz schools are structured to foster much more co-operative behaviour than the European-style schools of surrounding Israeli cities. Children traditionally live together in a children's house, though they would maintain regular contact with their families. In recent years, however, there has been a clear trend toward family-style living arrangements. There are a number of possible implications for children's peer relations. First of all, the collective upbringing and extensive contact with caregivers rather than their parents may affect their early parental attachment relationships, which may in turn have repercussions in subsequent interpersonal relationships. Secondly, it is interesting to chart the degree to which the surrounding collectivistic atmosphere is mirrored in the children's play relations and social contacts. [. . .]

A number of observational studies have included systematic comparisons of the social play of kibbutz and non-kibbutz preschoolers. Levy-Shiff and Hoffman (1985) compared the social play of urban and kibbutz youngsters in free-play settings. All participants in both settings were Israeli-born children of European cultural origin. Kibbutz children displayed far more developed group interaction skills, and much less competition, than their city counterparts. At the same time, kibbutz children displayed far less emotion and less warmth. They replaced physical aggression with verbal confrontation. Levy-Shiff and Hoffman suggested that these play patterns foreshadow the social adjustment patterns of adult kibbutzniks, which are stereotypically characterized as more group-orientated in general, with a certain degree of emotional distance.

According to an observational study conducted by Hertz-Lazarowitz *et al.* (1989), kibbutz primary school children display similar high levels of interactive behaviour. Their level of social interaction was higher than that of city children in both traditional classrooms and classrooms which afforded greater opportunities for active participation by pupils. Shapira and Madsen's (1974) study involved kibbutz and city youngsters aged 4–11 years. They used the marble-pull task described earlier in this chapter. Kibbutz children at all age levels were less competitive than their city counterparts. While they did become more competitive as they got older, this increase occurred later than in the city children. At age 11, kibbutz children were still extremely cooperative while performing this task. Sharabany (1982), using a questionnaire method, determined that while kibbutz preadolescents had many more social contacts than Tel Aviv youngsters of the same age, the kibbutz group displayed less concern regarding peer group sanctions and lower identification with the peer group. Another study in which structured self-report instruments were used indicates that anxiety with regard to social relations – or, indeed, general manifest anxiety – appears to be no higher or lower among kibbutz children and preadolescents (Ginter *et al.*, 1989). These findings further corroborate the general picture of greater peer involvement but also greater emotional distancing from peers by kibbutz children that several researchers have portrayed.

The collective economy of the kibbutz may not be the only aspect of kibbutz culture which impacts on children's social competence. For instance, Eron and Huessman (1987) studied the relations between children's television watching, peer ratings of aggressiveness and peer popularity among Israeli kibbutz youngsters and Israeli city youngsters, as well as children in Australia, the United States, Finland and Poland. There were many findings common to all these samples. Children's aggressiveness as rated by peers was highly stable over a 3-year period, and was a negative correlate of popularity in all samples. On the other hand, there was considerable cross-cultural variability in the degree to which exposure to television, particularly violent television, predicted aggressiveness. This correlation was particularly weak for kibbutz children, quite possibly because the kibbutzim regulate the amount of violent television the children watch. *Metaplot* typically discuss the social implications of violence after the children watch television programmes of this sort. Another plausible explanation of the findings is that the effects of violent television are attenuated by the general collectivistic nature of the kibbutz. [. . .]

Value judgements as to whether kibbutzim produce children with better or worse social development contribute little to our understanding of the influence of this collectivistic setting. However, the kibbutz research strongly suggests that such an emphatically collectivistic subculture has profound effects on the peer relations of children raised in it. [. . .]

Peer and school experiences of Pumehana adolescents

In addition to the above-mentioned studies conducted with preschoolers, the social behaviour of adolescents raised in subcultures more collectivistic than the surrounding majority culture has received attention. One of the most dramatic examples is Gallimore, Boggs and Jordan's (1974) study of the adolescents of 'Aina Pumehana, a community in Hawaii. This study employed a combination of in-depth interviews and observations of the children's behaviour at school.

There may be few cultures in which adolescents assign a fundamental importance to peer relations as do the Pumehana youth. Only two of the fifty adolescents interviewed expressed the desire to spend their leisure time on their own. Half could think of *no* leisure-time activity that they would enjoy doing by themselves. Conversations appear to focus almost exclusively on shared activities and acquaintances, with little mention of non-shared experiences or one's own perspective. The peer network is a highly supportive one. An individual could easily drift away from contact with a friend or group of friends, but be fully accepted should he decide to drift back. Displays of inequality were scrupulously avoided. A football coach noticed that younger players did not really try their best in order to avoid depriving the football heroes of the school's graduating class of their last year of glory. Friends were expected to be helpful, friendly and modest. In fact, when asked by the interviewer what qualities they admired or 'looked up to' in friends, many of the respondents indicated that they did not think friends should be admired or looked up to; everyone should be equal. They considered friendliness as among the most important qualities. While some of the youths, particularly boys, were physically aggressive, much of their aggression, indeed all the aggression which they regarded as serious, would be directed at outsiders or their property. Outsiders were seen as meriting little kindness.

Peer group discussions were characterized by much participation and latitude. The youths maintained that they were free of pressures to conform, though, as discussed above, belonging to the peer group was crucially important to them. In most groups, there was only an identifiable leader in very exceptional circumstances. Nonetheless, there were some cases of bullies dominating by force. Those youths who had gravitated to the more delinquent sub-groups nonetheless subscribed to the common premium placed on friendship and mutual support. They conceived their superficial roughness as horseplay occurring among potential friends.

As one might imagine, the teachers of these children, who were not members of the Pumehana community, were among the outsiders who served as targets. Pumehana high schools were virtual battlegrounds. Even one of the researchers was physically attacked. Some teachers managed a modicum of control by being highly authoritarian but emphatically fair, others by adopting a stance similar to that of an older brother or sister left in charge of younger siblings. In either case, strict consistency and avoidance of hostile verbal interactions – or even nonhostile but protracted negotiation procedures – were the only roads to peaceful coexistence with the class.

At home, total, unquestioned compliance with parental authority was expected. Sanctions for disobedience by children or wives might include physical beatings, though domestic violence seems to have been more talked about than practised. Discussion or negotiation with parents were rare. Older children were very heavily involved in raising their younger siblings; this may well relate to their propensity toward affiliative behaviour. It would be simplistic to attribute the complex social behaviour of Pumehana adolescents at school solely to a clash between a collectivistic subculture in an individual-istic context. The highly cohesive adolescent peer group can be seen as engaging in collective rebellion against both the strict authoritarianism of its parents and the incursions of other cultural groups. The adolescent peer culture has norms for aggression which differ markedly from those of the school authorities. This may in some way relate to the fact that authoritarian relationships at home were cemented with at least the spectre of physical violence. The youngsters bring to school little experience with authority figures who are reasonable and compromising, and unfortunately often leave school early, having gained little skill at dealing with authority figures in more mature ways. If there is a single enduring message to be learned from this study, it is that prediction of behaviour from broad cultural character-istics must take into account the interplay of a variety of environmental forces, and must be fine-tuned enough to account for differences across situ-ations. While most collectivistic societies are non-aggressive, collectivism may also be expressed as collective aggression in some situations.

Cultural dimensions of childhood aggression

Adult and child aggression in Zapotec communities

Just as cultures and subcultures differ in terms of normative levels of co-operation, there are important differences in levels of violence and aggression. The Zapotec communities in Oaxaca, Mexico, provide interesting opportun-ities for examining the possible links between adult aggressiveness in a com-munity and children's aggressive behaviour in peer contexts. Most of the Zapotec are engaged in agriculture and live in relatively small communities. Interestingly, there are enormous differences between the communities in terms of the rates of adult aggression, with annual homicide rates reported to range from under 4 to 123 per 100,000 inhabitants in the twenty-four com-munities which have been studied (Paddock, cited in Fry, 1988). Attitudes toward violence differ markedly from community to community. In the non violent communities, young children are discouraged from even play fight-ing. In the more aggressive communities, there is frequent horseplay even among adults and greater use of corporal punishment with children.

Fry (1988) conducted an observational study of the behavioural inter-actions of children in two Zapotec communities that differed markedly in normative violence. Twenty-four children in each community participated in the study: their ages ranged from 5 to 8 years. The observation code was limited to serious fighting, play fighting and threats. The rate of play aggres-sion was fully twice as high in San Andres (a pseudonym), the more violent community, than La Paz: an average of 6.9 incidents per hour in comparison with 3.7. There was far less serious aggression in both communities, but, again, the rate was twice as high in San Andres, 0.78 incidents per hour versus 0.39. Perhaps more important are the age differences. In San Andres, the older children engaged in more serious play fighting than the younger ones, whereas in La Paz, serious aggression was lower for the older children in the sample. Correlations between serious and play fighting were marginal.

Fry's results suggest that while aggressive behaviour among childhood peers occurs across cultures and may have some evolutionary function, the immediate cultural context plays a striking role in at least the maintenance of aggressive tendencies. The findings also lend credence to Smith's (1989) contention that play fighting is a means by which children prepare for the roles they will assume in their cultures as adults.

'Gentleness' in Tahitian culture and Tahitian children's peer relations

The classic example of a culture characterized by low levels of hostility is that of Tahiti. [. . .] According to Levy (1978), Tahitians believe in a cult of 'passive optimism' – that individuals should accept the 'natural ordering' of things, rather than strive to influence the status quo. Aggression is defined as an attempt to upset the natural ordering of things. Timidity is actively encouraged. While children may express aggression at times without excessive sanction, they may be warned that nature will get even with them. Tahitians believe that hostility is dangerous to one's body, but by expressing it briefly and appropriately one will minimize the somatic consequences. Wrestling is a very popular pastime. However, anything more enduring than a transient display of anger is considered a shameful indicator of weakness.

According to Levy, Tahitian infants are fussed over, coddled and spoiled. Adoption is very normal – Levy's observations indicate that approximately half of all children were adopted, when their biological parents felt unready to raise them. In early childhood (3–5 years), limits are abruptly set and the child is thrust into a social world of other children and a variety of caretakers and siblings. Given the norms for adopting children and group caretaking, children in Tahiti during the 1960s were very much children of their whole communities. Levy implicitly attributes the gentleness of the Tahitians to this collective socialization, the collectivistic economy and to the culture's reverance of 'natural' forces over individual impulse. [. . .] Tahitian society has changed since the 1960s, with greater Western inroads and some degree of political unrest. If these recent tensions have in any way compromised the gentleness of Tahitian peer relations, this may be a transitory phenomenon as in previous periods of collective stress. It should be noted that a number of other Polynesian societies have been studied and are characterized by the same cooperativeness and helpfulness (Graves & Graves, 1983; Tietjen, 1986). [. . .]

Different priorities for children—cultural differences in the perceived importance of peer relations

Socialization of adolescent boys by southern Italians and their emigrant cousins

Young and Ferguson (1981) conducted a careful and comprehensive study of 120 adolescent boys in southern Italy, as well as emigrants from the same communities who had settled in Rome ($n = 123$) and Boston ($n = 96$). The subjects in all three sites shared essentially a common cultural heritage, though their immediate social, economical and family environments varied considerably. According to the authors (p. 11), the relatively homogeneous Italian regions of Sicily, Calabria, Puglia, Campania, Lucania and Abruzzi were selected because there is some indication that these regions are characterized by fairly homogeneous genetic composition, as established by distribution of blood groups, prevalence of colour blindness and gene frequency of A, B and Rh D, and are thought to differ from the rest of Italy in these respects. The researchers elected to study males only because they believed that in a culture which maximizes protection of adolescent girls, there might be some difficulty in generating an appropriate female sample. The subjects were followed from early adolescence through early adulthood. At the time the data were collected in the 1950s and 1960s, economic conditions in southern Italy were markedly less favourable than in Rome or Boston for individuals of similar socioeconomic level. The southern Italian communities lagged behind in terms of nutrition and health care, opportunities for physical exercise at school, extracurricular activities at school, psychological counselling and many other services.

A structured interview regarding parents' socialization of their sons was conducted at all three sites. The Boston parents were clearly more permissive in almost all respects than either Italian sample, allowing their adolescent sons significantly more freedom in choice of friends, activities and school programme. There were some interesting differences in the parents' instructions regarding the boys' aggression toward peers. The Boston parents tended to advise that their sons defend themselves physically against an aggressive peer, while the Italian parents tended to allow the child to decide how he would respond or, alternatively, exhort the child to respond in a non-aggressive fashion. The Italian-American families were characterized by a more reciprocal communication style, with sons discussing their own needs and participating in group decisions to a far greater extent. The Italian-American parents regarded their sons' friendships as immensely more important than both parent samples in Italy. Fully 40 per cent of the Boston parents mentioned aspects of human relations as among the most important things a boy should learn to do; this response was rare in Italy. There was far more participation in group activities with other adolescents by the Boston boys (64 per cent) than either Italian sample (26 per cent in Rome and 10 per cent in Palermo). Virtually all the Boston parents (99 per cent) indicated that they were pleased that the boy had friends, while as many as 34 per cent of the Palermo parents were not pleased; many Italian parents preferred that their son spend his free time at home.

These differences in the parents' values with respect to peer affiliation and aggression were very clearly mirrored during interviews with the boys at age 14–16 years. The Boston boys were overwhelmingly more oriented to social relations than the Italian adolescents, a third of which expressed a preference for having a few friends rather than many, compared with only 4 per cent in Boston. Only 2 per cent of the boys interviewed in Boston said that they had no friends or only one, compared with 20 per cent of the Italian boys. About one-sixth of the Palermo boys indicated a preference for playing alone, a response which was virtually unknown in Boston or Rome. Eight per cent of the Palermo boys felt that their parents did not wish them to have friends, another response virtually unknown among the other samples. Despite these differences in affiliativeness, the samples were quite similar in patterns of liking and disliking of peers. Classroom sociometrics revealed similar proportions of classmates nominated for positive and negative roles.

With regard to their responses to a physically aggressive peer, there were differences in the boys' responses as to what they were *expected* to do. The vast majority of the Italian boys said that their parents expected a non-violent response, as did a smaller majority of the Boston boys. A sizeable minority of the Americans indicated that their parents expected them to hit back. In any case, hitting back is what most of the boys in all three sites said they would in fact do, regardless of parental dictates. [. . .]

Parents' valuing of social competence in different cultures

Another, though less comprehensive, study of parental valuing of social competence was conducted by O'Reilly, Tokuno and Ebata (1986) in the Hawaiian islands. They compared parents of Japanese and European origin in terms of their priorities for their children. The Japanese-Americans placed highest emphasis on 'behaving well', followed by self-direction, then sensitivity to others. In contrast, the two highest-ranking values among American parents of European ancestry were self-direction and sensitivity to others' feelings. The researchers interpreted these findings as indicating the importance of the values of the culture of origin, especially since Japanese-Americans in Hawaii are known to constitute a distinct community within which children must initially function. Unfortunately, some potentially interesting data points were not included, such as comparisons with parents in Japan or Japanese-Americans living in communities where they constitute a proportionally smaller minority. It would also be interesting to know whether and how the parents attempt to transmit these values to their children, and whether such attempts are successful. Quite possibly, parents living in cultures where social competence is highly valued may make greater efforts to 'set the stage' for children to get together, arrange opportunities for children to interact, provide guidance and actively encourage their children in initiating social contacts. Cross-cultural comparisons of such parental behaviours would be very interesting.

Cultural differences in tolerance of atypical social behaviour

One fundamental dimension of cultural difference is the latitude of acceptable social behaviour. Different thresholds for tolerable child behaviour will likely lead to differential efforts by adults to reinforce or extinguish comparable withdrawn or aggressive behaviours by children. Weisz *et al.* (1988) systematically compared Thai and American parents' tolerance thresholds for both overcontrolled behaviour (i.e. shyness and fear) and undercontrolled behaviour (e.g. aggression). Thailand was selected because the core teachings of Thai Buddhism emphasize that everyone experiences some degree of dissatisfaction or unhappiness, but that these conditions should not be considered permanent or indicative of one's enduring personality. Two vignettes, each describing an exemplar of the behaviour patterns studies, were read by both Thai and American teachers and parents. They were then asked to rate the seriousness of the behaviour, how unusual it is, how concerned they would be if they were the protagonist's parent or teacher, and how likely it was that the behaviour would change. Respondents were also asked to indicate what they believed to be the likely cause of the behaviour and what they would do about it.

In comparison with American parents, Thai parents and teachers rated both over- and undercontrolled behaviours as less serious, less worrisome to a teacher or parent, less unusual and more likely to improve spontaneously. Importantly, these effects held up after statistical correction for the effects of age and education, a methodological safeguard often overlooked in cross-cultural research. Interestingly, Thai and American psychologists were about equally concerned about the 'problem' behaviours (more concerned than Thai parents and teachers, but much less concerned than American parents and teachers). Thais tended to attribute both the undercontrolled and overcontrolled behaviours to faulty child rearing more frequently than Americans, who more often attributed them to environmental stressors or internal conflicts. In both cultures, undercontrolled problems were considered more worrisome than overcontrolled behaviours. It would be most interesting to see if Thais and Americans – and individuals from other cultures – actually react differently in their homes and schools to similar child social behaviour.

A number of studies documenting cross-cultural differences in parents' child-rearing beliefs and practices have been less venturesome in speculating as to the theoretical origins of this diversity. Lambert, Hamers and Frasure-Smith's (1979) study of parenting is perhaps the most comprehensive and sophisticated methodologically. However, the ten nations studied were all highly literate and relatively advanced technologically. Therefore, the generalizability of the results is somewhat limited.

Less attention has been devoted to cross-cultural differences in school and teacher thresholds for acceptable social behaviour. Walker and Lamon (1987) compared the behavioural standards and expectations of American and Australian primary schoolteachers. Though most behaviours rated as problematic in American schools were also somewhat problematic to the Australian sample, American teachers were far more concerned about disruptive behaviour in their classrooms than about children's lack of positive social skills; this gap was not as wide in Australia. In comparison, Australian teachers seemed more preoccupied with the continuity of their lessons. They assigned very negative ratings to pupils' off-topic remarks during lessons. They assigned very negative ratings to pupils' off-topic remarks during classroom conversations. In both countries, teachers who work with handicapped or behaviour-disorded pupils were more accepting of atypical child social behaviour. While the comparison of these two countries is of interest, it would be useful to see these methods applied in a wider spectrum of cultures.

Cultural differences in gender segregation

North American studies of children's friendships have clearly illustrated a preference for same-sex friends from early childhood throughout adolescence (see reviews by Daniels-Beirness, 1989, and Hartup 1983). This finding emerges from studies using sociometric as well as observational methods. In addition, it has been found that school-age boys tend to play in larger groups while girls play in groups of two and three.

There are some indications that such gender segregation in children's groups is less marked in other cultures. Harkness and Super (1985) conducted an observation study with 152 children aged 18 months to 9 years in a rural community in Kenya. Agriculture is the major economic activity in Kokwet, Kenya. Children assist in looking after the cows, removing weeds and caring for younger siblings. This more collective upbringing may be related to the finding that gender segregation in children's play groups was less pronounced than in an American comparison sample, with the shift towards greater gender segregation occurring at later ages. Presumably, adolescent experiences foster the transition to the largely gender-segregated adult world in Kokwet, though the social development of adolescents in that community has not been systematically studied.

Cross-cultural comparison of sex differences in early social development was a major thrust of the very comprehensive Six Culture Project (Whiting & Edwards, 1988; Whiting & Whiting, 1975). This ambitious project featured very careful direct observation of children aged 2–10 years and their mothers in India, Okinawa, the Philippines, Mexico, Kenya and the United States. The precise observation scheme used by researchers familiar with each culture contributes greatly to the value of the study; mother–child interaction was coded as well as interaction among children. The two volumes describing the study detail each culture in terms of living arrangements, economic activity, children's responsibility, child-rearing norms and beliefs and social support network.

There were some important differences in social development among the cultures studied. For example, there was more extensive peer contact, with same-sex peers primarily, among school-age children in cultures with universal education. In contrast, interaction with peers was lowest in Nyansango, Kenya, where only one of the twenty-two children studied attended school. Aggression among peers during the observation intervals was rare in all samples, especially among girls, but the highest frequency of aggressive behaviour occurred in Khalapur, India, where children were subjected to the most physical punishment, and in Mixteca, one of the Mexican Indian communities characterized by high levels of adult aggression. Rough-and tumble 'horseplay' among boys was most typical of cultures which provided sex-segregated competitive school experiences. Nurturant behaviours with same-sex peers were highest in cultures where children had the most experience caring for younger siblings.

Despite these differences, there were a great many cross-cultural universal features of childrens social interaction. School-age children in all cultures associated mainly with peers of the same sex. Behaviours characterized as sociable were the most important aspect of the social play of both girls and boys. Rough-and-tumble games as well as dominance-related behaviours were the next most frequent categories for boys. In all cultures, girls were more nurturant than boys with same-sex peers, while boys engaged in more dominance-related behaviour. There were also a great many cross-cultural similarities in the ways mothers respond to their children. In their conclusion, Whiting and Edwards (1988) emphasized the role of universal biologically-prepared 'scripts' which interact with culture-specific environmental influences to determine children's social development. Nevertheless, one cannot conclusively determine from these data whether the sex segregation of children's groups is attributable to genetically-based aspects of children's social behaviour or to seemingly universal sex-role socialization by parents.

Cultural differences in the relative influence of context elements

As illustrated above, investigators have compared the values, beliefs and practices of parents of various cultures in socializing their children's peer relations. There has also been some cross-cultural comparison of schools and of peer group values. Research rarely accommodates the very genuine possibility that the total impact of the family, school or peer group context may be much greater in some cultures than others, depending upon the structure and value system of the society. The relative importance of these contexts may vary somewhat across cultures as well. There may also be cultural differences in children's overall susceptibility to the influences of other persons. Chu (1979) compared the responses of 180 elementary school children in Taipei and 180 New Mexico children of the same age to a task designed to measure sensitivity to interpersonal influence. Two classmates participated in the study at the same time – one designated as model, the other as recipient of modelling. In one experimental condition the model's 'status' was raised by the experimenter, who passed on compliments which supposedly had been heard from the teacher. In another condition, the model's 'status' was enhanced in the same way. The subjects were asked to select a picture to represent the best answer to a series of questions whose solution was ambiguous. The designated model completed the task first. In a competence-manipulation paradigm, the model was told that his or her answers were right or wrong for the model-competent and model-incompetent conditions, respectively. In some conditions, a token prize was added for 'correct' answers. The modelling recipient completed the task after the designated model was finished. Imitation of the model's choices was used as a measure of susceptibility to peer influence.

Chu's results were somewhat complex. Chinese students gave answers indicative of either complete imitation of the model or total anticonformity, i.e. giving the opposite responses. American children displayed a pattern of responding more independent of the model. Chu interpreted these differences as indicating that Chinese children are more susceptible to peer influence – with such influence operating both ways. The various manipulations of reward and 'status' yielded non-significant findings. It would be interesting to see whether children of these and other cultures respond to parent or other adult models in the same way. As well, it would be useful to determine whether these processes operate outside the confines of a contrived laboratory situation. Nevertheless, Chu's findings do confirm at least that there may be important cultural differences in susceptibility to peer influence. [. . .]

Conclusions: culture and children's social competence

On the whole, the evidence for cultural influences on the emergence of children's social competence appears quite fragmented. Also, the methodology used in many of the scattered studies inspires only limited confidence in the findings. Robust, multimethod assessment of social competence is relatively rare in the literature. In considering many if not most of the studies discussed above, it is very appropriate to wonder whether the results would replicate if an attempt at replication were made. Where larger, more complex societies are studied, there is little compelling reason to believe that the conclusions are valid across socioeconomic strata and other internal distinctions.

Nevertheless, some of the studies do appear to document logical links between characteristics of cultures and patterns of children's social behaviour. There would seem to be enough data to accept, at least, that the broad dimension of cultural individualism/collectivism is associated with more co-operative interaction of children. Of course, the argument might be raised that these cross-cultural differences in both adult collectivism and children's co-operativeness are both attributable to genetic influence. However, some of the studies provide clear refutation of this hypothesis. For example, there is little reason to suspect a substantially different gene pool for Israeli children raised in kibbutzim and in cities, for southern Italians in Italy and immigrants from the same regions in Boston, or for Zapotec Indians in different villages within the same Mexican state.

If one subscribes to the view that development is a function of both cultural influences and universal aspects of maturation, it is imperative to consider both in designing research. At the very least, it would be useful to track developmental differences when conducting cross-cultural comparisons, the importance of which has been illustrated at several points in this chapter (cf. Young & Ferguson, 1981). Whiting and Whiting (1975) inferred that by age 6, children have internalized many important elements of the value system of the adult culture. While this does suggest that the study of the socialization of younger children is of paramount importance, socialization does continue and may change as both children and parents encounter new developmental challenges. Furthermore, the adult values internalized by age 6 may have different impact on the social behaviour of individuals at different stages of development.

This literature has been repeatedly criticized as atheoretical. Shortage of suitable theoretical vantage points cannot possibly be responsible for atheoretical forays into the cross-cultural comparison of children's social development, if this criticism is indeed valid. Most of the studies reviewed in this chapter did specify a theoretical rationale, often quite elaborate. However, the link between the theory and the data may be quite weak. For example, the finding that the correlates of children's sociometric acceptance and rejection tend to be similar across cultures has been invoked to support a number of theoretical positions. Weisfeld, Weisfeld and Callaghan (1984) suggested that the tendency of boys in different cultures to value physical prowess may relate to an inherent need to preserve the species by selecting the best hunters. This position cannot be reconciled with the repeated finding that aggressive children are socially rejected by their classmates (Coie, 1985). Another explanation of the cross-cultural similarities in the correlates of peer acceptance might emanate from social learning theory, because children could come to internalize an appreciation of behaviours they have seen reinforced in others. That might well have occurred for both the Hopi and Afro-American samples in Weisfeld, Weisfeld and Callaghan's study, both of which had access via the media to American professional sport. A social-learning explanation would equally suit other correlates of peer acceptance, such as academic achievement, which would seem to have few ethological implications. Several other theories can and have been used quite validly in explaining cross-cultural similarities in distributions of sociometric data. While multiple explanations of findings are interesting, research that is only superficially informed by theory is only slightly more valuable than atheoretical research. Hopefully, more sophisticated research designs will be developed to better differentiate among explanations for cross-cultural similarities and differences in children's social behaviour.

Life-span developmentalists are increasingly focusing on cultures, social contexts and historical cohorts in explaining specific developmental patterns as opposed to general, universal patterns of development (Silbereisen & Eyferth, 1986). Many of the societies which have welcomed researchers in the past are undergoing profound change at this moment. Collective ideology is waning in Eastern Europe and elsewhere. Impending changes within the European community will result in increased contact between highly different peoples. North American Indians, whose culture has been widely studied, are becoming increasingly conscious of their identities and insisting on educational environments that will foster them. Israeli kibbutzim are largely abandoning collective housing for children in favour of more traditional family sleeping arrangements. Each of these changes represents an important opportunity for researchers to document the impact of societal change on children's social relations.

Our knowledge about cultural influences on children's social competence may also have implications for improving relations between diverse cultural groups brought into contact because of migration. Collett (1971) found that sharing this information was useful in enhancing Englishmen's understanding of Arabs and their culture. A parallel approach might help teachers, neighbours and children understand the social behaviours of culturally different children new to their communities.

References

Argyle, M. (1983). *The psychology of interpersonal behaviour*, New York: Penguin.

Argyle, M., Furnham, A., & Graham, J. A. (1981). *Social situations*. Cambridge: Cambridge University Press.

Argyle, M., Henderson, M., Bond, M., Contarello, A., & Iuzuka, Y. (1986). Cross-cultural variations in relationship rules. International Journal of Psychology, 12, 287–315.

Bachtold, L. M. (1984). Antecedents of caregiver attitudes and social behavior of Hupa Indian and Anglo-American preschoolers in California. *Child Study Journal*, 13, 127–233.

Biesanz, R., Biesanz, K. Z., & Biesanz, M. H. (1982). *The Cost Ricans*. Englewood Cliffs, NJ: Prentice-Hall.

Chu, L. (1979). The sensitivity of Chinese and American children to social influences. *The Journal of Social Psychology*, 109, 175–186.

Coie, J. D. (1985). Fitting social skills intervention to the target group. In B. H. Schneider, K. H. Rubin, & J. E. Ledingham (Eds.), *Children's peer relations: Issues in assessment and intervention* (pp. 141–156). New York: Springer-Verlag.

Collett, P. (1971). On training Englishmen in the non-verbal behavior of Arabs: An experiment in intercultural communication. *International Journal of Psychology*, 6, 209–215.

Corsaro, W. A. (1985). *Friendship and peer culture in the early years*. Norwood, NJ: Ablex.

Corsaro, W. A. (1988). Routines in the peer culture of American and Italian nursery school children. *Sociology of Education*, 61, 1–14.

Daniels-Beirness, T. (1989). Measuring peer status in boys and girls: A problem of apples and oranges? In B. H. Schneider, G. Attili, J. Nadel, & R P. Weissberg (Eds.), *Social competence in developmental perspective*. Dordrecht: Kluwer.

DeRosier, M. (1989). *Costa Rican children's perceptions of their social networks*. Paper presented at the biennial meeting of the Society for Research in Child Development, Kansas, MO, April 1989.

Edwards, C. P. (1986). *Promoting social and moral development in young children: Creative approaches for the classroom*. New York: Teachers College Press.

Eron, L. D., & Huesmann, L. R. (1987). The stability of aggressive behavior in cross-national comparison. In C. Kagitcibasi (Ed.), *In growth and progress in cross-cultural psychology* (pp. 207–217). Lisse, Netherlands: Swets.

Fry, D. P. (1988). Intercommunity differences in aggression among Zapotec children. *Child Development*, 59, 1008–1019.

Furman, W., & Buhrmester, D. (1985). Children's perceptions of the personal relationships in their social networks. *Developmental Psychology*, 21, 1016–1024.

Gallimore, R., Boggs, J. W., & Jordan, C. (1974). *Culture, behavior and education: A study of Hawaiian Americans*. Beverly Hills: Sage.

Ginter, E. J., Lufi, D., Trotzky, A. S., & Richmond, B. O. (1989). Anxiety among children in Israel. *Psychological Reports*, 65, 803–809.

Graves, N. B., & Graves, T. D. (1983). The cultural context of prosocial develop-ment: An ecological model. In D. L. Bridgeman (Ed.), *The nature of prosocial development* (pp. 243–264). New York: Academic Press.

Gudykunst, W. B., & Ting-Toomey, S. (1988). *Culture and interpersonal communication*. Newbury Park: Sage.

Harkness, S., & Super, M. (1985). The cultural context of gender segregation in children's peer groups. *Child Development*, 56, 219–224.

Hart, D., Lucca-Irizarry, N., & Damon, W. (1986). The development of self-understanding in Puerto Rico and the United States. *Journal of Early Adolescence*, 6, 293–304.

Hartup, W. W. (1983). Peer relations. In P. H. Mussen (Ed.), *Handbook of child psychology*, 4th edition (pp. 103–196). New York: Wiley.

Hertz-Lazarowitz, R., Fuchs, I., Sharabany, R., & Eisenberg, N. (1989). Students' interactive and noninteractive behaviors in the classroom: A comparison between two types of classrooms in the city and the kibbutz in Israel. *Contemporary Educational Psychology*, 14, 22–32.

Hewstone, M., Bond, M., & Wan, K. (1983). Social facts and social attributions: The explanation of intergroup differences in Hong Kong. *Social Cognition*, 2, 142–157.

Hofman, T. (1985). Arabs and Jews, Blacks and Whites: Identity and group relations. *Journal of Multilingual and Multicultural Development*, 6, 217–237.

Hofstede, G. (1979). Value systems in forty countries. In L. Eckensberger, W. Lonner, & Y. Poortinga (Eds.), *Cross cultural contributions to psychology*. Lisse, The Netherlands: Swets & Zeitlinger.

Hofstede, G. (1980). *Culture's consequences: International differences in work-related values*. Beverly Hills, CA: Sage.

Hofstede, G. (1983). Dimensions of national cultures in fifty countries and three regions. In J. Deregowski, S. Dzuirawiec, & R. Annis (Eds.), *Explications in cross-cultural psychology*. Lisse, The Netherlands: Swets & Zeitlinger.

Hofstede, G. (1984). Hofstede's culture dimensions: An independent validation using Rokeach's value survey. *Journal of Cross-Cultural Psychology*, 15, 417–433.

Kupersmidt, J. B. & Trejos, L. (1987). *Behavioral correlates of sociometric status among Cost Rican children*. Paper presented at the biennial meeting of the Society for Research in Child Development, Baltimore, MD, April 1987.

Lambert, W. E., Hamers, J. F., & Fasure-Smith, N. (1979). *Child rearing values*. New York: Praeger.

Levy, R. I. (1978). Tahitian gentleness and redundant controls. In A. Montagu (Eds.), *Learning non-aggression* (pp. 222–235). New York: Oxford University Press.

Levy-Shiff, R., & Hoffman, M. A. (1985). Social behavior or urban and kibbutz preschool children in Israel. *Developmental Psychology*, 21, 1204–1205.

Madsen, M. C. (1971). Developmental and cross-cultural differences in the co-operative and competitive behavior of young children. *Journal of Cross-Cultural Psychology*, 2, 365–371.

Madsen, M. C. & Shapira, A. (1970). Cooperative behavior of urban Afro-American, Anglo-American and Mexican village children. *Developmental Psychology*, 3, 16–20.

McGuire, W., McGuire, C., Child, P., & Fujioka, P. (1978). Salience of ethnicity in the spontaneous self-concept as a function of one's ethnic distinctiveness in the social environment. *Journal of Personality and Social Psychology*, 36, 511–520.

Miller, A. G., & Thomas, R. (1972). Cooperation and competition among Blackfoot Indian and Urban Canadian children. *Child Development*, 43, 1104–1110.

Moore, H. A., & Porter, N. K. (1988). Leadership and nonverbal behaviors of Hispanic females across school equity environments. *Psychology of Women Quarterly*, 12, 147–163.

Ogbu, J. U. (1981). Origins of human competence: A cultural-ecological perspective. *Child Development*, 52, 413–429.

O'Reilly, J. P., Tokuno, K. A., & Ebata, A. T. (1986). Cultural differences between Americans of Japanese and European ancestry in parental valuing of social competence. *Journal of Comparative Family Studies*, 17, 87–97.

Philips, S. V. (1972). Participant structures and communicative competence: Warm Springs children in community and classroom. In C. B. Cazden, V. P. John, & D. Hymes (Eds.), *Functions of language in the classroom* (pp. 370–394). New York: Teachers College Press.

Shapira, A., & Madsen, M. C. (1974). Between and within group cooperation and competition among kibbutz and non-kibbutz children. *Developmental Psychology*, 10, 1–12.

Sharabany, R. (1982). Comradeship: Peer group relations among preadolescents in kibbutz versus city. *Personality and Social Psychology Bulletin*, 8, 302–309.

Silbereisen, R. K., & Eyferth, K. (1986). Development as action in context. In R. K. Silbereisen, K. Eyferth, & G. Rudinger (Eds.), *Development as action in context* (pp. 3–16). Berlin: Springer-Verlag.

Smith, P. K. (1989). The role of rough and tumble play in the development of social competence: Theoretical perspectives and empirical evidence. In B. H. Schneider, G. Attili, J. Nadel, & R. P. Weissberg (Eds.), *Social competence in developmental perspective* (pp. 239–255). Dordrecht: Kluwer.

Thompson, L. (1950). *Culture in crisis*. New York: Russell & Russell.

Tietjen, A. (1986). Prosocial reasoning among children and adults in a Papua New Guinea society. *Developmental Psychology*, 22, 861–868.

Walker, H. M., & Lamon, W. E. (1987). Social behavior standards and expectations of Australian and U.S. teacher groups. *The Journal of Special Education*, 21, 56–82.

Weisfeld, G. E., Weisfeld, C. C., & Callaghan, J. W. (1984). Peer and self-perceptions in Hopi and Afro-American third and sixth graders. *Ethos*, 12, 64–84.

Weisz, J. R., Suwanlert, S., Chaiyasit, W., Weiss, B., Walter, B. R., & Anderson, W. W. (1988). Thai and American perspectives on over- and undercontrolled child behavior problems: Exploring the threshold model among parents, teachers, and psychologists. *Journal of Consulting and Clinical Psychology*, 56, 601–609.

Whiting, B. B., & Edwards, C. P. (1988). *Children of different worlds: The formation of social behavior*. Cambridge, MA: Harvard University Press.

Whiting, B. B., & Whiting, J. W. M. (1975). *Children of six cultures: A psychocultural analysis*. Cambridge, MA: Harvard University Press.

Young, H. B., & Ferguson, L. R. (1981). *Puberty to manhood in Italy and America*. New York: Academic Press.

Part II

Conflict and cooperation

Chapter 5

The state of play in schools*

Peter Blatchford

Children's play has been studied by historians, biologists, sociologists, folk-lorists, educationalists, and psychologists. The more specific topic of play in schools has also received a good deal of study and attention. This chapter examines issues concerning play in schools but deliberately avoids reviewing the overall role of play in the school curriculum and learning, which has been dealt with elsewhere (see Moyles, 1989; Smith, 1990). Instead, it concentrates on children's play in the context of informal experiences that take place not in the classroom but outside the school building, usually in the playground. In particular, it will focus on what we know about play and games during school breaktimes; until recently, this has been largely taken for granted and not studied. It draws largely from a recent British programme of research at the University of London Institute of Education, which includes a national survey of breaktime in schools and a focus on pupil perspectives on breaktime. Of all aspects of school life, breaktime in schools is the area perhaps most opaque to adults. Pupils alone are the participants at breaktime – the experts, as it were – and often the only witnesses of what goes on then.

Though relatively neglected by researchers and policy, there are more recent signs of a growing appreciation that much can be learned about children from studying their behaviour and experiences at breaktime (see Blatchford & Sharp, 1994; Hart, 1993; *Journal of Research in Childhood Education*, 1996; Smith, 1994). The playground is a useful research site because breaktime is one of the few occasions when children interact in a relatively safe environment, free of adult control, and when their play and social relations are more their own (Smith, 1994). There has also been growing recognition of its negative and positive contribution to school progress (see Blatchford, 1994; Pellegrini, 1995; Pellegrini & Smith, 1993).

A main theme of this chapter is that the prevalence of a negative view about breaktime in schools is leading to more deliberate management and

---

* This is an edited version of a paper that appeared in *Child Psychology & Psychiatry Review*, Volume 3, No. 2, 1998.

supervision of breaktimes, and a reduction in their duration. At its most forceful, a negative view can be expressed in a deliberate anti-breaktime viewpoint (an anti-recess movement has been identified in the United States by Pellegrini, 1995), but recent changes appear to be occurring because breaktime in schools is taken for granted and not – understandably given teachers' other concerns – seen as a priority. It is argued that the consequences of these recent changes for pupils' social development need to be considered carefully.

The chapter has five sections: it examines, first, current views about play and behaviour in schools; second, characteristics of breaktime in schools, as revealed in a recent national survey; third, the nature of play and games at breaktime, and some selected issues; fourth, positive aspects of breaktime experiences; and fifth, supervision arrangements at breaktime. It ends with conclusions concerning the role of breaktime in schools, and school approaches to it.

A note about terms: in Britain the term 'playtime' is often used at primary level (4–11 years) whereas the term 'breaktime' is preferred at secondary (11–16 years). I prefer to use the term 'breaktime' for all breaks, including lunchtime, because it is more inclusive and indicates that breaktime issues are of relevance through all the school years. Both are interchangeable with 'recess', which is the term preferred in the United States and some other countries, though recess is only likely to be experienced by the younger primary grades in US schools.

Views on play in school

Although difficult to quantify, the dominant view of children's behaviour at breaktime appears to be negative, with a stress on unacceptable behaviour that can occur then. Several areas of concern have fuelled this negative view. One is a growing appreciation in recent years of the extent of bullying in schools and the harm that it can do to the victims. Initially inspired by the work of Olweus (1993), there have now been a number of studies and initiatives in Britain (e.g. La Fontaine, 1991; Sharp & Smith, 1994; Smith & Sharp, 1994; Tattum & Lane, 1989). Views have also been influenced by violent incidents such as the murder of a British Asian boy in a Manchester secondary school playground. This incident led to the setting up of a public enquiry, because it showed how violence, possibly racially motivated, could erupt in school playgrounds. In interviews conducted with primary teachers and headteachers in 13 Local Education Authorities (LEAs) in the South East of England, one concern was with what was seen as a large amount of needlessly aggressive behaviour. Sometimes this was seen as a major problem because of the way it could set the tone for the school (Blatchford, 1989).

A more general influence has been concern about behaviour in schools, particularly expressed by the Teacher Unions and the press, which gathered momentum over the 1980s and culminated in the reporting of the Elton Committee of Enquiry into Discipline in Schools, (DES, 1989). The Committee identified the lunchbreak as 'the single biggest behaviour-related problem that (staff) face'. Less dramatically, many in schools are aware of lower-level but more common problems that can arise at breaktimes and that can spill over into the school. It is felt that problems can arise particularly during the long lunchbreak (Blatchford, 1989). In a national survey of staff views about breaktime (Blatchford & Sumpner, in press), staff in primary schools appeared to be making more effort than those in secondary schools to improve behaviour, and this might explain why they felt behaviour at break-time had improved over the past 5 years. Nevertheless, in one in four schools, both primary and secondary, the view was that behaviour at breaktime had declined. There was a perception at both primary and secondary schools of less respect toward authority and the environment, an increase in aggression, and more individual pupils with difficult behaviour. There was also a clear view that behaviour *out of school* had declined in the last 5 years.

There is an allied concern with the quality of outside play – a general perception that children are not as constructive in their play as they once were. In interviews with teachers, concern was expressed about children idling around the playground – not seeming to know what to do with themselves – and play being described as low level, and, for the boys, mainly tests of physical prowess (Blatchford, 1989). Traditional playground games were commonly seen to be in decline. One head felt that children had 'lost the vocabulary of outside play', and felt it appropriate to 'teach' children supposedly forgotten outside games.

Characteristics of breaktime in schools

Before pupils' play and activities at breaktime are discussed. I want to look at what we know about basic characteristics of breaktime, the main setting within which play occurs. Surprisingly, we could locate no systematic infor-mation on this neglected part of the school day and so we recently conducted a national questionnaire survey about breaktimes, with returns from 6 per cent of all primary and secondary schools in England (a response rate of 61 per cent). Results are summarised here for what they tell us about basic character-istics of breaktime (see Blatchford & Sumpner, 1996, 1998, for full details).

We are interested, first, in the duration of breaktime – how much of the school day does it take up? We found that the total average time for morning and afternoon breaks and lunchtime was 93 minutes at the infant stage, 83 minutes at the junior stage, and 77 minutes at the secondary stage. We estimated the proportion of the school day allocated to breaktime, as a per-centage of the school day, to be 24 per cent, 21 per cent, and 18 per cent for the infant, junior, and secondary stages respectively. There was a clear tendency for the youngest children in school to experience the longest breaktimes. There was a tendency for the afternoon break to have been abolished, though this was again related to the age of child; 87 per cent of secondary schools, 58 per cent of junior schools, and 30 per cent of infant schools had no afternoon break.

We found that in more than half of the primary schools (56 per cent) and slightly fewer secondary schools (44 per cent) there had been changes to the length of breaktime over the previous 5 years (that is, from the 1990/91 to the 1995/96 school years). The main change was a reduction in time spent at lunchtime, along with the abolition of the afternoon break. The overwhelming reason given by school staff was to increase the amount of time spent on teaching to meet the new requirements of the National Curriculum. A second reason was to reduce behaviour problems in school. Conversely, the survey also showed that over the last 5 years there was a tendency for the length of the school day to have increased.

So, along with a negative view of breaktime, there appears to have been a growing reduction in breaktime in schools that has led to growing restrictions on opportunities for informal social experiences and play, and less opportunity for meeting peers and developing friendships in school. This has also been noted in the US (see Pellegrini, 1995) and in Australia (Evans, unpublished).

Alongside this have been changes in the opportunities for peer interaction *outside* school. There are signs in England and elsewhere that children of primary school age (5–11 years) have fewer opportunities out of school for interacting freely with peers (Hillman, 1993), and for developing friendships and social skills. For example, children are far more likely to be driven to school, rather than walk. This emphasises the likely importance of interaction at breaktime in schools, which for a growing number of pupils may be the main opportunity for them to interact and develop friendships.

The nature of play and games at breaktimes

This section looks at what is known about play and activities at breaktime. There is not space for a comprehensive review and readers are referred to Blatchford (1994, 1998), Boulton (1992), Evans (1989), Pellegrini (1995), and Smith (1994) for a full account.

Sutton-Smith (1982) has argued that 'the most important thing to know about peer culture is what is going on there. That is, that we might learn more of the structure and more of the function if we first studied *what the action is* (that is) the performances that are central to children . . .' (p. 68). We know surprisingly little about the nature of breaktime 'performances' and peer relations. One influential description of children's outside play is that provided by the Opies (Opie & Opie, 1969). They provided a detailed catalogue and analysis of games and language, and a portrayal of childrens play culture from the pupils' own perspectives. They argued that control of games has to be with children themselves; adults have no role in this culture. The world of childhood games is passed on from child to child, and is restricted to the primary years, disappearing as children become self-conscious about the games. Though influential, the Opies' research was mostly not based on events in school playgrounds, which they dismiss as a 'restricted environment', and they could not be called social scientists ('folklorists' is a preferred term).

Other studies have taken a sociological or ethnographic perspective, using qualitative methods. Sluckin's (1981) pioneering study was exclusively concerned with the school playground. He argued that the playground offers children the opportunity for peer interaction in the context of which many lessons relevant to adult life are learned. More recently Grudgeon (1993) has argued that playground games and language contribute to gender identity, and, for girls, a form of empowerment against boys. Thorne (1993) has provided a thoughtful analysis of the degree to which boys and girls in school can be said to have separate cultures and argues that gender identity needs to be seen not as abstract and fixed but as it arises in school contexts. Gender relations can differ in school and in the playground.

There have been few psychological studies directly focused on breaktime behaviour, although studies in the areas of friendship development, social skills and competence, and popularity and rejection are relevant. For example, playground behaviour has been studied in research on social competence and social status (Dodge, Coie, & Brakke, 1982), and on peer rejection (e.g. chapters in Asher & Coie, 1990). Interest has been in the playground behaviour of rejected and popular children, with popular children tending to engage in more prosocial, and rejected children in more aggressive, behaviour (see review by Williams & Gilmour. 1994). Research reported in Ladd and Price (1993) used a short-term longitudinal design to show that playground behaviour of preschool children early in the school year (for example, cooperation and arguing) is predictive of social status later in the year. There are exceptions (e.g. Ladd & Price, 1993), but playground behaviour has been used as an outcome measure rather than being of interest in its own right.

Descriptions that do exist point to the vigour and involvement shown in the play of primary school children at breaktime. Boulton (1992) found that sociable contact between children, and rule games such as football, rounders and tiggy, as well as rough-and-tumble play, were common activities. Blatchford, Creeser, and Mooney (1990), in a study based on 11-year-old pupil reports of games and breaktime activities, found a wide variety of games played but a domination by active games, with the most popular activities being ball games and chasing games. The most popular game of all was football, played by 60 per cent of children, boys more than girls (84 per cent of boys, 36 per cent of girls). Other ball games such as netball, basketball, and cricket were played by 32 per cent of children. The most common chasing game by far was the basic game of 'it', 'had', or 'he' (46 per cent of children). Seeking games (17 per cent), catching games (16 per cent), racing games (12 per cent), and skipping games (9 per cent with a rope, 6 per cent with elastic) were also noted. Of activities other than games, talking to friends (48 per cent), walking and hanging around (32 per cent), and just sitting down (28 per cent) were the most common.

Some issues regarding breaktime play and activities

Age changes

Activities at breaktime show a main difference between primary and secondary stages (Blatchford, 1996). In a follow-up study at 16 years of children studied at 11 years (see above) the main change was that games other than football had all but disappeared; football was now played by only 26 per cent of pupils, and only 1 pupil mentioned a chasing game. Other ball games had declined by 16 years. By 16 years the most popular activity was talking to friends, hanging around, and socialising (72 per cent). As at 11 years, there was a significant difference between boys and girls in reported breaktime activities. Boys were more likely to report playing football, other ball games, and cards and chess. Girls were more likely to talk to friends and socialise, do school work, and listen to music.

The active nature of primary school breaktimes contrasts with the more covert and sometimes apparently unfocused activities of the last years at school, but one needs to be cautious about concluding that secondary breaktimes are of less value. As they move through secondary school, pupils' social lives become important in new and deeper ways and are vital to their developing sense of who they are and what they want to do. In consequence, social concerns are not so tied to location and activity, and, in contrast to social activities during the primary school stage, are not so visible to staff.

A closer study of changes in the playground games of 8- to 9-year-olds over the first year after entry to junior school showed a gradual narrowing of the range of games, and the emergence of a few dominant ones (Blatchford, 1998). The influence of developmental and school influences on games was examined. Connections with friendship and social network formation were suggested, indicating that the nature of play should be considered in terms of social relations and situational factors within a particular school, as well as in terms of more general developmental factors.

The quality of outside play

As we saw earlier, it is the view of some teachers that traditional games and the quality of play are in decline. Elsewhere we have considered evidence concerning historical changes in the quality of outside play (Blatchford *et al.*, 1990). The point I wish to make here is that consideration of social and contextual issues makes the debate over general trends in the quality of play more complex. It may be more profitable to consider the quality of play behaviour not in a general or historical way but in terms of forces within schools, for example, the influence of other pupils such as particular 'key players'; connections between breaktime activities, particularly games, and friendship formation; and the influence of the school's informal culture. As we have seen, the 'quality' of breaktime pursuits of 16-year-olds may seem to be low-level but may in fact be subservient to other social ends such as the formation of friendships. Any consideration of, and judgement about, the general quality of outside play and games would need to consider these factors.

Individual differences in breaktime activities and play

As described above, there is considerable evidence now on the correlates of social status categories such as 'rejected' and 'popular'. Ladd and Price (1993) report that rejected children are less likely to play with friends, have less consistency in play partners, gravitate to younger play partners, and play preferences are less likely to be reciprocated. Social status and friendship categories are likely to overlap with being left out of games, and having more limited social networks, but these possible associations need closer investigation. Such information will be of value to schools in considering difficulties faced by some pupils at breaktime. Boulton (1992) found that some children habitually spend large amounts of playground time alone, and that it is possible that such children can be overlooked by supervisors. Recent case studies of junior age children at breaktime indicated that rejected players had fewer or no friends, were seen by peers as not cooperative, and friendship choices were not reciprocated. Again, boys and girls seemed to differ, with girl rejected players having low peer relation self-concepts and boys being seen by others as more aggressive (Blatchford, 1998).

Parker and Asher (1987), in a widely cited review, have identified the long-term consequences of peer difficulties (in terms of peer acceptance, aggressiveness, and shyness/withdrawal) on later personal adjustment (in terms of dropping out of school, criminality, and psychopathology). Strongest support was for a link between peer adjustment, in terms of aggressiveness and peer acceptance, and later adjustment in terms of dropping out of school and criminality. The relevance of these findings is that one of the main settings in school for peer rejection and peer difficulties is breaktime. This does not necessarily mean that breaktime experience, including peer rejection that may take place then, is causally related to later peer experiences. Moreover, it does not follow that one solution to later difficulties would be in reducing breaktime and therefore opportunities for earlier social rejection; rejection may still occur in other settings. An alternative implication is that for some children much could be gained from closer attention by teachers and supervisors to their breaktime experiences, because it may help reveal more about the nature and extent of difficulties with peers.

There is a more positive side to individual differences in breaktime experiences. In a study already cited (Blatchford, 1998), the role of a few 'key players' in suggesting, maintaining, and terminating games was suggested. Case studies indicated that such key players were likely to be popular, to be seen by peers as group leaders, and have older sisters, but differences within this group were also apparent, particularly between boys and girls. Boys seemed to have a key role because of physical prowess, girls because of social skills and imagination, possibly associated with academic progress. But small numbers of children in this study mean these suggestions need further testing. In a similar way, research by Haslett and Bowen (1989, reviewed in Erwin, 1993) classified differences in social skills of 5-year-olds in terms of three categories: 'agenda setters', who tended to initiate and dominate play, and to be active physically and verbally; 'responders' who reacted appropriately to play bids and maintained interaction without establishing the play agenda or initiating change; and 'isolates' who responded inappropriately and were insufficiently persistent and often overlooked. Given the seeming importance of lack of success in game involvement and social skills for later social development, there is likely to be considerable practical benefit from more research on differences between children in their play involvement at breaktime.

Aggression and peer relations

The current concerns with bullying and aggression at breaktime have already been mentioned. It is important to make the point that some children do have difficulties at breaktime, and that bullying, intimidation, and violence need to be dealt with promptly and thoroughly in schools. There is some indication from pupil accounts that schools can differ in the extent to which pupils attach value to aggression and dominance in terms of physical prowess (Blatchford, 1998). There has also been concern about teasing and name-calling and the extent to which it can make children's lives miserable and used to bully and intimidate them. Mooney, Creeser, and Blatchford (1991) showed the pervasive nature of teasing and name-calling in primary schools. Kelly (1988) has drawn attention to the extent of racist name-calling in the playground, and to racist and sexist harassment that can take place on school playgrounds (Kelly, 1994).

Without wishing to downplay the negative effects of some behaviours, it is also possible that the extent of unacceptable and aggressive behaviour can be overestimated. Part of the problem is that there can be considerable difficulties for adults in judging the nature and ill effects of breaktime behaviour. Boulton (1996) has shown how adults, particularly lunchtime supervisors, can overestimate the extent of aggressive behaviour, confusing rough-and-tumble play for aggression. The research of Boulton (1994), Pellegrini (1995), and Humphreys and Smith (1987) on rough-and-tumble play has offered valuable guidance on how to recognise and separate this behaviour from true aggression. Though superficially similar, rough-and-tumble play tends to take place between friends and is nonaggressive in intent and outcome.

Another problem has been a tendency to see certain behaviours such as teasing and name-calling in a fixed way as signs of negative behaviour such as bullying, when the interpretation and meaning of behaviour to the part-icipants will vary according to a number of factors, including relationships between pupils; the same form of words, for example, can have a very diff-erent meaning when the participants are friends as opposed to nonfriends (Blatchford, 1998). I return to the issue of teasing and name-calling in the next section.

Positive aspects of breaktime

Having examined the negative view of breaktime activities, and some issues concerning breaktime activities and play, I now look at possible positive effects of breaktime for pupils.

In a powerful statement, which runs counter to the negative climate of thought about breaktime in many schools, Sutton-Smith (1990) concludes that:

> the school playground festival is one of the few places where a distant and non-intrusive supervision is possible so that children's political rights can be guaranteed consistent with an adult concern with their safety. The school playground still provides the one assured festival in the lives of children.

What does research suggest about a more positive side to breaktime experiences and play? In this section several themes are identified. A starting point is the well-established view that peer relations have particular value for social and even cognitive development. In an influential book, Youniss (1980) adapted the theories of Piaget and Sullivan to show how peer relations were qualitatively different from adult–child relations. In contrast to adult–child relations, peer relations are characterised by equality, cooperation, reci-procity, and mutuality – all of which make a contribution to social develop-ment. Youniss did not argue that adult–child and peer relations were better or worse than each other; rather that they served different functions and had different effects. Piaget's theory – not usually seen as stressing the social context of development – has been recently painstakingly re-evaluated in order to highlight the role of peers in cognitive development (DeVries, 1997). This general position regarding the value of peer relations for social relations underlies much social developmental psychology (see Hartup, 1992). The link with breaktimes has been studied by Pellegrini and Smith (1993):

> In both correlational and longitudinal research, children's recess behaviour is related, in theoretically predictable ways, to both cognitive and social outcome measures . . . Thus, it seems to have educational value and certainly has considerable educational relevance.

Pupils' positive views about breaktime

Longitudinal research at the Institute of Education with pupils of 7, 11, and 16 years of age has shown that breaktime is a significant and generally enjoyable time for them – the great majority of pupils throughout their school careers expressed a positive view about breaktime (Blatchford, 1998). This was despite their recognition, especially at secondary level, of the sometimes unsatisfactory nature of the physical environment provided for breaktimes. Despite the difficulties faced by some children at breaktime, therefore, we should not lose sight of the large vote of confidence from most of the participants involved. Main reasons for a positive view were similar at primary and secondary school: they liked the opportunity to socialise with their friends, and having a break from work. At primary level the other main reason for liking breaktime was the opportunity it gave for playing games. By the end of secondary school, breaktime was appreciated because of the opportunities it provided for independence from adults. Pupils' accounts showed how valuable breaktime and lunchtime could be for talking openly about school and teachers in a way that would not be possible in lesson time, and for allowing them to behave in ways freed from the constraints expected in school. Breaktime can therefore be of value to pupils throughout the school years, though the nature of the value changes from primary to secondary (Blatchford, 1998; Blatchford et al., 1990).

Friendship development and breaktime

Studies of the development of children's friendships are too numerous to be covered here (see reviews in Dunn, 1993: Hartup, 1992; Parker & Gottman, 1989). There has been progress in understanding the significance of friendship for young children (Davies, 1982; Goodnow & Burns, 1985), the importance of friendship as a support in adjusting to school (Ladd, Kochenderfer, & Coleman, 1996; Savin-Williams & Berndt, 1990), in social and communicative skills, and in school work (Faulkner & Miell, 1993). For primary-aged children, play has been credited with a central role in friendships (see Dunn, 1993).

Although evidence is still unclear, it is likely that breaktime has a main role to play because it is at breaktime that friends, perhaps not in the same class at school, have a chance to meet. Given the difficulties children may face in meeting out of school, breaktime may be the main setting within which friendships are formed and develop.

More specifically, in the study of 8- to 9-year-olds over the first year after entry to junior school, breaktime games and children's friendships and social networks in school were interconnected (Blatchford, 1998). One function of games soon after entry to school was the facilitation and support provided for entry into social relationships, whereas at a later point in the school year the social function changed to one of supporting and maintaining friendship groups. The early days in a new school can be a time of uncertainty for children and it seems likely that new friendships, developed in the context of play and games, can help reduce uncertainty and thus help adjustment to school. This view is consistent with research showing that children's friendships are supportive at the time of adjustment to a new school (Davies, 1982; Ladd *et al.*, 1996). Davies (1982) has also commented on the connections between play and friendships, and has argued that much of the building of shared understandings that lies at the heart of friendships develops through play. She describes how the compulsive dynamic of a game can draw children in, aiding friendship formation, and providing access to a shared children's culture.

Conflict at breaktime: Positive effects?

As discussed earlier, the playground is a setting where aggression and conflict between pupils can take place. Given the density of pupils and the often vigorous nature of their play, there is the potential for falling out and for conflict. But there is much evidence now on the differences between aggression and conflict and the positive role of the latter in peer relations. The extent to which earlier laboratory-based studies overestimated aggression has become more apparent as researchers have studied children in natural settings. Aggression and conflict are best seen as ways children negotiate and seek to solve their differences (Hartup & Laursen, 1993: Shantz & Hartup, 1992), and the playground is a main arena within which this takes place.

One form of breaktime behaviour studied in the Institute of Education longitudinal study was teasing. Interviews with pupils at 7, 11, and 16 years showed the ubiquitous place of teasing in peer interactions throughout school. The majority of children at all ages said that teasing occurred. On occasions teasing could really upset pupils, and the effects could be harmful emotionally, and could adversely affect school progress. But one needs to be careful not to see all teasing and name-calling in a negative light. Pupils were keen to say that much teasing was understood not to be hurtful, but more a part of everyday banter, often between friends. Some teasing no doubt serves a social purpose, helping to denote limits, helping to define and consolidate friendships, showing off sharpness in social discourse, and jostling for status. Pupils showed that considerable skill could be required in determining what form of teasing was appropriate with particular people.

Pupil accounts showed the importance of considering teasing in the context of more general social relations between peers; it is, in other words, subservient to the intent and purpose of peer relations, both affiliative and aggressive. This point is made well by Troyna and Hatcher (1992), who have pointed to the way peer cultures express tensions between a desire for domination as well as equality, and how they can support racial teasing even when children themselves are not racist.

Conflict, then, is a normal part of social relations including that between peers. One function of breaktime, therefore, is its role in allowing pupils to develop strategies for the management of difficulties. What can be noticeable about fighting and aggression in primary schools is the extent to which pupils will go, and the sometimes skilful methods they employ, to *avoid* fights (Evans, 1989: Sluckin, 1981). This highlights the appropriate role of the school in the extent of control over breaktime life and we return to this theme in the conclusions.

Peer culture at breaktime

Researchers from disciplines other than psychology have been more ready to conclude that at breaktime children can acquire and develop a distinctive and vibrant culture, separate from the school culture, and not easily recognised by adults. Pollard (1985) argued that pupils' interests and rules vary according to school situation. Peer culture may appear more informal than the parallel school culture but it nonetheless has its own hierarchy, rules, and criteria of judgement. Different pupil subgroups – which Pollard called 'goodies', 'joker', and 'gang' groups – vary in the degree to which they draw on peer cultures, and therefore the degree to which they run counter to classroom-based school culture.

Sutton-Smith (1990, p. 5) has analysed more specifically the nature of breaktime culture and concludes:

> there is a culture of school playground play, just as there is a culture of schooling . . . Further, the school-playground child culture is apparently one of the most important as far as the children are concerned.

More recently, Grudgeon (1993) argued that playground culture is as complex, structured, and rule-bound as that of the classroom, and that the culture is learned from other children. Like Sluckin (1981), she sees the playground as a site of cultural transmission and socialisation into adult roles, though she more clearly shows that the culture of the playground, and the socialisation processes, are different for boys and girls.

In the case study already referred to there was evidence that in their play pupils were acquiring a distinctive culture, with particular activities and rules of engagement, that were particular to the school, though, interestingly, seemingly independent of staff (Blatchford, 1998).

The value of breaktime, therefore, can be in the opportunities it provides – probably rarer in children's lives than they once were – for control over play and social activity to rest with children themselves, and for the acquisition and development of a distinctive children's culture.

Social skills and competence

One assumption in some studies of breaktime play and activity is that life in the playground can help in the acquisition of many subtle social skills essential to later life (e.g. Sluckin, 1981). This notion of recess play as preparation for adulthood has been called a 'socialisation model' (see Pellegrini, 1995). Sutton-Smith (1982) cautions against an extreme version of this view because of the way it can detract from a recognition of the value of interaction to pupils here and now. More specifically, Boulton (1992) has drawn attention to the skilful way that children can form large (and sometimes very large) groups, and form their own social order when engaged in playground games, and how this is likely to benefit social development.

The implication of much developmental psychological research discussed here is that pupils with poor or inadequate social skills are more likely to behave inappropriately during breaktime play and activities and are more likely to be rejected or isolated. It is arguable, however, whether simply cutting back on breaktime will help such pupils. Breaktime is the time when their actions have possibly negative social consequences, but also when their difficulties are likely to be revealed. There is much work that can be done within schools to encourage social skills and skills in friendship building (see Roffey, Tarrant, & Majors, 1994), but as we have seen, pupils' social relations and culture can be very different at breaktime and it is likely that effective work in this area will be limited if it does not take account of breaktime experiences as well.

Supervision at breaktime

In the national questionnaire survey, information was collected on supervision arrangements at breaktime. At primary level, ancillary staff were the main supervisors, outnumbering teachers by 6 to 1, and this presence had increased over the last 5 years, while at secondary level about the same number of teachers, ancillary, and support staff were involved. We found that school teaching staff had concerns about the ability of supervisors to maintain discipline, their lack of training, and the quality of supervision provided. But, as described in Blatchford (1989), there is a danger of blaming supervisors, who themselves face considerable difficulties (on very low pay levels), when we should be considering, more fundamentally, the basis of supervision provided in school. The survey indicated that training of non-teaching supervisory staff relied on relatively informal arrangements such as informal discussion with teaching staff, and discussion of job description, school policy, or staff hand-book. In only a minority of schools was training provided by the LEA or outside group, or regular meetings held with senior teachers. The involve-ment of non-teaching staff in decision making regarding breaktime (see Blatchford & Sumpner, 1996) appeared limited and relatively superficial.

There were signs, seen in answers to the questionnaire, of recent initiatives at primary level with regard to supervision. Moreover, school staff, especially at primary level, thought that supervision had improved over the past 5 years. There is also a problem for school staff with regard to the turnover of ancillary staff, and difficulties of getting them involved in training and discussion. But in general, the supervision of breaktime, like breaktime itself, has tended to be marginalised and dealt with in an *ad hoc* way. It appears to us that the whole area of supervision at breaktime needs to be reconsidered funda-mentally, and that this should include examination of resources, training, and involvement in decision making.

Conclusion

It has been argued in this chapter that the playground is a site for peer inter-action that has both a negative and positive side. This presents dilemmas for school management. A main problem arises out of a tendency toward grow-ing restrictions on pupils' unsupervised activities within school, on the one hand, and the likely benefits of these activities for their social development, on the other. There is a tension, in other words, between a greater control of pupil behaviour, and the likely value of pupil independence. An important part of a school's position with regard to this tension between control and independence, as it bears on school breaktimes and play, largely hinges on the stance taken with regard to a main question: What is the appropriate role of adults with regard to breaktime? There are two extremes of view. The first, which might be called an 'interventionist' view, involves more deliberate management of pupils' behaviour at breaktime, and playground environment changes. In a similar vein, in some primary schools the supposed decline in traditional games has been approached by teaching children games. At the other extreme is an alternative, what might be called a 'non-interventionist' view. The Opies were very clear that adults had no role at all in children's play activities, no matter how well-meaning their intentions. In a strong warning the Opies (1969, p. 16) said:

> If children's games are tamed and made part of the school curricula, if waste-lands are turned into playing-fields for the benefits of those

who conform and ape their elders, if children are given the idea that they cannot enjoy themselves without being provided with the 'proper' equipment, we need blame only ourselves when we produce a generation who have lost their dignity, who are ever dissatisfied, and who descend for their sport to the easy excitement of rioting, or pilfering, or vandalism.

Both extremes have difficulties. The interventionist stance, which is probably gaining dominance, risks over-running pupils' freedoms and the positive aspects identified above, whereas the non-interventionist stance risks allowing anti-school cultures to develop and dominate, and have a destructive effect on school learning.

Recently, there have been a number of initiatives concerning school playgrounds and breaktimes (see Blatchford & Sharp, 1994). School grounds are being improved and opportunities for environmental education have been encouraged by organisations such as Learning Through Landscapes (Lucas, 1994). Sheat and Beer (1994) have described ways of involving pupils in the design and improvement of play grounds. In an effort to reduce bullying, there are initiatives to improve the school grounds in a collaborative way with pupils (Higgins, 1994). Titman (1994) has described ways of changing and developing school grounds based on awareness of pupils 'readings' of the school grounds.

Picking up what was said in the last section about supervision arrangements, another direction of recent work has been the introduction of a number of schemes to train supervisory staff and improve dialogue between lunchtime and teaching staff (see Fell, 1994; Sharp, 1994). A main message underlying recent breaktime initiatives (see especially Ross & Ryan, 1994) is that breaktime improvements should involve the whole school, that is, they should as far as possible involve all in schools – teaching staff, of course, but also ancillary staff, pupils, and parents – and they should also be whole-school approaches, in the sense that what is discussed and decided with regard to breaktime is consistent with what goes on in the school. Expectations about behaviour that are not seen to operate once pupils go outside to the playground are unlikely to be effective (Sharp & Blatchford, 1994).

As well as initiatives directed at breaktime and the playground, there have also been more specific initiatives to help and encourage interpersonal relations between pupils. These include techniques such as collaborative conflict resolution, peer counselling, and assertiveness training, which have been used as part of preventive work to reduce conflict and bullying (Sharp, Cooper, & Cowie, 1994; Sharp & Cowie, 1994).

These and other developments are to be welcomed. An important challenge facing schools, therefore, is getting the balance between the two polarities right, that is, the balance between control and independence. Is it possible to reconcile the value to pupils of free assembly, outside play, and social contact, with the understandable wish of schools to ensure control over behaviour and learning? One problem is that classroom-based initiatives (and even those on the playground) can still leave pupils' breaktime experiences and peer culture untouched, and separate. Elsewhere (Blatchford, 1998) I have attempted to develop some principles that could help inform a school's approach. In brief there is much that can be achieved from:

1   better descriptive information on, and better understanding of, the meaning and value of pupils' breaktime experiences;
2   more involvement of pupils in decisions concerning breaktime;
3   a more active role in facilitating in a sensitive way breaktime play and activities; and
4   working toward a moral context for breaktime activities and social relations, at both primary and secondary level.

I end by stressing again the positive as well as the negative side to breaktime play and experience. There are few signs of an appreciation in schools that breaktime may be the context for fundamental social processes that have value in social development. Current changes and developments in education are affecting breaktime experiences and there is little regard for something as marginal as breaktime. The danger is that we may recognise the value of breaktime to pupils long after changes have severely altered or reduced it.

References

Asher, S. R., & Coie, J. D. (1990). *Peer rejection in childhood*. Cambridge: Cambridge University Press.

Blatchford, P. (1989). *Playtime in the primary school: Problems and improvements*. Windsor, UK: NFER-NELSON (now London: Routledge).

Blatchford, P. (1994). Research on children's school playground behaviour in the UK: A review. In P. Blatchford & S. Sharp (Eds.), *Breaktime and the school: Understanding and changing playground behaviour*. London: Routledge.

Blatchford, P. (1996). ' We did more then': Changes in pupils' perceptions of breaktime (recess) from 7 to 16 years. *Journal of Research in Childhood Education*, 11, 14–24.

Blatchford, P. (1998). *Social life in school: Pupils' experiences of breaktime and recess from 7 to 16 years*. London: Falmer.

Blatchford, P., Creeser, R., & Mooney, A. (1990). Playground games and playtime: The children's view. *Educational Research*, 32, 163–174. Reprinted in M. Woodhead, P. Light, & R. Carr (Eds.) (1991). *Growing up in a changing society*. London: Routledge/Open University.

Blatchford, P., & Sharp. S. (Eds.) (1994). *Breaktime and the school: Understanding and changing playground behaviour*. London: Routledge.

Blatchford, P., & Sumpner, C. (1996). *Changes to breaktime in primary and secondary schools*. Final Report to Nuffield Foundation.

Blatchford, P., & Sumpner, C. (1998). What do we know about breaktime? Report on a National Survey of Changes to breaktime and lunchtime in primary and secondary schools. *British Educational Research Journal*. 24, 79–94.

Boulton, M. (1992). Participation in playground activities at middle school. *Educational Research*, 34, 167–182.

Boulton, M. (1994). Playful and aggressive fighting in the middle school playground. In P. Blatchford & S. Sharp (Eds.), *Breaktime and the school: Understanding and changing playground behaviour*. London: Routledge.

Boulton, M. (1996). Lunchtime supervisors' attitudes towards playful fighting, and ability to differentiate between playful and aggressive fighting: An intervention study. *British Journal of Educational Psychology*, 66, 367–381.

Davies, B. (1982). *Life in the classroom and the playground: The accounts of primary school children*. London: Routledge & Kegan Paul.

DES (Elton Report). (1989). *Discipline in schools: Report of the Committee of Enquiry*. Chaired by Lord Elton. London: HMSO.

DeVries, R. (1997). Piaget's social theory. *Educational Researcher*, March, 4–17.

Dodge, K., Coie, J. D., & Brakke, N. P. (1982). Behaviour patterns of socially rejected and neglected preadolescents: The roles of social approach and aggression. *Journal of Abnormal Child Psychology*, 10, 389–410.

Dunn, J. (1993). *Young children's close relationships: Beyond attachment*. Newbury Park. CA: Sage.

Erwin, P. (1993). *Friendship and peer relations in children*. Chichester, UK: Wiley.

Evans, J. (1989). *Children in play: Life in the school playground*. Geelong, Australia: Deakin University.

Evans, J. (unpublished). *Cutting playtime in response to behaviour problems in the playground*. Deakin University, Australia.

Faulkner, D., & Miell, D. (1993). Settling into school: The importance of early friendships for the development of children's social understanding and communicative competence. *International Journal of Early Years Education*, 1, 23–45.

Fell, G. (1994). You're only a dinner lady! A case study of the 'SALVE' lunchtime organiser project. In P. Blatchford & S. Sharp (Eds.), *Breaktime and the school: Understanding and changing playground behaviour*. London: Routledge.

Goodnow, J., & Burns, A. (1985). *Home and school: A child's eye view*. Sydney: Allen & Unwin.

Grudgeon, E. (1993). Gender implications of playground culture. In P. Woods & M. Hammersley (Eds.), *Gender and ethnicity in schools: Ethnographic accounts*. London: Routledge.

Hart, C. H. (Ed.) (1993). *Children on playgrounds: Research perspectives and applications*. Albany, NY: State University of New York Press.

Hartup, W. W. (1992). Friendships and their developmental significance. In H. McGurk (Ed.), *Childhood social development: Contemporary perspectives*. Hove, UK: Lawrence Erlbaum.

Hartup, W. W., & Laursen, B. (1993). Conflict and context in peer relations. In C. H. Hart (Ed.), *Children on playgrounds: Research perspectives and applications*. Albany, NY: State University of New York Press.

Higgins, C. (1994). Improving the school ground environment as an anti-bullying intervention. In P. K. Smith & S. Sharp (Eds.) (1994). *School bullying: Insights and perspectives*. London: Routledge.

Hillman, M. (1993). One false move . . . In M. Hillman (Ed.), *Children, transport and the quality of life*. London: Policy Studies Institute.

Humphreys, A. P., & Smith, P. K. (1987). Rough and tumble, friendship, and dominance in schoolchildren: Evidence for continuity and change with age. *Child Development*, 58, 201–212.

Journal of Research in Childhood Education (1996). Special edition: The role of recess in schools. 11, No. 1.

Kelly, E. (1988). Pupils, racial groups and behaviour in schools. In E. Kelly & T. Cohn, *Racism in schools – New research evidence*. Stoke-on-Trent, UK: Trentham.

Kelly, E. (1994). Racism and sexism in the playground. In P. Blatchford & S. Sharp (Eds.), *Breaktime and the school: Understanding and changing playground behaviour*. London: Routledge.

Ladd, G. W., Kochenderfer, B. J., & Coleman, C. C. (1996). Friendship quality as a predictor of young children's early school adjustment. *Child Development*. 67, 1103–1118.

Ladd, G. W., & Price, J. M. (1993). Playstyles of peer-accepted and peer-rejected children on the playground. In C. H. Hart (Ed.), *Children on playgrounds: Research perspectives and applications*. Albany, NY: State University of New York Press.

La Fontaine, J. (1991). *Bullying: The child's view*. London: Calouste Gulbekian Foundation.

Lucas, B. (1994). The power of school grounds: The philosophy and practice of learning through landscapes. In P. Blatchford & S. Sharp (Eds.), *Breaktime and the school: Understanding and changing playground behaviour*. London: Routledge.

Mooney, A.. Creeser, R., Blatchford, P. (1991). Children's views on teasing and fighting in junior schools. *Educational Research*, 33, 103–112.

Moyles, J. R. (1989). *Just playing: The role and status of play in early childhood education*. Milton Keynes, UK: Open University Press.

Olweus, D. (1993). *Bullying at school: What we know and what we can do*. Oxford: Blackwell.

Opie, I., & Opie, P. (1969). *Children's games in street and playground*. London: Oxford University Press.

Parker, J. G., & Asher, S. R. (1987). Peer relations and later personal adjustment: Are low-accepted children at risk? *Psychological Bulletin*. 102, 357–389.

Parker, J. G., & Gottman, J. M. (1989). Social and emotional development in a relational context: Friendship interaction from early childhood to adolescence. In T. J. Berndt & G. W. Ladd (Eds.), *Peer relationships in child development*. New York: Wiley.

Pellegrini, A. D. (1995). *School recess and playground behaviour: Educational and developmental roles*. Albany, NY: State University of New York Press.

Pellegrini, A. D., & Smith, P. K. (1993). School recess: Implications for education and development. *Review of Educational Research*. 63, 51–67.

Pollard, A. (1985). *The social world of the primary school*. London: Holt, Rinehart & Winston.

Roffey, S., Tarrant, T., & Majors, K. (1994). *Young friends: Schools and friendship*. London: Cassell.

Ross, C., & Ryan, A. (1994). Changing playground society: A whole-school approach. In P. Blatchford & S. Sharp (Eds.), *Breaktime and the school: Understanding and changing playground behaviour*. London: Routledge.

Savin-Williams, R. C., & Berndt, T. J. (1990). Friendship and peer relations. In S. S. Feldman & G. R. Elliott (Eds.), *At the threshold: The developing adolescent*. Cambridge, MA: Harvard University Press.

Shantz, C. U., & Hartup, W. W. (1992). *Conflict in child and adolescent development*. Cambridge: Cambridge University Press.

Sharp, S. (1994). Training schemes for lunchtime supervisors in the United Kingdom: An overview. In P. Blatchford & S. Sharp (Eds.), *Breaktime and the school: Understanding and changing playground behaviour*. London: Routledge.

Sharp, S., & Blatchford, P. (1994). Understanding and changing school breaktime behaviour: Themes and conclusion. In P. Blatchford & S. Sharp (Eds.), *Breaktime and the school: Understanding and changing playground behaviour*. London: Routledge.

Sharp, S., Cooper, F., & Cowie, H. (1994). Making peace in the playground. In P. Blatchford & S. Sharp (Eds.), *Breaktime and the school: Understanding and changing playground behaviour*. London: Routledge.

Sharp, S., & Cowie, H. (1994). Empowering pupils to take positive action against bullying. In P. K. Smith & S. Sharp (Eds.), *School bullying: Insights and perspectives*. London: Routledge.

Sharp, S., & Smith, P. K. (1994). *Tackling bullying in your school*. London: Routledge.

Sheat, L. G., & Beer, A. R. (1994). Giving pupils an effective voice in the design and use of their school grounds. In P. Blatchford & S. Sharp (Eds.), *Breaktime and the school: Understanding and changing playground behaviour*. London: Routledge.

Sluckin, A. (1981). *Growing up in the playground: The social development of children*. London: Routledge & Kegan Paul.

Smith, P. (1990). The role of play in the nursery and primary school curriculum. In C. Rogers & P. Kutnick (Eds.), *The social psychology of the primary school*. London: Routledge.

Smith, P. (1994). What children learn from playtime, and what adults can learn from it. In P. Blatchford & S. Sharp (Eds.), *Breaktime and the school: Understanding and changing playground behaviour*. London: Routledge.

Smith, P. K., & Sharp, S. (Eds.) (1994). *School bullying: Insights and perspectives*. London: Routledge.

Sutton-Smith, B. (1982). A performance theory of peer relations. In K. M. Borman (Eds.), *The social life of children in a changing society*. Hillsdale, NJ: Lawrence Erlbaum.

Sutton-Smith, B. (1990). School playground as festival. *Children's Environments Quarterly*. 7, 3–7.

Tattum, D., & Lane, D. (Eds.) (1989). *Bullying in schools*. Stoke on Trent: Trentham.

Thorne, B. (1993). *Gender play: Girls and boys in school*. Buckingham: Open University Press.

Titman, W. (1994). *Special places, special people: The hidden curriculum of the school grounds*. Godalming, UK: World Wildlife Fund for Nature/Learning Through Landscapes.

Troyna, B., & Hatcher, R. (1992). *Racism in children's lives: A study of mainly-white primary schools*. London: Routledge.

Williams, B. T. R.. & Gilmour, J. D. (1994). Annotation: Sociometry and peer relationships. *Journal of Child Psychology and Psychiatry*, 35, 997–1013.

Youniss, J. (1980). *Parents and peers in social development: A Sullivan-Piaget perspective*. Chicago, IL: University of Chicago Press.

Chapter 6

Relationships of children involved in bully/victim problems at school*

Peter K. Smith, Louise Bowers, Valerie Binney and Helen Cowie

For a child at school, perhaps the most important and salient aspects for happiness will be the quality of relationships with peers. This is not to deny the importance of early relationships with parents, generally thought to be crucial in the early years (e.g. Bowlby, 1988), and indeed to have continuing influence on the extent and quality of peer relationships. But, and especially if relationships with parents are reasonably satisfactory, by middle childhood peer relationships will occupy much of a child's time. This appears to be increasingly so through to adolescence; and the quality of friendships during these years is likely to affect later indicators of social adjustment, such as criminality, and mental health problems (Kupersmidt, Coie, & Dodge, 1990; Parker & Asher, 1987). Correlational evidence certainly supports such links, and various causal models have been proposed (Parker & Asher, 1987).

Most of the evidence on peer relationships in middle childhood comes from studies in schools. In modern urban societies, schools provide a prominent forum for same-age peer interaction, and for about 25 percent of the typical school day, children are engaged in playtime or dinner break activities, which allow for fairly unstructured peer interactions. The majority of such peer *interactions* are, in general terms, amicable and supportive, or playful; the majority of peer *relationships* are friendly or neutral. Observations in playgrounds indicate that actual fights between pupils are rare, taking up usually less than 1 percent of playground time (Humphreys & Smith, 1987; Pellegrini, 1989a).

Nevertheless some interactions are hostile, and some relationships are far from friendly. Psychologists have long been interested in aggressive interactions (for a review, see Parke & Slaby, 1983). However, many aggressive interactions are transient ways of dealing with immediate conflicts that may arise between two individuals. Probably more insidious for children's developing relationships are situations in which a child (or children) *persistently* harasses or causes hurt to another child. In this more relationship-oriented

---

* This is an edited version of a chapter that appeared in *Learning about relationships*, Newbury Park, CA: Sage Publications, 1993.

mode, we may think of "bullies" (who harass others) and "victims" (who are the recipients of this harassment). Research on bully/victim relationships does often tend to become a study of bullies or victims as individuals (and the evidence for stability of these categories across time [Olweus, 1991] goes some way to justify this), but the relationship concept is implicit in the definition.

The study of bully/victim relationships and associated problems in schools has shown a recent upsurge in interest in Scandinavia, the United Kingdom, North America, continental Europe, and Japan. These relationships appear to be prevalent and serious (Olweus, 1991; Smith, 1991b). In the United Kingdom, a survey of 6,758 pupils in Sheffield, based on anonymous pupil questionnaires, reported 27 percent of junior/middle school children and 10 percent of secondary school children were being bullied "sometimes" or more often; more frequent bullying of "once a week" or more was reported by 10 percent of junior/middle school children and 4 percent of secondary school children (Whitney & Smith, 1993). Comparable figures are available from Ireland, Spain, the Netherlands, and Japan; lesser but still significant figures are available from Scotland and Norway.

Bullying can have a devastating effect on the lives of victims. They suffer continuing loss of confidence and self-esteem in social relationships. They may resort to absenteeism to escape torment at school (Reid, 1983), and in the most severe cases victims have been known to commit suicide. For the child who bullies, too, an increased incidence of later problems of alcohol abuse, domestic violence, and violent crime in the community has been reported (Lane, 1989; Olweus, 1991).

School-based interventions to combat the problem have been implemented and have had some degree of success (Olweus, 1991; Smith, 1991b). But it is also important to understand why some children become bullies or victims and others do not. What part do child and family characteristics have in this matter? Also the nature of peer relationships that bullies and victims have is an area of interest and debate. Do bullies lack social skills, in some sense? Are bullying behaviors, by contrast, adaptive in some ways? Are bullies developing status and reputation in the peer group?

In this chapter we review these issues. First, however, we consider further what is meant by *bullying* and its relationship to such behaviors as teasing and playful fighting.

Definitions of bullying, teasing, and playful fighting

Bullying, and related terms such as *harassment,* can be taken to be a subset of aggressive behavior (e.g., Manning, Heron, & Marshall, 1978; Price & Dodge, 1989). As with aggressive behavior generally, bullying intentionally causes hurt to the recipient. This hurt can be both physical and psychological; although some bullying takes the form of hitting, pushing, and taking money, it also may involve telling nasty stories or social exclusion. It may be carried out by one child or a group.

Three further criteria particularly distinguish bullying. First, the hurt done is <u>unprovoked</u>, at least by any action that would normally be considered a provocation. (Being clumsy, for instance, might invoke some bullying but would not normally be considered a legitimate provocation.) Second, bullying is thought of as a <u>repeated action</u>; something that happens only once or twice would not be called bullying. Third, the child doing the bullying is generally thought of as <u>being stronger or is perceived as stronger</u>; at least, the victim is not (or does not feel him- or herself to be) in a position to retaliate very effectively (Smith, 1991b).

Teasing provides a category of behavior that overlaps with bullying, being persistently irritating but in a minor way or such that, dependent on context, it may or may not be taken as playful. Pawluk (1989) provides a useful analysis of how teasing may be construed. She draws attention to three factors: (a) the *commentary*, particularly how the teaser signals intent and the relation of the tease to prior events or context; (b) the *recipient response*, whether the person teased takes it in a serious or lighthearted way; and (c) the *audience response*, whether anyone else witnessing the teasing evaluates it as playful or hurtful.

In our own work on self-reports of bullying or being bullied, we have included <u>nasty teasing</u> as bullying. This inclusion emphasizes the importance of commentary or of recipient response and the finding from interviewing children that they, too, distinguished playful and more hurtful kinds of teasing (Ahmad & Smith, 1990).

Playful fighting is usually different from bullying

Playful teasing might be signaled by laughing or smiling to mark what might otherwise be an ambiguous remark or action. This action has clear parallels with what happens in play fighting. Play fighting and chasing, or "<u>rough-and-tumble play</u>," is a typical form of behavior in children, taking up some 10 percent of playground time in middle childhood (Humphreys & Smith, 1987; Pellegrini, 1989a). It looks in many respects like real fighting but is clearly distinguishable in a number of respects by children and by trained adult observers (Boulton, 1991a; Costabile *et al.*, 1991). It is often indexed by laughter or smiling. Play fighting and chasing normally show self-handicapping and restraint; participants do not fight or chase at full strength. This forbearance allows friendly play to continue, even between unequally matched partners. It often is characterized by reversal of roles, as first one child is on top, then the other.

Unlike bullying and nasty teasing, *play fighting* and *play chasing* seem generally to be activities often enjoyed and participated in by friends. A study of 5-, 8-, and 11-year-olds in England and in Italy found that about half of the children said they enjoyed play fighting, and over 80 percent said they enjoyed play chasing (Smith, Hunter, Carvalho, & Costabile, 1992). Smith and Lewis (1985) found that observed play partners for play fighting in 3- and 4-year-olds tended to be ranked as highly liked and that "best friends" participated in a greater number of play fighting episodes than expected by chance. Similarly Humphreys and Smith (1987) found that at 7, 9, and 11 years, play fighting partners ranked each other above chance for "liking," both when the points of view of the initiator and of the recipient of the play fighting bout were considered. Boulton (1991b) found that 8- and 11-year-olds liked play fighting partners at above chance levels.

There is evidence that play fighting can provide some benefits to the play participants. The two most frequently hypothesized benefits are that it may provide practice in fighting skills (Humphreys & Smith, 1987) and that it practices social skills (Pellegrini, 1988).

The hypothesis that play fighting improves fighting skills (which it resembles in form) would be consistent with children choosing friends as play partners but also would predict that children would chose partners matched for fighting ability. Humphreys and Smith (1987) found that although this was not the case at 7 and 9 years of age, there was evidence for this at 11 years. Boulton (1991b) reports that play fighting partners were closely matched for strength at both 8 and 11 years.

The hypothesis that play fighting advances social skills is supported by work with parent–infant physical play (MacDonald & Parke, 1984; Power & Parke, 1981), as well as peer–peer play (Pellegrini, 1988). It is argued that such forms of play develop communication skills of encoding and decoding (as in displaying or understanding play signals), the ability to regulate emotional display and strength of physical action (as in restraint), and the ability to take turns and to understand another's point of view (as in role reversals and self-handicapping).

Parke et al. (1987) reported correlational evidence to suggest that father–infant physical play correlates with emotional decoding ability; MacDonald (1987) found that children who were sociometrically neglected at nursery school had less parent–infant physical play at home; rejected children had more physical play at home, but it was characterized by overstimulation or avoidance of stimulation. These findings are patchy, but the general hypothesis that physical play and play fighting develop social skills is supported by corresponding findings from Pellegrini (1988) on peer play fighting. He found that, for popular children, frequency of play fighting correlated with a social skills measure. Also, popular children are best able to distinguish play fighting from real fighting on videotape episodes presented to them (Pellegrini, 1989b).

Play fighting can turn into fighting and bullying

Just as teasing can be ambiguous, so too can play fighting. The conventions of handicap and self-restraint normally are recognized in play fights, but cheating may occur. This possibility was pointed out by Fagen (1981); a participant might take advantage of the "play convention" to actually harm another when that other has "consented" to be in an inferior position in a play bout. Some reports on play fighting in young children have found very low frequencies of such cheating (Fry, 1987; Humphreys & Smith, 1987; Smith & Lewis, 1985), but instances were reported by Neill (1976) in a sample of 12- to 13-year-old boys. He reported that play fighting might be used as

> a means of asserting or maintaining dominance; once the weaker boy has registered distress the bond can be maintained by the fight taking a more playful form, but if he does not do so at the start of the fight, the stronger boy may increase the intensity of the fight until he does.
>
> (Neill, 1976, p. 219)

The sociometric status of children (Coie, Dodge, & Coppotelli, 1982) is another relevant factor here. Pellegrini (1988) found that play fighting seldom led to real fighting in most 5- to 9-year-old children but that it often did so in children who were sociometrically *rejected*. The actual nature of the rough-and-tumble bouts was not described in Pellegrini's study, however, so it is not certain what aspects of the rejected children's play fighting bouts led so often (in 25 percent of cases) to fighting or whether "cheating" was involved. However, rejected children are overrepresented among children nominated by peers as bullies and victims.

Bullies, victims, and social relations with peers

Overall, both bullies and victims tend to be disliked by peers, but the picture is by no means a simple one. On sociometric tests, our own studies suggest that bullies tend to be either *controversial* or *rejected* (Boulton & Smith, 1994; Smith & Boulton, 1991). Thus they are collecting mainly "liked least" nominations from peers, but also, in the case of controversial children, some "liked most" nominations; they have a high social impact. On behavioral nominations (as used by Coie *et al.*, 1982), bullies tend to be nominated often as "starting fights," and "disrupting" others, but sometimes as high in "leadership" (Boulton & Smith, 1994; Whitney, Nabuzoka, & Smith, 1992). Some bullies can be quite liked and be leaders within their own network or gang (Cairns, Cairns, Neckerman, Gest, & Gariepy, 1988; Sluckin, 1981). Olweus (1991) also found that bullies were not necessarily less popular than other children. Using the Harter Self-Perception Profile (Harter, 1985), our own studies suggest that bullies do not have low self-esteem, except perhaps (accurately!) so far as the *behavioral conduct* scale is concerned. [. . .]

Victims tend to be *rejected* on sociometric tests and to be nominated as "shy" and "seeking help" (Boulton & Smith, 1994; Whitney *et al.*, 1992). The perceived shyness of victims may be reflected in such measures as how often the children are alone and how lonely they report feeling. More victims than nonvictims report feeling lonely at school (Olweus, 1991). For some victims, at least, a natural tendency to withdraw may be a contributory factor. [. . .] Other victims may wish to associate with others but, through factors such as prejudice, may be unable to do so as much as they wish. [. . .]

Typically victims of bullying appear to have a low opinion of themselves and to be anxious and insecure (Olweus, 1991), as do many socially withdrawn children (Rubin *et al.*, 1990) and rejected children (Patterson *et al.*, 1990). We found that victims generally perceived themselves as being less *physically competent* than did bullies and noninvolved children and that female victims perceived themselves as being less *well accepted* by their peers than did the other two groups (Boulton & Smith, 1994).

There is good evidence for a distinction between *passive* or *withdrawn victims*, who do not often start fights or disrupt others, and *provocative victims* or "bully/victims," who do often start fights and tend to be the least liked children of all (Smith & Boulton, 1991). This distinction corresponds to that of Pikas (1989) between innocent victims and provocative victims and to corresponding categories in Stephenson and Smith (1989). Our findings suggest that these bully/victims (who often are nominated as both bullies and victims by classmates) are seen as the least cooperative children. Bully/victims, like bullies, do not seem to show low self-esteem (Smith & Boulton, 1991) despite their objective unpopularity; however, given the disturbed nature of many of these children, it is possible that self-esteem tests such as the Harter are eliciting defensive or idealized responses. [. . .]

Bullying and peer relationships

One influential group of theorists (Dodge *et al.*, 1986) see the cause of many problems in peer relationships as lying in a lack of appropriate social skills. Following an information-processing model of social interaction, they hypothesize that some children may interpret social signals incorrectly or have only a very limited range of response options available. Thus *aggressive children* may overreact to ambiguous signals and more readily select aggressive response options in a provocative situation. On the other hand, *withdrawn children* may lack the social skills of group entry. The evidence for the social skills deficit approach is mixed, however, and this approach leaves open the question of why some children lack these social skills (leaving aside cases of clear cognitive disability).

Applied to bullies and victims, the social skills approach would suggest that bullies have deficits similar to those of aggressive children, while victims may lack social skills of assertiveness and group entry. For bullies, however, the "deficit" label may be inappropriate. Rather than misinterpreting signals or having a limited range of response options, some bullies may simply be choosing goals of dominance and status reputation by aggressive and domineering means. [. . .] Two sources of evidence – attributions of others' behavior, and "cheating" in play fighting – are relevant here.

Attributions made by bullies and victims

Developing the ideas of Dodge and Frame (1982) that rejected and aggressive children may perceive ambiguous stimuli differently from other children, we have examined the way bullies, victims, and control children (who were neither bullies nor victims) perceived a videotape of fighting and bullying and described the feelings of the participants. Participating were 45 children, aged 9–11 years, 15 each of bully, victim, or control status, determined from peer nomination. They were shown a videotape depicting two incidents of physical fighting in the playground; in the second, another child intervened to stop it. They then were interviewed about how they interpreted these scenes, how the participants might have felt, whether they had experienced similar events, and why the children might be behaving that way.

When viewing the videotape, both bullies and victims tended to describe the two episodes as "bullying," whereas controls tended to describe it as "fighting." Other results suggested that bullies differed from both the victims and the controls in a number of respects. Most of the bullies (80 percent), but few of the controls or victims (30 percent), described the bullies in the videotape episodes as feeling "happy"; few of the bullies (27 percent), but most of the controls or victims (53 percent), described the victim as feeling "unhappy." Many bullies (47 percent), but few controls or victims (13 percent), thought that the bullying was happening because of some relatively unchangeable characteristic of the victim (such as physical appearance or color). Most bullies (67 percent) also thought that the bullying in the videotape was due to provocation and that if they themselves bullied others it was due to provocation.

In general, this and more detailed qualitative analysis of the interviews suggest that many bullies see little wrong in their bullying behavior; they are happy doing it; the playground is a tough place; and, though they show little awareness of the victim's feelings, they assert that the victim in one way or another often deserved the bullying.

"Cheating" in play fighting

Pellegrini (1988) found that, for rejected children, play fighting often "went wrong," turning into real fighting. Rejected children are often aggressive

(Coie *et al.*, 1982), and a lack of social skills could contribute to this aggression if playful signals or ambiguous contexts are mistakenly interpreted as aggressive. Evidence supports this scenario, both from ethnographic reports of playground behavior (Sluckin, 1981) and from the finding that rejected, aggressive children do interpret ambiguous cues as aggressive in test situations (Dodge & Frame, 1982). Such examples of play fighting going wrong might be thought of as "honest mistakes" (Fagen, 1981) if a signal is genuinely misunderstood.

But the alternative "cheating" hypothesis implies a different and more deliberate causation that Neill's (1976) observations, cited earlier, are more consistent with. Here, play fighting appears to be a context in which "cheating," and hence a public humiliation of the play partner, may be used to display dominance and, perhaps, to increase the status or reputation of the cheat or bully with the immediate peer group. Such ideas would link with the suggestion from many ethnographic and sociological writings that children who are aggressive or antisocial may have their own cliques or networks of allies (Cairns *et al.*, 1988; Hargreaves, 1967) and may be establishing or managing a reputation as a tough and dominant person in this network (Emler & Reicher, 1993; Sluckin, 1981).

There may be an adaptive value for some children to achieve a "tough" reputation, in terms of their likely later career paths (Emler & Reicher, 1993). [. . .] Whether or not this particular adaptive hypothesis is correct, it may be useful to think of aggressive, cheating kinds of play fighting, and bullying more generally, to be for some children a particular developmental pathway that may have advantages and that does not necessarily reflect lack of social skills in any narrow sense (Smith, 1991a).

Peer relationships and family circumstances

Belsky, Steinberg, and Draper (1991) hypothesize a link between aggressive peer relationships and family-rearing experience at the level of adaptive significance rather than immediate causal pathways. Other theories are more relevant to causal links. Most of the relevant research has looked at correlates with high aggressiveness in children, rather than at bullying *per se* (and the background factors predisposing to being a victim are even less well explored). Two broad approaches are evident here.

One approach stems from attachment theory and especially from recent developments of the concept of *internal working models*. Following Bowlby (1969, 1988), theorists such as Bretherton (1985) and Main (1991) argue that a child develops internal working models of relationships that may be secure or insecure (avoidant, ambivalent, or disorganized). Unless there are changes in life circumstances (or an internal cognitive reevaluation that is thought unlikely to happen before adolescence), these patterns of attachment are hypothesized to show continuity into secure and insecure (dismissing, dependent/preoccupied, and controlling/disorganized) relationships in middle childhood and adulthood.

Insofar as the internal model of relationships developed with primary caregivers is generalized to others, these patterns may be expected to affect relations with peers as well as parents. Some evidence for this influence has appeared in the last few years – for example, linking child–mother attachment to qualities of friendship (Park & Waters, 1989) and to sociometric status at school (Cohn, 1990).

One study has made a specific link to bully/victim relationships. Troy and Sroufe (1987) characterized 38 children as having either a secure, anxious-avoidant, or anxious-resistant attachment with their mothers; when the children were 4–5 years old, they were assigned to same-gender play groups. All cases of bullying occurred when a child with an avoidant attachment history (the bully) was paired with a child with an anxious attachment history (the victim). Children who had been securely attached were able to distance themselves and to avoid bullying or being bullied. [. . .]

The theoretical background to this approach is most thoroughly worked out by Renken et al. (1989). They suggest that children with avoidant-insecure attachment relationships lack trust and expect hostility and thus may develop aggressive patterns of interaction with peers. By contrast, children with ambivalent-insecure attachment relationships with parents are likely to be getting haphazard care and to doubt their own effectiveness in influencing the caregiver. While staying somewhat dependent, they lack self-esteem and confidence in their own worth and are thus susceptible to being victimized by peers. Renken et al. (1989) report some (limited) confirmation of these associations.

This approach does not put so much emphasis on social skills as on the child's internal model of relationships. Social withdrawal, however, will in itself lead to less practice in important peer social skills, so many withdrawn children and many victims might indeed lack some social skills even if this may not be a primary cause for their condition.

The second approach is represented by a body of work on parenting styles not closely related to attachment theory. For example, Manning et al. (1978) reported that children with overcontrolling or dominating parents were found to harass other children more often at school. Using path analysis, Olweus (1980) reported that four factors contributed significantly to peer-rated aggression of boys: the boy's temperament (active, hot-headed), the mother's negativism (lack of warmth), the mother's permissiveness of aggression, and the parents' use of power-assertive methods. Loeber and Dishion (1984) found that parents who practiced inconsistent or highly aversive discipline techniques, coupled with physical punishment, were more likely to have a child who was aggressive toward others. Dishion (1990) used path analysis to show that ineffective parental discipline (rather more than lack of parental monitoring) led to antisocial behavior. These studies suggest that children growing up in such families are having aggressive behaviors modeled for them, and, in the absence of effective discipline and perhaps monitoring by parents, these behaviors develop and are used subsequently in peer interactions. [. . .]

Patterson *et al.* (1989) have elaborated a developmental path-way embodying these ideas. Poor parental discipline and monitoring practices are presumed to lead to childhood conduct problems (such as aggression), in turn leading to academic failure and rejection by normal (nondeviant) peers. These outcomes, in turn, result in children who more frequently have commitment to a deviant peer group and who subsequently get involved in delinquent behavior.

These two approaches both focus on familial determinants of peer aggressiveness but have different emphases – one on internal models of relationships, and one on parental management and discipline practices. Are they reconcilable? [. . .]

Rubin *et al.* (1990) also have gone some way to integrate conceptual aspects of the two research traditions, basically proposing an integrative pathway model. They suggest a set of developmental pathways linking familial circumstances, infant temperament, mother–infant attachment, child-rearing techniques, self-esteem, and peer relationships. From this general model they postulate two main "deviant" pathways – one leading to aggressive or provocative peer problems, the other leading to passive/withdrawal problems and difficulties in initiating and maintaining relationships. The first pathway is linked to dispositional and temperamental traits in the child, such as being fussy and difficult to soothe, and to insecure-avoidant attachment patterns, leading to hostility, peer rejection, and externalizing problems. The second pathway is linked to dispositional and temperamental traits in the child, such as shyness, and to insecure-ambivalent attachment patterns, leading to anxiety, lack of social success, and internalizing problems such as withdrawal.

The first pathway might lead to bullying behavior, though the concept is not synonymous with high aggression. The second pathway might lead to being a victim. Anxiety and withdrawal may increase vulnerability to bullying, further lowering the individual's self-esteem, making him or her a still easier victim in the peer group. A vicious cycle can be set up, reinforced by the child's reputation in the peer group.

A study of family influences from different perspectives

The integrative models proposed are promising, but it is by no means certain that different factors – such as attachment relationships or parental management practices – have equal impact. Also the research is mostly on children defined by sociometric status, aggression, and withdrawal. In our own research, we are investigating aspects of family relationships from several points of view (Bowers *et al.*, 1992, 1994). We have focused on the family as perceived by the child; the child's own subjective view of relationships may reveal best his or her working models of relationships and relate most strongly to peer relationships (Patterson *et al.*, 1990; Schaefer, 1965). We have related family characteristics to children nominated as bullies, victims, bully/victims (children nominated both as bullies and victims), and controls.

Children aged 8–11 years were selected from nine classes in three Sheffield middle schools, a total sample pool of about 200 children. On the basis of peer nomination, 20 bullies, 20 victims, 20 bully/victims, and 20 control children were chosen from this pool. These four subgroups were reasonably balanced for age, gender, and ethnicity and did not differ in mean family size/ number of siblings. Children were interviewed individually using standard interview measures such as the Family Relations Test (FRT) (Bene & Anthony, 1957); the Parental Style Questionnaire (PSQ) (a measure of parental warmth and discipline modified from Parker, Tupling, & Brown, 1979) and a family sculpt task, the FAST, in which family figures are represented on a spatial plot (Gehring & Wyler, 1986).

The findings from the FRT on the total sample indicated that, for these children, who were approaching adolescence, the predominating role of parents in the child's life was moderated not only by friends and peers outside the family but also by siblings and other family members who are seen as within the family (such as aunts, grandparents). Siblings and some other family members captured a great deal of the involvement expressed by the children. Involvement with siblings was reasonably balanced but with appreciable negative elements; involvement with other family members, as also with mother and father but often with less intensity, was generally positive.

The results from the FRT, when combined with those from the PSQ and the FAST, yielded clear and interesting differences between the four subgroups of bullies, bully/victims, victims, and controls. Children involved in bullying others, whether bullies or bully/victims, shared some characteristics: They were more likely not to have a father at home, but to have another family member at first involvement rank (this was not just an artifact of absent fathers; only two of the nine children who ranked another family member first, lacked a father), and in the FAST test they more often marginalized one or more family members by putting them into a corner of the plot.

Bullies and bully/victims, however, differed in other respects. Bullies particularly indicated a lack of cohesion on the FAST test, by spreading out the figures widely, and a concern with power. Their FRT results indicated high ambivalent involvement with siblings and others, and the FAST results indicated that they saw siblings and others as powerful. Although poor relationships with parents often have been suggested as a factor in children's aggressiveness, these data highlighted the apparently relatively negative relationships with those siblings or other family members who often elicit high involvement at this age – in general, a family system lacking cohesion and warmth and with marked power relationships.

Bully/victims, by contrast, indicated on the PSQ more troubled relations directly with parents; they perceived parents lowest for accurate monitoring and warmth, yet highest for overprotection and for neglect, thus indicating inconsistent discipline/monitoring practices untempered by warm affection. This description is actually more similar to the picture of parental antecedents of bullying from Olweus (1980); in addition, however, these bully/victims indicated some increased obsession with self, both in terms of involvement (FRT) and power (FAST). Although they tended to put more power blocks under themselves and saw their mothers as relatively lacking in power, they also gave more negative items to themselves on the FRT. This distribution suggests an ambivalence about themselves that bears out the suggestion from other evidence (Stephenson & Smith, 1989) that bully/victims may be the most at risk of the four subgroups.

The picture for victims is different again from that of bully/victims; it is one of high and positive involvement with other family members, but perhaps to the extent of an enmeshed family structure. Victims tended to clump all figures together without separation on the FAST test; to have a parent more often at first or second involvement rank on the FRT, apparently unusual at this age; and to show high positive involvement generally with siblings and other family members.

Finally the control children represented their families as cohesive on the FAST test, but not as clumped as did the victims, and they did not have such high involvement with parents as victims did. They also perceived their parents as highest on accurate monitoring and lowest on both neglect and punitiveness. Mothers were seen to have equal power to fathers. In general, these parents seemed to be providing a warm, secure environment without being overinvolved with their children. [. . .]

Overview of bullies' and victims' relationships with others

It is clear that bullies and victims differ from other children in their peer relationships and in their family relationships; from what little evidence we have, this is true of bully/victims (or provocative victims) too. These differences (and the differences of rejected and aggressive children, who often overlap with the victims and bullies) can be described from various perspectives: in the case of peer relationships, social information-processing and deficit models, or models based on manipulation of conventions and management of reputation; in the case of family relationships, models based on internal working models and attachment, or parental management styles.

It is tempting to say that all of these models may represent facets of the truth, at least for certain subgroups of children. Such a view may have something to recommend it; for example, the different approaches to family relationships may look primarily at different aspects of a complete system, as our own study indicates. However, models and theories can sometimes use-fully confront each other, and, notably, it is difficult to reconcile the social skills deficit approach to evidence that some bullies are deliberately pursuing goals that humiliate others publicly and downplay others' feelings, possibly for their own advantage.

The social skills deficit model may have most relevance to victims of bullying who are shy and withdrawn. They may be enmeshed in overintense or overinvolved family systems, consistent with dependent or preoccupied types of attachment relationships. It is possible that they thereby get less practice in the rougher sorts of social interaction, the teasing and play fight-ing that (both in family and peer contexts) actually may enhance social skills, and the control and interpretation of emotional expression.

So far as bullies are concerned, both our attributional data and our family data suggest that, by middle childhood, they are developing a general model of relationships as lacking warmth and concerned with power, consistent with the dismissing relationships postulated by attachment theorists, This involvement with power relations and lack of cohesion in families of bullies is, by 8.11 years of age, perceived as much or more with siblings and other family members as with parents. Furthermore, some bullies are, if not popu-lar, at least controversial in the peer group; that is, they have their own friends and may be dominant and influential in the peer group. Rather than lacking social skills, they may be able to manipulate situations to their own ends; they do, however, seem to ignore unhappiness of victims and do not readily accept responsibility or blame for their own actions.

Bully/victims appear to form a clear subgroup with a distinct identity from children who just bully others or from children who are just victims, a subgroup that deserves more attention in future research. So far, we have found this subgroup to overlap considerably with the aggressive-rejected subset of children from sociometric studies, who appear to have a distinct profile also from this tradition of research (Patterson *et al.*, 1990). In contrast to bullies, the location of such bully/victims' own perceived problems in middle childhood continues to lie with lack of accurate monitoring and discipline practices of parents; and bully/victims are more likely to be involved with themselves in an ambivalent way. This ambivalence possibly could be linked to disorganized attachment patterns, if further research con firms the usefulness of attachment theory in this area.

Finally it is worth noting that these arguments are not just academic ones. Given the problems associated with peer group bullying noted earlier, implications for treatment are important. The social skills approach already has led to associated training programs for highly aggressive children, though with only moderate success (Akhtar & Bradley, 1991). Insofar as parental management is important, working with parents would be appropriate (Patterson *et al.*, 1989). Links to attachment problems might suggest, by middle childhood at least, the usefulness of counseling approaches to work through issues of relationships (Pikas, 1989). Finally, insofar as some children may be following strategies that are adaptive in terms of dominance and status, approaches may include not only moral development programs but also creating an institutional and peer environment that sanctions against, rather than ignores or condones, the kinds of continuing hurtful actions that occur in bully/victim relationships (Olweus, 1991; Smith & Thompson, 1991).

References

Ahmad, Y., & Smith, P. K. (1990). Behavioral measures: Bullying in schools. *Newletter of the Association for Child Psychology and Psychiatry*, 12, 26–27.

Akhtar, N., & Bradley, E. J. (1991). Social information processing deficits of aggressive children: Present findings and implications for social skills training. *Clinical Psychology Review*, 11, 621–644.

Belsky, J., Steinberg, L., & Draper, P. (1991). Childhood experience, interpersonal development, and reproductive strategy: An evolutionary theory of socialization. *Child Development*, 62, 647–670.

Bene, J., & Anthony, J. (1957). *Manual for the Family Relations Test.* London: National Foundation for Education Research.

Boulton, M. J. (1991a). A comparison of structural and contextual features of middle school children's playful and aggressive fighting. *Ethology and Sociobiology*, 12, 1119–1145.

Boulton, M. J. (1991b). Partner preferences in middle school children's playful fighting and chasing. *Ethology and Sociobiology*, 12, 177–193.

Boulton, M. J., & Smith, P. K. (1994). Bully/victim problems in middle school children: Stability, self-perceived competence, peer perceptions, and peer acceptance. *British Journal of Developmental Psychology*, 12, 315–329.

Bowers, L., Smith, P. K., & Binney, V. A. (1992). Cohesion and power in the families of children involved in bully/victim problems at school. *Journal of Family Therapy*, 14, 371–387.

Bowers, L., Smith, P. K., & Binney, V. A. (1994). Family relationships as perceived by children involved in bully/victim problems at school. *Journal of Personal and Social Relationships*, 11, 215–232.

Bowlby, J. (1969). *Attachment and loss.* New York: Basic Books.

Bretherton, I. (1985). Attachment theory: Retrospect and prospect. In I. Bretherton & E. Waters (Eds.), *Growing points of attachment theory and research* (Monographs of the Society for Research in Child Development, Vol. 50, Serial No. 209, pp. 3–35). Chicago: University of Chicago Press.

Cairns, R. B., Cairns, B. D., Neckerman, H. J., Gest, S. D., & Gariepy, J. (1988). Social networks and aggressive behavior: Peer support of peer rejection. *Developmental Psychology*, 24, 815–823.

Cohn, D. A. (1990). Child–mother attachment at six years and social competence at school. *Child Development*, 61, 152–162.

Coie, J. D., Dodge, K. A., & Coppotelli, H. A. (1982). Dimensions and types of social status: A cross-age perspective. *Developmental Psychology*, 18, 557–569.

Costabile, A., Smith, P. K., Matheson, L., Aston, J., Hunter, T., & Boulton, M.

(1991). Cross-national comparison of how children distinguish serious and playful fighting. *Developmental Psychology*, 27, 881–887.

Dishion, T. (1990). The family ecology of boys' peer relations in middle childhood. *Child Development*, 61, 874–892.

Dodge, K. A., & Frame, C. L. (1982). Social cognitive biases and deficits in aggressive boys. *Child Development*, 53, 620–635.

Dodge, K. A., Pettit, G. S., McClaskey, C. L., & Brown, M. M. (1986). Social competence in children. *Monographs of the Society for Research in Child Development*, 51(1, Serial No. 213).

Emler, N., & Reicher, S. (1993). *A social psychology of adolescence and delinquency*. Oxford, UK: Blackwell.

Fagen, R. (1981). *Animal play behavior*. New York: Oxford University Press.

Fry, D. P. (1987). Differences between playfighting and serious fights among Zapotec children. *Ethology and Sociobiology*, 8, 285–306.

Gehring, T. M., & Wyler, I. L. (1986). Family Systems Test (FAST): A three-dimensional approach to investigate family relationships. *Child Psychiatry and Human Development*, 16, 235–248.

Hargreaves, D. (1967). *Social relations in a secondary school*. London: Routledge & Kegan Paul.

Humphreys, A. P., & Smith, P. K. (1987). Rough and tumble, friendship, and dominance in schoolchildren: Evidence for continuity and change with age. *Child Development*, 58, 201–212.

Kupersmidt, J. B., Coie, J. D., & Dodge, K. A. (1990). The role of poor peer relationships in the development of disorder. In S. R. Asher & J. D. Coie (Eds.), *Peer rejection in childhood* (pp. 274–305). Cambridge, UK: Cambridge University Press.

Loeber, R., & Dishion, T. J. (1984). Boys who fight at home and school: Family conditions influencing cross-setting consistency. *Journal of Consulting and Clinical Psychology*, 52, 759–768.

MacDonald, K. B. (1987). Parent–child physical play with rejected, neglected, and popular boys. *Developmental Psychology*, 23, 705–711.

MacDonald, K. B., & Parke, R. (1984). Bridging the gap: Parent–child play interaction and peer interactive competence. *Child Development*, 55, 1265–1277.

Main, M. (1991). Metacognitive models, metacognitive monitoring, and singular (coherent) model of attachment: Findings and directions for future research. In C. M. Parkes, J. Stevenson-Hinde, & P. Marris (Eds.), *Attachment across the life cycle* (pp. 127–159). London: Routledge.

Manning, M., Heron, J., & Marshall, T. (1978). Styles of hostility and social interactions at nursery, at school, and at home: An extended study of children. In L. A. Hersov, M. Berger, & D. Shaffer (Eds.), *Aggression and antisocial behavior in childhood and adolescence* (pp. 29–58). Elmsford, NY: Pergamon.

Neill, S. R. St.-J. (1976). Aggressive and nonaggressive fighting in 12- to 13-year-old preadolescent boys. *Journal of Child Psychology and Psychiatry*, 17, 213–220.

Olweus, D. (1980). Familial and temperamental determinants of aggressive behavior in adolescents – A causal analysis. *Developmental Psychology*, 16, 644–660.

Olweus, D. (1991). Bully/victim problems among schoolchildren: Basic facts and effects of a school-based intervention program. In K. Rubin & D. Pepler (Eds.),

The development and treatment of childhood aggression (pp. 441–448). Hillsdale, NJ: Lawrence Erlbaum.

Park, K. A., & Waters, E. (1989). Security of attachment and preschool friendships. *Child Development*, 60, 1076–1081.

Parke, R. D., & Slaby, R. G. (1983). The development of aggression. In P. Mussen (Ed.), *Handbook of child psychology* (4th ed., Vol. 4, pp. 547–642). New York: John Wiley.

Parker G., Tupling, H., & Brown, L. B. (1979). A parental bonding instrument. *British Journal of Medical Psychology*, 52, 1–10.

Parker, J. G., & Asher, S. R. (1987). Peer acceptance and later personal adjustment: Are low-accepted children "at risk"? *Psychological Bulletin*, 102, 357–389.

Patterson, C. J., Kupersmidt, J. B., & Griesler, P. C. (1990). Children's perceptions of self and of relationships with others as a function of sociometric status. *Child Development*, 61, 1335–1349.

Pawluk, C. J. (1989). Social construction of teasing. *Journal for the Theory of Social Behavior*, 19, 145–167.

Pellegrini, A. D. (1988). Elementary school children's rough-and-tumble play and social competence. *Developmental Psychology*, 24, 802–806.

Pellegrini, A. D. (1989a). Elementary school children's rough-and-tumble play. *Early Childhood Research Quarterly*, 4, 245–260.

Pellegrini, A. D. (1989b). What is a category? The case of rough-and-tumble play. *Ethology and Sociobiology*, 10, 331–341.

Pikas, A. (1989). The common concern method for the treatment of mobbing. In E. Roland & E. Munthe (Eds.), *Bullying: An international perspective* (pp. 91–104). London: David Fulton.

Power, T. G., & Parke, R. D. (1981). Play as a context for early learning. In L. M. Laosa & I. E. Sigel (Eds.), *Families as learning environments for children* (pp. 147–178). New York: Plenum.

Price, J. M., & Dodge, K. A. (1989). Reactive and proactive aggression in childhood: Relations to peer status and social context dimensions. *Journal of Abnormal Child Psychology*, 17, 455–471.

Reid, K. (1983). Retrospection and persistent school absenteeism. *Educational Research*, 25, 110–115.

Renken, B., Egeland, B., Marvinney, D., Mangelsdorf, S., & Sroufe, L. A. (1989). Early childhood antecedents of aggression and passive-withdrawal in early elementary school. *Journal of Personality*, 57, 257–281.

Rubin, K. H., LeMare, L. J., & Lollis, S. (1990). Social withdrawal in childhood: Developmental pathways to peer rejection. In S. R. Asher & J. D. Coie (Eds.), *Peer rejection in childhood* (pp. 217–249). Cambridge, UK: Cambridge University Press.

Schaefer, E. S. (1965). A configurational analysis of children's reports of parent behavior. *Journal of Consulting Psychology*, 29, 552–557.

Sluckin, P. K. (1981). *Growing up in the playground: The social development of children.* London: Routledge & Kegan Paul.

Smith, P. K. (1991a). Hostile aggression as social skills deficit or evolutionary strategy? *Behavioral and Brain Sciences*, 14, 315–316.

Smith, P. K. (1991b). The silent nightmare: Bullying and victimization in school peer groups. *The Psychologist*, 4, 243–248.

Smith, P. K., & Boulton, M. J. (1991, July). *Self-esteem, sociometric status, and peer-perceived behavioral characteristics in middle school children in the United Kingdom.* Paper presented at the Eleventh Meeting of ISSBD, Minneapolis, MN.

Smith, P. K., Hunter, T., Carvalho, A. M. A., & Costabile, A. (1992). Children's perceptions of playfighting, playchasing, and real fighting: A cross-cultural interview study. *Social Development*, 1, 211–229.

Smith, P. K., & Lewis, K. (1985). Rough-and-tumble play, fighting, and chasing in nursery school children. *Ethology and Sociobiology*, 6, 175–181.

Smith, P. K., & Thompson, D. A. (Eds.). (1991). *Practical approaches to bullying.* London: David Fulton.

Stephenson, P., & Smith, D. (1989). Bullying in the junior school. In D. P. Tattum & D. A. Lane (Eds.), *Bullying in schools* (pp. 45–57). Stoke-on-Trent: Trentham.

Troy, M., & Sroufe, L. A. (1987). Victimization among preschoolers: Role of attachment relationship history. *Journal of the American Academy of Child and Adolescent Psychiatry*, 26, 166–172.

Whitney, I., Nabuzoka, N., & Smith, P. K. (1992). Bullying in schools: Mainstream and special needs. *Support for Learning*, 7, 3–7.

Whitney, I., & Smith, P. K. (1993). A survey of the nature and extent of bullying in junior/middle and secondary schools. *Educational Research*, 35.

Chapter 7

Children in Need
The Role of Peer Support*

Helen Cowie

> The most important bit is just sitting down and listening to the person in general and seeing what their problem is. And use your eyes to concentrate on them. Let them know that you are listening.
>
> (Peer supporter)

The importance of friendships

Peer relationships are of critical importance to young people since it is through these interactions that so much can be learned about self, others and the social world. Being close to someone, sharing experiences, having disagreements, and resolving differences are all part of growing up. If these experiences of peer relationships are, on balance, good ones, the child grows up with a positive outlook on life and the expectation of being liked and valued by those who matter to him or her. They also gain invaluable opportunities to take the perspective of others. But if the experiences are less favourable, then the long-term outlook for emotional well-being is likely to be bleak. Being amongst a group of peers who apparently have no difficulty in relating to one another with confidence and enjoyment can be immensely dispiriting and undermining to the child who is often ignored, deliberately left out, who is derided or rejected. Here are some common answers which young people gave to the question, 'Why are friends important to you?'

> I can talk to her about my feelings.
> When my dog died and I was upset he helped me.
> We phone each other up for a chat.
> We share things.
> It is fun to be in her company.

* Source: Paper presented at the European Conference on Initiatives to Combat School Bullying, 15–16th May 1998, The Barbican, London. The content of this chapter is developed in Sharp, S. and Cowie, H. (1998) Understanding and Supporting Children in Distress, London, Sage

We have lots of laughs.

We teach each other to do things like games.

We look out for each other. He protects me and I protect him.

I feel safe when I'm around my friends in lessons and all that, but I find I'm unsafe when I'm by myself – (when) there is not a lot of people around me.

The themes which recur concern closeness and intimacy, mutuality and sharing, and learning together (e.g. about peer relationships, social rules and how to avoid danger).

Children who find it hard to form close affiliations with their peers (for example, those who are neglected or rejected for whatever reason) may develop behaviour patterns which in turn perpetuate the difficulty. They may become timid and unresponsive in groups; they may have angry outbursts; they may become provocative and attention-seeking; they may develop a downcast demeanour which distances them from others. In each case, the long-term effects can persist right into adult life (Farrington, 1993; Olweus, 1993; Rivers, 1997).

Dealing with bullying behaviour: bystanding or standing by

A crucial aspect of social relationships concerns *power*. We cannot dispute the fact that power differentials exist in social groups. Some children are more talented, stronger, more expert or more fun to be with than others. It is important during development that children and young people learn to affirm their own and others' strengths and weaknesses and to acknowledge the richness which diversity of difference has to offer. Problems arise, however, when that power differential is abused, for example, when the stronger person uses that strength to intimidate or put down a peer, or promotes their own interests at the expense of others. This kind of behaviour is broadly defined as bullying, and is a major source of emotional distress among young people. It is a complex social phenomenon involving onlookers and bystanders as well as bullies and victims.

Surveys of children's perspectives on bullying (e.g. MacLeod and Morris, 1996) show that most children dislike it and that a teacher can count on the majority of children in a class to be opposed to it. But paradoxically, researchers such as Rigby and Slee (1991) in Australia, Menesini, Fonzi and Genta (1996) in Italy, Morita (1996) in Japan and Eslea and Smith (1996) in the UK have all found that bullies can usually find allies who despise weaker or more helpless peers. Those who are 'non-committal' – the bystanders – can also be perceived by the victims as acting in collusion with the bullies. Pepler's (1996) observational studies of Toronto school playgrounds provide supportive evidence that bullying is indeed a social event and that this social context has a powerful influence on whether bystanders act responsibly or remain 'neutral'. She found that peers were present in 85 per cent of the bullying episodes in playground and classroom and that peers adopted a number of roles: co-bullies, supporters, audience and 'seldom intervenors'.

Salmivalli, Lagerspetz, Bjorkvist, Osterman and Kaukiainen (1996) argue that it is possible to assign a participant role to 87 per cent of the pupils present at a bullying episode. The most common of these participant roles are 'assistant', 'reinforcer', 'outsider', and 'defender'. *Assistants* join in the bullying, though they do not instigate it; they help the bully by, for example, holding the victim down. *Reinforcers* act as audience to the bullying incident, laugh at the victim and incite the bully to do more. They are likely to be excited by the incident and to call others over to view the fun with comments like, 'Come on over. There's a fight! Someone's being done!!' They take overt pleasure in the distress of their peer. *Outsiders* stay outside the situation, remain inactive and pretend not to notice what is happening. Typically when they see a peer in distress they say, 'I'm all right and that's all that matters' or 'it's none of my business'. They are likely to claim that they know nothing of the person's unhappiness and so remain, as they see it, neutral, unaware that, by their inaction, they appear to the victim to be colluding with the actions of the bullies. *Defenders* comfort the victim, tell an adult about what is happening, or even attack the bully; they may also go out of their way to be friends with the victim afterwards and encourage the victim to seek help in some way. They are more likely to confront the bullies and the reinforcers by asking them to stop or by running to get others to help stop the harassment. After the incident, they are the ones who will stay behind to comfort and support the victim and who will encourage the victim to tell an adult. They may well also promise to keep the victim company and devise ways of making sure that the victim is safe.

The authors noted that boys are more likely to be actively involved in the bullying process and their most frequent participant roles are of Assistant and Reinforcer. By contrast, girls are most commonly found to be in the roles of Outsider and Defender. These findings are confirmed in other studies. For example, Osterman et al (1997) found strong gender differences in conflict resolution behaviour, with girls significantly more likely to be pereceived by peers to use constructive conflict resolution techniques than boys.

The discrepancy between what children say and what they actually do when faced with a bullying situation suggests that there are conflicts taking place within them, with implications for their emotional well-being as well as that of the more active participants. Hazler (1996) argues that bystanders fail to take action for one of the following basic reasons:

they do not know what to do;

they are fearful of becoming the brunt of the bullies' attacks;

they might do the wrong thing which could cause even more problems.

The safest line of action in these circumstances is likely to be non-intervention. But this avoidance of involvement on the part of a bystander has its own form of anguish.

Inaction can give bystanders a sense of powerlessness similar to that being experienced by the victim. The victim's loss of self-esteem amongst the peer group is clear to perpetrators and those who played a less active part. But the consequences for bystanders, he argues, are also negative:

> An adrenalin rush may well come with watching someone be victimised, but there is no pride or self-respect in knowing you are an ineffective bystander in someone else's tragic situation. Regaining the self-respect and confidence that goes with feeling in control does not have to come by accident. It can also be conscientiously fostered by counselors, educators, and parents.
>
> (Hazler, 1996, p. 15)

There are longer-term consequences arising from the failure to take action when faced with a peer in distress. Many young people become desensitised to others' suffering the longer they are exposed to situations where intervention does not take place (Safran and Safran, 1985).

It seems likely that adults wishing to initiate peer-led interventions to combat bullying turn to defenders, the young people who spontaneously 'stand by' the victim rather than 'bystand'. The interventions which I describe indicate the active part which adults can play in building on this potential for help and providing the training, guidance and supervision which can channel it into effective action to help children and young people who are at risk.

Befriending

This approach encompasses a number of forms but is essentially about building on the natural helping skills which children learn through the process of everyday interactions with friends and in the family. In some cases, this help is of a purely practical nature. Konet (1991) and Demetriades (1996) describe the value of after-school clubs where students as befrienders offer companionship, activities and refreshments to peers who would otherwise be miserable and alone. Such systems may not require intensive training, simply the presence of friendly young people with a willingness to help others. To a vulnerable child, the existence of this system, run by friendly, supportive peers, can offer an essential lifeline.

Here are some examples. Kaye and Webb (1996) describe a system through which sixth formers were given personal responsibility for small groups of pupils new to the school. In their groups, they facilitated discussion around issues such as feelings of loneliness, making friends, dealing with bullying behaviour, learning to share. The well-being of the younger students was enhanced and the helpers gained greatly in confidence and a belief in their own efficacy. Bourgault (1991) also trained senior students in active listening, assertiveness and leadership; they were then ready to implement helpful interventions to support students new to the school by facilitating small group discussion of issues like managing homework, coping with peer group pressure and becoming aware of their sexuality. There were immediate and long-term effects which were beneficial to both younger students and peer helpers.

There is evidence that peer helpers have the potential to help young people in the midst of very difficult life experiences. Demetriades (1996) showed that peer partners, in the setting of an after-school club, were able to offer effective support to young people who had been severely traumatised by war, had experienced the loss of close family relationships and were trying to rebuild their lives in a strange country. She points out that peer support did not replace professional intervention but that it provided a crucial emotional and social safety net for very vulnerable young people. It is significant that many of those who were helped became in turn peer partners in the scheme.

Mediation and conflict resolution

Peer mediation is more structured than most befriending schemes but, like them, can be adapted to a wide range of school settings. It is reported to result in a substantial decrease in the incidence of aggressive behaviour (Stacey, 1996). The skills can be learned by pupils from around 9 years of age through to adolescence. The peer mediation method has evolved from the 'no-blame' position that one of the most effective ways of resolving conflict is to create a 'win-win' outcome. One of the problems with conflict is that, too often, the outcome is that one wins and the other loses. Common interpersonal and intergroup problems – bullying, racist name-calling, fighting and quarrelling – may well escalate if unresolved, while punishing wrong-doers can leave feelings of resentment, and the behaviour may become even more entrenched. Peer mediation, by contrast, offers a non-punitive solution.

How does peer mediation work? Typically, two trained peer mediators work as a team to encourage problem-solving between people who are in disagreement. The mediators meet with the disputants, each disputant tells his or her story and how he or she feels about the incident, the mediators listen without passing judgement, disputants are each asked what they would like to happen next, and finally they are involved in exploring what might be done to ensure that each participant in the dispute comes away from the mediation with a positive 'win-win' feeling and the sense that the outcome is fair to both sides.

The mediation process can be carried out where the dispute occurs – often in the playground. Students receive a highly-structured programme of training which equips them with specific skills for mediating in disputes, including active listening, the expression of feelings, clarification of meaning through clear, unambiguous terms, appropriate sensitivity to the meaning of non-verbal communication and different ways of asking questions. A key aspect involves the mediators encouraging those in dispute to give 'I' messages owned by the speaker. For example, they are encouraged to say 'I am very angry right now' or 'When you said that you hurt my feelings' rather than using vague generalisations like 'Everyone knows that he is a bully' or 'What do you expect when someone insults you?'. Role-play is used a great deal to help mediators practice newly-learned skills, such as intervening in a playground quarrel which has got out of hand, or mediating between a child who bullies and a child who is victimised (Cowie and Sharp, 1994).

Peer support: counselling-based approaches

Peer support systems more directly modelled on a counselling approach vary widely in emphasis, encompassing issues like bullying, loneliness, adjusting to a new school and dealing with separation and loss (Cowie and Sharp, 1996). But there are some common elements in these counselling-based programmes of support, including the teaching of basic skills of active listening, empathy, problem-solving and supportiveness. First, they involve direct response to a request for help with regard to a specific problem. They are generally implemented through a formal system of referral soon after the request for help has occurred. Second, they all involve giving the peer helpers skills and strategies for enabling the young people involved in the situation to find a resolution to the problem. Third, though the direct action is taken by the peer helpers, adults retain a supportive and supervisory role without imposing solutions. Fourth, they are non-punitive interventions which do not seek to apportion blame but to offer clear and genuine channels of communication amongst those involved in the situation. Counselling-based interventions of this kind recognise that pupils themselves have the potential to assume a helpful role in tackling a problem.

Once training has taken place, students are regularly supervised in their work and have follow-up sessions to review special issues as they arise. This will in turn often lead to requests for further training. In all cases, it is recommended that training should be experiential, whatever the orientation of the trainers may be. The most effective training seems to be that which gives trainees the opportunity to share their own experiences, to practice the skills of listening and responding appropriately in a safe environment, and to be trained by adults who model good practice and a sensitive awareness of young people's issues.

Evaluating peer support: the benefits

In most studies, both peer helpers and teachers consistently report a general improvement in the ethos of the school.

> It creates a symbiotic ethos, feeling safer. People are looking out for one another. We're quite together as a school.
>
> (Counsellor, secondary school, quoted in Cowie 1998)

Pupils in the school as a whole become more open to the idea that a problem could be profitably shared with another rather than keeping it to themselves. Where bullying was the focus, the peer helpers and teachers also report that pupils became more likely to view 'telling a teacher' about a bullying incident as a positive action rather than a betrayal of peer values. The benefits of peer support can be summarised as follows:

- children in need are given support and confidence;
- a safer climate is created in schools;
- bystanders are given a structure within which to offer help;
- young people are offered training in valuable skills of helping,
- communication and empathy for others;
- vulnerable children are helped to make friends;
- there is an opportunity to practice citizenship in the real-life setting of
- the school;
- the practice of peer support provides a preparation for the roles and
- responsibilities of adult life.

Over time, these systems appear to improve the social climate of the school (Naylor and Cowie, 1998). One teacher put it this way:

> I think it creates an atmosphere of caring for each other, being concerned about why somebody is unhappy, why they are under-performing, and wanting to help support them through and reach a solution if that's possible, or at least with coping and coming to terms with the difficulty.

Following the introduction of a peer support programme in one school, it became more acceptable for all pupils (not only the peer helpers) to report bullying incidents when they saw them; a sample of pupils who were interviewed about their perceptions of bullying in their school reported that the atmosphere in the school had changed and that it 'felt safer to tell' (Sharp, Sellors and Cowie, 1994). Overall, research seems to show that the establishment of a peer support service can benefit children in need and the school as a whole.

The findings for peer helpers are also consistent and clear (Cowie, 1998). Training in peer support improves self-confidence, gives young people useful skills, enhances their sense of social responsibility and gives them a useful opportunity to act pro-socially in their school. As one teacher in a sixth form college put it:

> Actually, it's beneficial both for the people who are taking advantage of the system, but also for the students themselves who are involved in the counselling, because . . . they take responsibility for things and participate too.

These enhanced personal qualities seemed to arise from a number of sources. First, there is involvement in teamwork as an integral part of planning, advertising and publicising the service, implementing it and talking about the experience in school assemblies and to external bodies. Interview responses give a clear indication of the value to these young people of addressing a real problem in their school community and being given the opportunity to tackle it. In some cases the publicity goes beyond the school to the outside community and attracts considerable media attention:

> It generally improves communication skills from speaking to small groups to up to a few hundred people . . . It is a challenge.
> (Boy peer supporter, quoted in Cowie, 1998)

The young people appreciate public awareness of their action.

Second, peer supporters consistently comment favourably on the value of the communication skills they learn in the course of training. These skills include active, empathic listening, summarising and reflecting back the accounts and narratives of peers in the role of 'clients', allowing space and time for the expression of emotions, learning not to offer advice too early, and collaborating with a peer to develop a problem-solving stance towards interpersonal issues. As one sixth form girl peer helper put it:

> It's what I want to do when I finish my degree. It's sort of like work experience and its sort of training as well, and I like helping people. I like trying to solve their problems, and things.

The value of this kind of experience cannot be under-estimated since the skills can be transferred to other aspects of the young person's relationships with others.

Third, there are indications from secondary school peer helpers that the process of supervision is a beneficial one in terms of developing a vocabulary to capture the nuances of emotion and in developing a reflective stance towards the interpersonal difficulties of themselves and others. This would confirm findings from other studies that young people trained to reflect on their actions in relation to others develop social intelligence and metacognition. In other words, they move more quickly through the levels of understanding of their social world. This process involves the increasingly complex capacity to step mentally outside themselves in order to take a 'second-person' perspective on their own thoughts, actions and feelings, and, at a higher level, to step outside the immediate interaction with another to take deeper and more abstract perspectives on relationships (Osterman et al., 1997).

Evaluating peer support: difficulties arising

The implementation of peer support in schools is, however, often hampered by ambivalent attitudes on the part of staff and students. A survey in 65 schools with a peer support system in place (Naylor and Cowie, 1998) revealed a dearth of men teachers and boy pupils in peer support systems; there was opposition to these systems from some teachers and from some male members of the peer group.

Sceptical teachers typically express anxiety that the pupils will lose motivation, that they lack appropriate training and even that they may do damage. Peer helpers typically perceived such statements as indicative of adult reluctance to share power:

> There was initial resistance from the staff. They were unwilling to give students the responsibility. The staff didn't really understand what we were doing, so we gave a small presentation in a staff meeting which helped to rectify this. But communication with staff has been a big problem.
>
> (Secondary school boy peer helper, quoted in Cowie, 1998).

Some peers too undermine the peer helpers' belief in their own competence by deriding them as 'wimps', 'grasses', 'teachers' pets', or, as in one boys' school, 'queer supporters'. Boys seem to be especially vulnerable to this kind of criticism and it is notable that, in peer systems in mixed sex schools, the girls typically outnumber boys at all stages of the process from application through selection, training and practice. Cowie (1998), in a study of peer support services in nine schools, found that participation could open peer helpers to teasing or taunts from others. Male peer supporters in particular reported problems in integrating the prevailing 'macho' image of their peer group with a caring, helpful role. A minority of boy peer helpers seemed to be able to withstand this peer group pressure and acknowledge the benefits, but at every point, from recruitment through training and implementation, boys were under-represented and were most likely to drop out. The adults in charge of the peer support services were keenly aware of the need to involve boys as peer supporters but were unable to find a solution. If we reflect back on the findings of Salmivalli and her colleagues, this is not surprising. The helpers, we suggest, are largely drawn from 'defenders' who, according to the research, are more likely to be girls.

There is also some evidence of peer group pressure against making use of a peer support service. For example, MacLeod and Morris (1996), the authors of a UK survey sponsored by ChildLine (a children's telephone support service), asked children about the policies which were in place in their schools to counteract bullying. These authors noted the "startlingly little use" made of peer-led interventions, including 'bully lines, bully boxes, peer counselling, mentoring or mediation schemes' (p. 85). Yet the children in their sample talked frequently about the value to them of having someone to talk to about their troubles.

Charlton and David (1997) express surprise that so few schools make use of peers to offer personal and educational support to others and link this reluctance to an unwillingness to share power and give opportunities for responsible action in real-life settings:

> As ample evidence is now at hand showing clearly that this 'peer' resource can make valuable contributions to schools' efforts to improve their children's all-round performance, it is surprising that so few schools make use of it. Furthermore, this neglect becomes more bewildering given a growing recognition of children's right to be listened to.
>
> (Charlton and David, 1997, p. 22)

A recurring issue noted by Cowie (1998) concerns the low allocation of time and resources to underpin the efforts of the adults and young people involved in peer support services. Very little time was allowed for the teachers to manage the services and to organise the necessary supervision. Consequently, this was usually done voluntarily during lunchtimes or after school. The question of the cost of training arose frequently. So too did the issue of the supplying of private space for individual work with the young people who sought help. Cowie and Naylor (1998) also expressed concern that insufficient attention was paid by schools in their survey to the key role of supervision in supporting the work and the personal well-being of the peer supporters themselves. Although in all the schools in their study the head teachers expressed their commitment to the establishment of the peer support schemes, it could be argued that they had under-estimated the extent of the financial and resource requirements needed for such a service to be maintained over time.

Bullying and peer support in the context of children's rights

I would like to conclude by considering the issue of peer support against bullying in a wider context. The United Nations Convention on the Rights of the Child, 1989, proposes an international perspective on the rights of children to life itself and to a reasonable quality of life. This document gives nations the opportunity to define human rights standards for children, to identify gaps in the provision for those rights, and to set this in the context of an international binding agreement (UN 1991). The fifty-four Articles in the Convention cover a range of children's rights which have been categorised (Children's Rights Development Unit, 1993, p. 6) as:

protection: from abuse, torture and armed conflict;
provision: of the right to life, state care, education, health services and social security;
participation: in decision-making on matters affecting the child, with due consideration for the age and maturity of the child; in judicial and administrative proceedings affecting the child, either directly or through a representative.

By emphasising non-discrimination, acting in the best interests of the child, and listening to the views of the child, the UN Convention built on earlier legislation by specifying not only children's rights to protection from physical and mental violence, and provision of certain medical, educational and social services, but also their rights to participation – so recommending some political voice for children.

The issue of bullying is one critical test of a society's willingness to take serious account of children's rights in relation to those who bully, those who are bullied and those who are bystanders. Some frameworks have been developed in schools to facilitate the process of democratic participation in school contexts while at the same time creating a balance between the rights of the individual child on the one hand and the constraints inherent in operating in a community. The Elton Report (DES 1989), for example, advised that schools should create environments where quality of relationships and a sense of responsibility were valued. It was recommended that teachers should listen to pupils and incorporate their opinions into school policies, especially those concerned with behaviour and school ethos in a context where pupils and teachers might begin to develop a process of negotiation of responsibilities and rights on both sides.

However, very little has been done in the UK to facilitate the process of greater participation on the part of children in the decisions which affect their lives. For many, childhood continues to be characterised by 'low status, little power and almost no control over the outcomes of their lives' (Children's Rights Development Unit, 1994, p. xiv). At present, children have no rights in law to be consulted or to be taken into account on any matter concerning their individual rights within the educational system. Nor is there any formal requirement to hear the views of an individual child concerning any issue relating to their education or problems in school, such as bullying and harassment (Dalrymple and Hough, 1995, p. 78).

The recommendations of the UN Convention are perceived by some as difficult to achieve. Many teachers underestimate children's potential to play a part in promoting positive values and a caring ethos in the peer group. Many adults ignore the fact that the process of being involved in decision-making for change can be as valuable to the individuals involved as the outcomes. Much educational practice continues to ignore children's basic democratic rights (Lloyd, 1997), and, in fact, there is no requirement on schools in the UK to implement the recommendations of the UN Convention at all. But I would like to argue that the establishment of peer support systems in schools creates a valuable opportunity for adults and young people to work co-operatively to tackle a real-life problem. What better preparation for adult roles and responsibilities could there be than feeling empowered to challenge an injustice in your own school community?

Conclusion

Fortunately, there is a great deal of teacher and pupil enthusiasm for these schemes, not only as a way of challenging bullying, but as a way, in the long term, of changing the ethos of a school to one of care. But a number of key points need to be taken into consideration if this approach is
to be used to its full potential (Naylor and Cowie, 1998):

- all schools need to develop their strategies for systematically monitoring and evaluating the effectiveness of their peer support systems;
- mixed sex schools need to continue to find ways of involving more men teachers and boy pupils in their peer support systems;
- all schools need to work at eliminating the opposition of some teachers to peer support systems;
- all schools need to ensure that peer supporters are provided with frequent and regular opportunities for being debriefed/supervised about their work;
- peer supporters need on-going support from the school as a whole if they are to be successful in their own supporting roles.

References

Bourgault, G. (1991) Peer support in high schools: a programme to complement pastoral care strategies, *Pastoral Care*, 10 (1) 25–7.

Charlton, T. and David, K. (1997) Orchestrating success in personal, social and educational areas: using peer support. *Pastoral Care in Education*, March, pp. 22–29.

Children's Rights Development Unit (CRDU) (1993) 'The UN convention on the Rights of the Child'. London: UNICEF/Gulbenkian/UNA.

Children's Rights Development Unit (CRDU) (1994) 'UK Agenda for Children'. CRDU.

Cowie, H. (1998) Perspectives of teachers and pupils on the experience of peer support against bullying. *Educational Research and Evaluation*.

Cowie, H. and Sharp, S. (1994) Empowering pupils to take positive action against bullying. In P. K. Smith and S. Sharp (eds.) School Bullying: Insights and perspectives. London: Routledge.

Cowie, H. & Sharp, S. (eds.) (1996) *Peer Counselling in School: A Time to Listen*. London: David Fulton.

Dalrymple, J. and Hough, J. (1995) *Having a Voice: an Exploration of Children's Rights and Advocacy*. Birmingham: Venture Press.

Demetriades, A. (1996) Children of the storm: peer partnership. In H. Cowie, and S. Sharp, (eds.) *Peer Counselling in School: A Time to Listen. London: David Fulton.*

DES (1989) Discipline in Schools; Report of the committee chaired by Lord Elton. London: HMSO.

Eslea, M. and Smith, P. K. (1996) *If anybody hits you hit them back*! parent and pupil attitudes towards bullying in primary schools. Paper presented at the 14th meeting of the ISSBD Quebec, August 1996.

Farrington, D.P. (1993) Understanding and preventing bullying. In M. Tonry and N. Morris (eds.) *Crime and Justice: An Annual Review of Research*, vol. 17. Chicago: University of Chicago Press.

Hazler, R. (1996) Bystanders: an overlooked factor in peer on peer abuse. *The Journal for the Professional Counselor*, 11, 2, 11–21.

Kaye, P. G. and Webb, A. (1996) A little help from my friends: a secondary school peer support programme. *Pastoral Care in Education*, 14, 2, 23–25.

Konet, R. (1991) Peer helpers in the middle school. *Middle School Journal*, September, 13–16.

Lloyd, G. (1997) Can the law support children's rights in schools in Scotland and prevent the development of a climate of blame? *Pastoral Care in Education*, Sept 13–16.

MacLeod, M. and Morris, S. (1996) *Why Me?* London: ChildLine.

Menesini, E., Fonzi, A. and Genta, M-L (1996). Bullying behaviour and attitudes among Italian school children, Paper presented at the European Congress on Educational Research (ECER), Seville, September.

Morita, Y. (1996) Bullying as a contemporary problem in the context of increasing societal privatization in Japan. *Prospects*, XXVI, 2, June 1996. (Open file: Violence in the school. Guest editor: T. Ohsako.)

Naylor, P. and Cowie, H. (1998) The effectiveness of peer support systems in challenging bullying in schools: a preliminary account of findings from a UK survey. *Preliminary Report, The Prince's Trust Project 'Peer support as a challenge to school bullying'*. School of Psychology and Counselling, Roehampton Institute London.

Olweus, D. (1993) *Bullying in Schools: what we know and what we can do*. Oxford: Basil Blackwell.

Osterman, K., Bjorkvist, K., Lagerspetz, K., Landau, S., Fraczek, A. and Pastorelli, C. (1997) Sex differences in styles of conflict resolution: a developmental and cross-cultural study with data from Finland, Israel, Italy and Poland. In D. Fry and K. Bjorkvist (eds.) *Cultural Variation in Conflict Resolution.* Mahwah, NJ: Lawrence Erlbaum Associates.

Pepler, D. (1996) A peek behind the fence: what we have learned about bullying. Paper presented at the conference 'Putting the Brakes on Violence', York University, Toronto, August 1996.

Rigby, K. and Slee, P. (1991) Bullying among Australian school children: reported behaviour and attitudes to victims. *Journal of Social Psychology,* 131, 615–27.

Rivers, I. (1997) Violence against lesbian and gay youth and its impact. In M. Schneider (ed.) *Pride and Prejudice: Working with Lesbian, Gay and Bisexual Youth.* Toronto: Central Toronto Youth Services.

Safran, J. S. and Safran, S. P. (1985) A developmental view of children's behavioral tolerance. *Behavioral Disorders* 10, 2, 87–94.

Salmivalli, C., Lagerspetz, K., Bjorkvist, K., Osterman, K. & Kaukiainen, A. (1996). Bullying as a group process: participant roles and their relations to social status within the group. *Aggressive Behaviour,* 22, 1, 1–15.

Sharp, S., Sellors, A. and Cowie, H. (1994) Time to listen: setting up a peer counselling service to help tackle the problem of bullying in schools. *Pastoral Care in Education,* 12, 2, 3–6.

Stacey, H. (1996) Mediation in the schools does go! An outline of the mediation process. *Pastoral Care in Education,* 14, 2, 7–9.

United Nations (1991) The United Nations Convention on the Rights of the Child, 1989, Innocenti Studies, Florence. UNICEF.

Part III

Moral development in context

Chapter 8

Children's grasp of controversial issues*

Geoffrey Short

'Primary ideology' and the curriculum

This chapter deals with the role played by beliefs about children's capabilities for understanding social, moral and political issues in shaping teachers' willingness to address these issues within primary education. I examine the impact of theories and research in developmental psychology on educational practice during the past three decades, and conclude by considering the prospects for establishing controversial issues more firmly within the primary curriculum. The original version of this chapter was published in 1988. At that time I suggested that the general resistance to controversial issues during the 1960s and 1970s had been shaped by two powerful sets of beliefs: the first relating to the protection of young children's 'innocence'; the second concerned with respecting their 'readiness' to understand social, moral and political issues – otherwise known as 'sequential developmentalism'.

Acceptance of childhood innocence was part of an idealised construction of childhood emanating from the seminal writings of Rousseau and Froebel, that had become embedded in 'primary ideology' (Alexander, 1984). I suggested that it would have been natural for teachers who believed in childhood innocence to want to protect their pupils from the harsh realities of life. In support of this contention I commented on a couple of incidents witnessed by Ronald King (1978) in his observational study of three infant schools. The first involved a class teacher reinforcing a 6-year-old's faith in fairies offering financial compensation for lost teeth. She later remarked to King (1978: 13) 'it's not up to me to destroy his innocence'. On a subsequent occasion, staff were found removing infirm guinea pigs from the classroom, partly 'to prevent their deaths being witnessed by the children' (1978: 14). The concern shown by these teachers may well have reflected their training in institutions that to a greater or lesser extent embraced a form of child-centredness influenced by Rousseau: that influence has all but disappeared from con-

---

* Specially prepared for this Reader, based on a chapter that first appeared in *Children and Controversial Issues*, Lewes: Falmer Press, 1988.

temporary teacher training. Educational discourse has undergone a *volte face* since the 1960s and the progressive tide that reached its high-water mark with the publication of the Plowden Report in 1967 has effectively been reversed. Developments of a different kind, however, might also have helped puncture the rhetoric of innocence. I refer to the abduction and murder in 1993 of the toddler, Jamie Bulger by a couple of 10-year-olds and to well-publicised cases of bullying and violence, including a recent allegation of rape in a London primary school. One other factor that may have contributed to re-shaping teachers' conceptions of childhood has been the shift away from 'protection', in favour of 'participation', evident in the Children Act of 1989 and in Article 12 of the United Nations Convention on the Rights of the Child.

Change has also been evident in relation to the second facet of primary ideology which, ten years ago, I considered a major constraint on the teaching of contentious subject matter to young children. Alexander defined 'sequential developmentalism' as:

> the idea that the child passes through a naturally ordered sequence of physiological, psychological and social development where . . . the rate of development will vary from child to child [but] the sequence and stages will be the same. Linked with development [is] the notion of 'readiness' particularly in relation to reading – the idea that children's capacity to cope with specific sorts of learning is determined by the developmental stage they have reached.
>
> (Alexander, 1984: 22)

The theoretical roots of both developmentalism and readiness are, of course, linked most often with the name of Jean Piaget. It was he who provided the best-known (though certainly not the only) description of cog-nitive development as a series of discrete stages, each defined in terms of a specific cognitive structure (or unique way of understanding the world) and associated with an approximate age range. According to his account, most children under the age of 7 or so are incapable of logical thought, for they tend to be seduced by appearances and thus cannot conserve; nor can they regard experience from any point of view except their own – clearly an obs-tacle to the reversibility of thought required for logical reasoning. During the junior school years Piaget believed that the average child develops an ability to reverse actions mentally, though only insofar as they refer to 'concrete' situations. At this juncture, too, most children manage to focus their thought on more than one aspect of a situation simultaneously and are thus in a position to relate ideas to one another. However, it is not until the secondary phase of schooling that children can normally think in the abstract and so discuss political and other concepts without recourse to their own experience.

While our understanding of children's progression towards logical thought has obvious relevance for the teaching of mathematics and the natural sciences, our understanding of the development of moral thought has particular relevance for the teaching of controversial issues. Here, too, Piaget was active and in 1932 published a monograph mapping the developmental milestones *en route* to adult conceptions of morality. He maintained that until the age of approximately 4 children are in a pre-moral phase where they have no understanding of rules and possess arbitrary ideas about right and wrong. They then enter the stage of *moral realism* where rules are regarded as sacrosanct and punishment is thought to follow inevitably upon their contravention. In addition, ethical judgements are based on consequences rather than intentions. From the age of 9 or 10, children become capable of *moral subjectivism*. Rules are seen as arbitrary, the acceptance of immanent justice is less in evidence and intention assumes a more prominent role in moral judgement.

So long as primary school teachers accepted Piaget's views on children's cognitive limitations, it followed, *ceteris paribus*, that they would resist all exhortations to stretch, or otherwise test the limits of, their pupils' intellectual competence. At the time (the 1970s), circumstantial evidence in support of this speculation focused on the extent of under-expectation alleged to exist in primary schools (e.g. Nash, 1976; Sharp and Green, 1975); a charge which prompted Alexander (1984: 24) to link low expectations to an exaggerated commitment to sequential developmentalism. By way of illustration, he cited the following extract from the NUT's response to HMI's Primary Survey

> The Union would not agree with [HMI's] analysis of what is suitable in the teaching of history to young children; the passage of time is a very difficult concept for children of this age to grasp.
>
> (NUT 1979: 25)

Insofar as political and moral education was believed to demand a high level of abstract thought, teachers influenced by Piaget were unlikely to consider it a suitable subject for the primary curriculum. Probing the young child's grasp of controversial issues would have been expected to prove particularly unremunerative since the skills required to appreciate a range of arguments and to evaluate conflicting evidence are normally assumed within Piagetian theory to be unavailable prior to adolescence.

Learning about society: the case for sequential developmentalism

Regardless of whether primary ideology was as widespread as Alexander maintained, it is certainly true that developmental psychologists and educationists offered teachers little encouragement to challenge the fundamental validity of Piaget's conclusions until the late 1970s. Indeed, the emphasis he placed on the young child's intellectual grasp has been extended (in the form of various stage analyses) to areas that Piaget himself never considered. Selman (1980), for example, proposed a five-stage model of social-perspective taking, an intellectual function with self-evident implications for political education. He argued that children below the age of 6 or so adopt an ego-centric viewpoint in that they fail to distinguish their own interpretation of an event from what they consider to be true. Between the ages of 6 and 8 they become aware that others may have an alternative perspective and over the next two years learn that individuals can know about other people's thoughts and feelings. These early stages are then followed by a period of 'mutual role-taking' when children, usually aged between 10 and 12, acquire the ability to view an interaction from the standpoint of a third party such as a parent or friend. It is only when children are at secondary school that they finally come to terms with the full complexity of human behaviour and acknowledge, for instance, the impact of genetics, social class and other forces over which the individual has no control.

Other theorists whose work reflects Piaget's ideas on the growth of under-standing include Damon (1977), who studied children's changing notions of authority and Livesley and Bromley (1973) who did likewise in respect of person perception. The best-known extension of Piaget's own work has been undertaken by Lawrence Kohlberg (1958 *et seq.*). He charted the course of moral development into adolescence and adulthood but retained Piaget's stress on the core concepts of stage and sequence. His work, however, is not beyond reproach as I make clear below.

Researchers with a more direct interest in children's political literacy have sometimes nailed their theoretical colours to Piaget's mast (in the sense of prospecting for stages) and, in the process, may unwittingly have reinforced conventional beliefs concerning the 'right' age to teach politics. Leahy's (1983) study of how children understand social class is a case in point. In anticipating the nature of his data, he wrote:

> Cognitive-developmental theory suggests that the ordering of societal conceptions will be similar to the ordering of other kinds of social cogni-tion, such as moral judgement, person descriptions and attributions for achievement. This is based on the idea that intelligence is *organised* – that is, common structures will be applied to a variety of contents.
>
> (Leahy, 1983)

Essentially the same point was made by Furth (1979) who asserted that:

> Piagetian research and theory have been severely limited by an almost exclusive emphasis on strictly logical-mathematical thinking. If the theory is to be maximally useful, it is necessary to apply it to other areas.
>
> (Furth, 1979: 223)

In a manner fully consonant with Piagetian theory, Furth examined the way in which 5- to 11-year-olds understand money, societal roles and the concepts of community and government. In reviewing the cognate literature, he highlighted studies of national and ethnic identity (Jahoda, 1963; Hartley *et al.*, 1948) which, *prima facie*, confirm the young child's lack of political sophistication. Jahoda's subjects were aged between 6 and 11 and were drawn from both working- and middle-class schools in Glasgow. They were asked questions such as, 'Where is Glasgow?', 'Where is Scotland?', 'What is Scotland?' and 'What is Britain?'. Jahoda analysed and classified the children's responses in terms of a four-stage sequence. The least mature was characterised by a notion of Glasgow as 'some kind of vague entity' close to the children's actual geographical location. According to one 6-year-old: 'It's up by the park there – you go round the corner'. At this stage, the child's concept of Scotland is also somewhat nebulous. A 7-year-old said it was a street and when asked if there was a place called Scotland, added: 'Yes, Scotland the Brave, it's up in the Highlands'. Another 7-year-old claimed that 'Scotland is the capital of Edinburgh; it's in Glasgow'.

The majority of children at this point could say nothing at all about Britain and although Jahoda's second stage is distinguished principally by the realisation that Glasgow relates in some way to the immediate vicinity, the idea of a country remains ill-defined. One 7-year-old said of Britain: 'It's a city in England', and a 9-year old thought it 'a city in Scotland'. Superficially, children begin to understand the concept of a country during stage three. They possess the appropriate vocabulary but Jahoda believes it amounts to little more than empty rhetoric. He cites an 11-year-old as saying: 'Britain is a lot of different countries . . . . Glasgow, London, France'. The most advanced level of comprehension (stage four) is marked by an awareness of Britain as a composite unity. As one 6-year-old put it: 'Glasgow is in Scotland. Scotland is a country in Great Britain. Britain is some countries joined together'.

The struggle that many pre-adolescents apparently face in grasping the concept of nationality has also been observed in respect of ethnicity. In one of the earliest studies in the area, Hartley *et al.* (1948) examined children's perceptions of ethnic group membership and were particularly interested in 'the role of being Jewish in America'. Once the children (aged between 3½ and 10½) had identified themselves as either Jewish or American in reply to the question 'What are you?' they were asked, 'What does Jewish mean?' and 'What does American mean?' Responses to the definition of Jewishness included the following: 'It means Jewish people. God makes them. The whole world is Jewish (age 6:6). 'Jewish is people who don't go to church' (7:11). 'Jewish is a religion just like Christian. You go to Hebrew [school] . . . 'It means to believe in these things, to respect your parents. You shouldn't steal' (10:5). Comments relating to their understanding of the term 'American' revealed similar levels of understanding: 'I was an American when I had my gun, but when they took my gun away, I wasn't any more' (4:0). 'God makes us Jewish or American which is both the same, just that some people talk American instead of Jewish' (7:1). 'A nationality. A nation you come from. If you are a citizen born in America, you are American' (9:10). Hartley *et al.* summarised their data by suggesting that:

> Younger children, who characteristically define their life-space concretely in terms of activities, describe ethnic terms comparably. Older children are mentally mature enough to attempt the use of abstractions.
>
> (Hartley *et al.*, 1948: 389)

Thus far, I have attempted to show how a number of psychologists, working within the Piagetian tradition, *indirectly* bolstered, or at least did nothing to undermine, primary teachers' reluctance to broach controversial issues with their pupils. Other researchers went further, openly relating their findings to the classroom and, in particular, to the teaching of social studies. Hallam (1969), for example, discussed the secondary school history syllabus from the standpoint of Piaget's theory. He seemed chiefly concerned to demonstrate that if 'material is too advanced for the children they will either assimilate it without understanding, or will reject it with possible damage to their whole attitude to the subject' (1969: 8). To obviate this possibility, he recommended that:

> history taught in the early years of secondary school should not be over-abstract in form, nor should it contain too many variables . . . Used wisely, topics . . . can be arranged so that the younger children learn the less detailed history of early times, while the history of recent years, which contains important yet complex topics, can then be taught when the pupils are able to reason at a more mature level.
>
> (Hallam, 1969: 4)

While the evidence of children's thinking uncovered by Jahoda, Hartley *et al.* and Hallam follows from their method – abstract questioning under test-like conditions – the inferences drawn from these and related studies have been both misleading and damaging. For, if children are unable to cope with a given task administered in a specific way, it cannot *a priori* be assumed that they will encounter similar difficulties in an experimental or pedagogic setting that departs, however slightly, from the original. I elaborate on this point below when discussing the teacher's role in promoting intellectual development. It is the failure to appreciate the extent to which data generated in one context *cannot* generalise to others that has been responsible, at least to some degree, for the persistent belief in children's limited grasp of controversial issues. I turn now to consider the legitimacy of this belief in the light of recent critiques of Piaget's work.

Dethroning Piaget

Although criticism of Piaget's ideas stretch back more than half a century (e.g. Isaacs, 1930) it is only during the past couple of decades or so that his continued preeminence as an authority on cognitive development has been called into question. Essentially he stands indicted for reading too much into his own experiments and hence failing to realise that alternative procedures could yield very different results. Donaldson (1978) points out that some of Piaget's studies did not make 'human sense' to the children and consequently led to an underestimation of their abilities. In relation to egocentricity her own work has indicated that contrary to Piaget's conclusions, young children *under certain circumstances*, can envisage situations from a point of view other than their own. More recently Dunn (1988) has recognised the tension between Piagetian egocentrism and the evidence of children's social competence in the context of family relations. It will be recalled that Kohlberg's research was heavily influenced by Piaget. Not surprisingly, he too has been accused of failing to appreciate the intellectual maturity of his subjects as a result of presenting them with complex and unfamiliar material.

Other major criticisms can be levelled at Piaget's work, such as whether stages of development actually exist and whether children are able to understand the questions they are asked (Wood, 1998). However, it is Piaget's underestimation of children's cognitive abilities that is crucial as far as the introduction of controversial issues into the primary classroom is concerned. As a result of research focusing on a range of issues previously unexplored, or treated very differently, the reigning orthodoxy now recognises young children as less naive politically than has traditionally been assumed. Stevens (1982), for example, interviewed eight hundred 7- to 11-year-olds and concluded that:

> Seven year olds can be seen to have some cognitive contact with the political world [encompassing] political information, awareness and not least, interest. What comes across most strongly is the sense the children seemed to have of political power being limited, consented to and conditional upon results.
>
> (Stevens 1982: 38)

She found that concepts of democracy, leadership and accountability of government were accessible to 9-year-olds. She also found that some children of this age were able to consider alternative social and political arrangements and to justify them in terms of principles. As this ability is usually associated with the stage of formal operations, Stevens asked whether, in relation to social or political understanding, the stages either contract to some degree or overlap more than in other areas. Piaget, of course, attached far greater importance to the invariant sequence of development than to the average age of children at particular stages within the sequence and, to this extent, Stevens's findings cannot be seen as contradictory. Her work did, however, add further weight to the view that children may generally be more *au fait* with their socio-political environment than has traditionally been acknowledged especially by those working within a Piagetian paradigm. To emphasise the point, she noted that by the age of 11 children were able to

> [link] politics not only with roles, structures and policies, but with topics such as conservation, women's rights and an economic re-organization of the country.
>
> (Stevens 1982: 150)

When one considers the content of children's media (including soap operas televised before the 9 o'clock watershed) the evidence of social and political consciousness among 7- to 11-year-olds becomes all the more convincing. Juvenile comics, for example, not only deal regularly with questions of authority, hierarchy, social class and wealth, but as Dixon (1977) and others (Carrington and Short, 1984) have revealed, they promote racism, sexism and xenophobia as both natural and acceptable. Dixon (1977: 50) asserted that 'name-calling . . . national stereotyping [and] hatred of foreigners . . . is found nowhere so much as in comics published in the United States and Britain'. He might have added that the same sentiments are, from time to time, articulated in those sections of the tabloid press likely to be read by children of primary school age. (Witness the coverage of the football tournament Euro '96).

The socio-economic attitudes that comics purvey have also come in for criticism. Referring to stories where 'myths and illusions . . . blur the real issues', Dixon noted the prevalence of

> charity, which oils the wheels of the system and . . . alleviates . . . the distress of the poor and the guilt of the rich; the 'ladder' concept of society, which holds out the hope that . . . anyone can succeed [and] moral virtue which the unfortunate and the unsuccessful usually have.
>
> (Dixon 1977: 32)

The evidence for children's social awareness

I 'Race'

That very young children are racially aware in the sense of being able to distinguish black people from white will surprise no one. (Laishley, 1971; Marsh, 1970). However, the fact that 3- and 4-year-olds can express genuinely hostile racial attitudes is rather less obvious. Indications of racism in pre-schoolers were first reported by Horowitz as long ago as 1936. He found that:

> The development of prejudice against Negroes begins very, very early in the life of the ordinary child . . . boys, barely over five years of age, demonstrated a preference for whites . . . Some few attempts at testing special cases at three and four years of age elicited such comments as (from a three year old) 'I don't like black boys' and (from a four year old) 'I don't like coloured boys'.
>
> (Horowitz, 1936: 117–18)

The British study that offers the closest parallel to Horowitz's findings was conducted by Jeffcoate (1977) in a Bradford nursery school. It was undertaken in order to draw teachers' attention to the specious nature of the widespread and commonsensical view that primary school children are incapable of displaying animosity towards individuals *qua* members of a racial or ethnic group. Jeffcoate debunked the myth by showing that 4-year-olds are not only sensitive to racial differences but that they can also express racially abusive remarks. When the children were initially asked by their teacher to discuss pictures portraying black people in a 'variety of situations and in a respectful and unstereotyped way' the children's responses could not possibly be construed as racially offensive. However, when the same set of pictures were left casually around the room (but in locations close to concealed tape recorders), the comments made by the children were undeniably racist in tenor. Although this study confirmed the results of previous research into the early onset of anti-black sentiment in white children, it is, perhaps, more important in showing that, even at the nursery stage, children are cognizant of the taboo status of these feelings and of the need to conceal them in the presence of adult authority.

Children at the upper end of the primary age range have been shown in a number of studies to possess a sophisticated understanding of both individual and structural racism (e.g. Short, 1989; Troyna and Hatcher, 1992). Bruce Carrington and I have demonstrated that this understanding is also available to children living in an 'all-white' environment who, under normal circumstances may not construe the world in racial terms (Short and Carrington, 1987). Our case study of anti-racist teaching with a class of 10- to 11-year-olds was partly concerned to access their untutored knowledge of racism. To this end we asked them to imagine that they had recently entered Britain from either the West Indies or the Indian sub-continent and were writing a letter to a close relative or good friend who was planning to join them. The class discussion that preceded the writing was intended to excavate the ideas the children already possessed, no attempt at this stage being made either to refine them or to suggest more plausible alternatives. In their 'letters' the children referred to manifestations of racial violence, racist name-calling and discriminatory practices in housing and employment. The following extracts are representative:

> *John:* . . . us black people get beat up as soon as we get off the ship. Would you fancy having to take your luggage everywhere by yourself while people just look and laugh at you as you go from house to house trying to get a place to spend the night? Just guess what their reply was after me begging for a bed. It was, 'Sorry, it's been took', or just a simple 'No, get lost. We don't give rooms to niggers like you'. In the end, when you get a house, they throw you out just because you were not used to their terrible food that they call pasties. And what about the jobs you said were very good for someone like me? Oh, I got a job alright. It was a dishwasher in a rotten old fish and chip shop where the dishes must have been at least twenty years old. Then I got kicked out for dropping an old chipped plate by accident.

> *Clare:* . . . I never thought it would be like this as we all get on so well back in India. I advise you to stay at home and forget about Britain. The other day I decided to start looking for a job. As you know, I have plenty of skills. I thought even if nobody likes me I'll be sure to get a good decent job but I was wrong. Instead, I got an awful job cleaning toilets. Over here, that's all they seem to think we're good for. Anyway, I started this job today. It was horrible, people pushing you around. One person even flushed my head down the toilet. I wish I never brought Julian, our son, to school. All he ever does is get picked on. He came home the other day covered with bruises and cuts. I am having second thoughts about staying here. Most people are prejudiced.

> (Short and Carrington, 1987: 227)

Despite occasional strains on the credulity ('get beat up as soon as we get off the ship') these imaginative accounts provide unequivocal evidence of children's awareness of racism in its various guises. John's allusion to food is of particular interest in that it shows how some children of this age are able to grasp the relationship of racism to ethnocentrism. Clare's 'letter' is noteworthy in that it demonstrates some cognizance of stereotyping ('that's all they seem to think we're good for') a concept that had not been mentioned in the previous class discussion. It is also of interest because it refers directly to the gulf between the expectation and the reality of immigrant life in Britain.

2 National identity

In contrast to the literature on children's racial and ethnic identities, relatively little is known about their understanding of national identity. For teachers wishing to combat racism this gap in our knowledge is significant, for as Norman Tebbit's infamous 'cricket test' proposal made plain (*Sunday*

Times, 19 April 1990), notions of national identity can have racial overtones. In order to chart the development of this form of collective identity, Bruce Carrington and I recently carried out an ethnographic study involving 128 children aged between 8 and 11 (Carrington and Short, 1995).

In response to the question, 'What makes a person British?' almost the entire sample focused on the 'more tangible characteristics' of Britishness (Penrose, 1993). Among the youngest cohort (8- to 9-year-olds) 'being born in Britain' was the most frequent response although many also alluded to 'speaking English', 'having British ancestry' and 'living in Britain' as defining characteristics of Britishness. Among the 10- and 11-year-olds, country of birth was again the most popular response but there were far fewer references to the other characteristics.

When asked whether 'everybody who lives in this country is British' very few children defined nationality in racial terms. Just 9 per cent of the 8- to 9-year-olds and 8 per cent of the 10- to 11-year-olds did so. One 10-year-old, for example, said it was not possible for people of Chinese origin to be British because 'they don't look British'.

The question, 'Can you stop being British and become something else?' clearly had the potential to evoke a response couched in terms of cultural affiliation. Among the children answering affirmatively, references to culture increased with age, amounting to 15 per cent of the total among the 11-year-olds. The most frequent (affirmative) responses for the two younger age groups were moving to another country and learning the language. For the oldest children moving abroad was far more important than learning the language. Those who thought it was not possible to change one's nationality did so mainly because they considered birthplace to be crucial. This was particularly the case for the two older age groups. However, between 7 per cent (of the oldest children) and 13 per cent (of the youngest) considered cultural constraints an insuperable obstacle.

Asked if being British was important to them, about two-thirds of the 11-year-olds said it was, although their 'reasons' tended to be tautologous. One girl, for example, said it was important because 'it means that I am part of Britain and that is what country I am from'. Roughly a half of the two younger age groups claimed that their British identity was important to them, but their responses were more to do with the advantages of having *a* national identity rather than a specifically British one. This was again evident when the children were asked to reflect on the best and worst things about being British. The younger children were particularly prone to comment on the benefits of being able to speak the same language as every one else. The 10- and 11-year-olds, however, were more inclined to think in terms of social, political and economic issues. One said that the worst thing 'is having a government which is bad ... They are always arguing over different things and they are always putting taxes on everything'. Another stated that 'Britain's a nice place. I know there's a lot of crime but it has nice countryside and a nice heritage'. A number of the children made direct references to racism. (Carrington and Short, 1995).

3 Gender and sex-role stereotyping

Among the many similarities in the development of children's understanding of 'race' and gender is the age at which identification of self and others is made in terms of the two categories (i.e. male or female, black or white). For the majority of children this milestone is reached by the age of 3 although the foundations of racial awareness and concepts probably develop somewhat later and are more variable (Katz, 1983). A further similarity concerns the acquisition of stereotypes. Those relating to sex roles have been studied in a variety of ways including direct questioning. Kuhn et al. (1978), for instance, read statements such as 'I'm strong' and 'when I grow up I'll fly an aeroplane' to a group of 2- to 3-year-olds. The children were then required to select the doll (Lisa or Michael) most likely to have made the statement. The results not only revealed a high level of agreement with adult stereotypes, but also showed that the children thought positively about their own gender and negatively about the other.

There seems to be little doubt that by the age of 5 most children make few 'errors' in assigning sex-stereotyped labels to activities, occupations and playthings (Katz, 1983). The learning of sex-typed traits, however, appears to develop rather later. Best and his colleagues (1977) illustrated this developmental progression by asking 5-, 8-, and 11-year-olds whether particular attributes were more often associated with a male or female silhouette. They found that less than a quarter of their 5-year-olds responded above a chance level as compared with nearly three-quarters of the 8-year-olds and virtually all the 11-year-olds. The traits that children found easiest to differentiate by gender (such as aggression) were those with a relatively familiar concrete referent.

Studies which permit a 'both' or 'neither' response to stereotyped statements (e.g. Marantz and Mansfield, 1977) are generally marked by an increase in flexibility with age. Damon's (1977) research, though, suggests that the relationship may, in fact, be curvilinear. His sample comprised children aged between 4 and 9. After reading them a story about a little boy (George) who wished to play with dolls, despite his parents' protestations, he asked the following questions: 'Why do people tell George not to play with dolls? Are they right? Is there a rule that boys shouldn't play with dolls?' The 4-year-olds thought it quite legitimate for George to play with dolls if that is what he wanted. In contrast, the 6-year-olds thought it quite wrong, for as far as they were concerned, what boys and girls tend to do is synonymous with what they ought to do. The oldest children were able to recognise sex roles as a convention and could distinguish the latter from both laws and social values. One of the 9-year-olds said: 'Breaking windows you're not supposed to do.

And if you [boys] play with dolls, well you can, but boys usually don't' (Damon, 1977: 263).

My own work (Short, 1989) also highlights the growth in understanding of gender-related issues among children of primary school age. For example, in respect of occupational discrimination I found that 6- and 7-year-olds tended to have little awareness of the problem. By the age of 8 or 9 they were familiar with discrimination against women both in paid employment and in domestic labour; however, they lacked any appreciation of the power of stereotypes to generate inequality. This lacuna was no longer apparent among the majority of 10- to 11-year-olds.

This brief and selective review of the literature on children's understanding of 'race' national identity and gender lends powerful support to the Swann Committee's (DES, 1985) recommendations on political education.

> Some educationists have argued that school pupils are insufficiently mature and responsible to be able to comprehend politically sensitive issues . . . and to cope with them in a balanced and rational manner. Even primary-aged pupils, however, have views and opinions on various 'polit- ical' issues. . . . We believe that schools have a clear responsibility to provide accurate factual information and opportunities for balanced and sensitive consideration of political issues in order to enable pupils to reflect upon and sometimes reconsider their political opinions within a broader context.
>
> (DES, 1985: 336–7)

Children and controversial issues in the 1990s

Ten years ago I argued that if primary teachers accepted Piaget's explicit reservations regarding the value of formal instruction, they were unlikely to explore their pupils' capacity to understand controversial issues (Short, 1988). Because of the importance he attached to maturation, Piaget thought that teachers played an insignificant role in children's cognitive development. He certainly seemed to lack interest in what he disparagingly referred to as the 'American question', that is, the extent to which a child's progression through the stages can be accelerated. He acknowledged that the rate of progress could be hastened but only within narrow limits and some research findings supported this conclusion. However, other prominent psychologists, notably Vygotsky (1956) and Bruner (1960) have argued forcefully that the teacher's role in fostering cognitive development is crucial. Vygotsky stressed the social nature of learning and consequently viewed intellectual potential as a quality created in the process of upbringing and education. He dis- tinguished between children's existing and potential levels of understanding, defining the former by what they could do without adult assistance and the latter by what they could do with it. He referred to the gap between these two levels as the Zone of Proximal Development, a term indicating 'what the child is ready to master next on the basis of present achievements, given the best possible adult attention' (Sutton, 1983: 196).

One of the main changes in educational theory to have occurred over the last ten years has been the increasing influence on teachers of Vygotsky's views and the concomitant decline in Piaget's influence. Vygotsky's works have only been available in English since the 1960s. They have, however, inspired developmental psychologists to look more closely at the social processes that foster learning, at the way in which teachers can 'scaffold' their pupils' understanding of complex concepts and at how pupils can best be introduced to the discourse of moral and political debate. In short, the optimistic implications of Vygotsky's ideas have reinforced Bruner's (1960: 33) well-known dictum that 'any subject can be taught to any child of any age in an honest way'.

> Research on the intellectual development of the child highlights the fact that at each stage of development the child has a characteristic way of viewing the world and explaining it to himself. The task of teaching a subject to a child at any particular age is one of representing the structure of that subject in terms of the child's way of viewing things.
>
> (Bruner, 1960: 33)

In 1988, I concluded this chapter by urging primary teachers to 'acquire an immunity to ideological constraints' and discover for themselves the limits of their pupils' understanding of controversial issues. In 1998 these constraints are now less of an issue. Sequential developmentalism has continued to weaken its hold on teachers' thinking partly because of advances at a theoretical level and partly because of the publicity surrounding the government's concern to raise educational standards. The Chief Inspector of Schools has frequently reminded teachers of the importance of high expectations. For example, an influential discussion paper published in 1992 stated that 'standards of education in primary schools will not rise until all teachers expect more of their pupils' (Alexander, et al. 1992: para 3.8). For reasons discussed above, the notion of childhood innocence has likewise become less of an obstacle to the teaching of controversial issues to young children.

However, as the situation has improved in these respects it has worsened in others. Specifically, the National Curriculum, introduced in 1988 has meant that teachers now have little time to discuss with their pupils issues such as racism, sexism and homophobia. The system of assessment that accompanied the curriculum and the advent of published league tables (with all that they imply in terms of pressures on teachers) make it unlikely that schools will spend much time on anything that is not prescribed, least of all on contentious subject matter. Indeed, it has been suggested that the exclusion of such matter was one of the reasons behind the introduction of the National

Curriculum (Maclure, 1988). Social Studies is not part of the curriculum. The nearest to it is the (non-mandatory) cross-curricular theme of Citizenship. This has been described by Haste as supportive of the status quo (*Times Educational Supplement*, 12 July 1996) and by Carr (1991) as 'depoliticised'. It has also been criticised for promoting passivity.

> Education for democratic citizenship is not merely learning *about* social processes; it is, much more, a matter of learning to evaluate them and the practices and policies of those whose task it is to implement them on our behalf. More than education for citizenship, it must be education for *active* and *critical* citizenship.
>
> It is this crucial ingredient that is . . . lacking in the recommendations of [the document on citizenship]. For too many of these recommendations begin with 'pupils need to know about . . .' and 'areas of study might include . . . .'; and . . . none begin with 'pupils need to question . . .' or 'areas of *enquiry* might include'. . .
>
> There is nothing . . . which suggests that the most important aspect of education for democratic citizenship is challenge, evaluation and choice.
>
> (Kelly, 1995)

Clearly, the definition of political literacy implicit in the guidance on citizenship continues to pay scant regard to the political capabilities of young children.

References

Alexander, R. J. (1984) *Primary Teaching*, London: Holt, Rinehart & Winston.

Alexander, R. J., Rose, J. and Woodhead, C. (1992) *Curriculum Organization and Classroom Practice in Primary Schools. A Discussion Paper*, London: Department of Education and Science.

Best, D. L., Williams, J. E., Cloud, J. M., Davis, S. W., Robertson, L. S., Edwards, J. R., Giles, H. and Fowles, J. (1977) 'Development of sex-trait stereotypes among young children in the United States, England and Ireland', *Child Development* 48: 1375–84.

Bruner, J. (1960) *The Process of Education*, New York: Vintage Books.

Carr, W. (1991) 'Education for citizenship', *British Journal of Educational Studies*, 39: 373–85.

Carrington, B. and Short, G. (1984) 'Comics – a medium for racism', *English in Education* 18(2): 10–14.

Carrington, B. and Short, G. (1995) 'What makes a person British? Children's conceptions of their national culture and identity', *Educational Studies*, 21: 217–38.

Damon, W. (1977) *The Social World of the Child*, San Francisco CA: Jossey-Bass.

Department of Education and Science (1985) *Education For All: Report of the Committee of Inquiry into the Education of Children from Ethnic Minority Groups*, (Swann Report) Cmnd 9453, London: HMSO.

Dixon, B. (1977) *Catching Them Young 2: Political Ideas in Children's Fiction*, London: Pluto Press.

Donaldson, M. (1978) *Children's Minds*, Glasgow: Fontana/Collins.

Dunn, J. (1988) *The Beginnings of Social Understanding*, Oxford: Blackwell.

Furth, H. G. (1979) 'Young children's understanding of society', in H. McGurk (ed.) *Issues in Childhood Social Development*, London: Methuen.

Hallam, R. (1969) 'Piaget and the teaching of history', *Educational Research* 12: 3–12.

Hartley, E. L., Rosenbaum, M. and Schwartz, S. (1948) 'Children's perception of ethnic group membership', *Journal of Psychology* 26: 387–97.

Horowitz, E. L. (1936) 'Development of attitudes towards Negroes', in H. Proschansky and B. Seidenberg (eds) (1965) *Basic Studies in Social Psychology*, New York: Holt, Rinehart & Winston.

Isaacs, S. (1930) *Intellectual Growth in Young Children*, London: Routledge & Kegan Paul.

Jahoda, G. (1963) 'The development of children's ideas about country and nationality. Part 1: The conceptual framework', *British Journal of Educational Psychology* 33: 47–60.

Jeffcoate, R. (1977) 'Children's racial ideas and feelings', *English in Education* 11(1): 32–46.

Katz, P. A. (1983) 'Developmental foundations of gender and racial attitudes', in R. L. Leahy (ed.) *The Child's Construction of Social Inequality*, New York: Academic Press.

Kelly, A. V. (1995) *Education and Democracy: Principles and Practices*, London: Paul Chapman Publishing.

King, R. (1978) *All Things Bright and Beautiful? A Sociological Study of Infants' Classrooms*, Chichester: Wiley.

Kohlberg, L. (1958) 'The development of modes of moral thinking and choice in the years ten to sixteen', unpublished PhD thesis, University of Chicago.

Kuhn, D., Nash, S. C. and Brucken, L. (1978) 'Sex-role concepts of two-and three-year olds', *Child Development* 49: 445–51.

Laishley, J. (1971) 'Skin colour awareness and preference in London nursery-school children', *Race* 13(1): 47–64.

Leahy, R. L. (1983) 'The development of the conception of social class', in R. L. Leahy (ed.) *The Child's Construction of Social Inequality*, New York: Academic Press.

Livesley, W. and Bromley, D. (1973) *Person Perception in Childhood and Adolescence*, London: Wiley.

Maclure, S. (1988) *Education Re-formed*, London: Hodder & Stoughton.

Marantz, S. A. and Mansfield, A. F. (1977) 'Maternal employment and the development of sex-role stereotyping in five- to eleven-year old girls', *Child Development* 48: 668–73.

Marsh, A. (1970) 'Awareness of racial differences in West African and British children', *Race* 11: 289–302.

Nash, R. (1976) *Teacher Expectations and Pupil Learning*, London: Routledge & Kegan Paul.

NUT (National Union of Teachers) (1979) *Primary Questions: The NUT Response to the Primary Survey*, London: NUT.

Penrose, J. (1993) 'Reification in the name of change: the impact of nationalism on social constructions of nation, people and place in Scotland and the United

Kingdom', in P. Jackson and J. Penrose (eds) *Constructions of Race, place and Nation*, London: UCL Press.

Selman, R. L. (1980) *The Growth of Interpersonal Understanding*, New York: Academic Press.

Sharp, R. and Green, A. (1975) *Education and Social Control: A Study in Progressive Primary Education*, London: Routledge & Kegan Paul.

Short, G. (1988) 'Children's grasp of Controversial Issues', in B. Carrington and B. Troyna (eds) *Children and Controversial Issues*, Lewes, Falmer.

Short, G. (1989) 'Unfair discrimination: Age-related differences in children's understanding of 'race', gender and social class', unpublished PhD thesis, University of Newcastle-upon-Tyne.

Short, G. and Carrington, B. (1987) 'Towards an anti-racist initiative in the all white primary school', in A. Pollard (ed.) *Children and their Primary Schools: A New Perspective*, Lewes: Falmer Press.

Stevens, O. (1982) *Children Talking Politics: Political Learning in Childhood*, Oxford: Martin Robertson.

Sutton, A. (1983) 'An introduction to Soviet developmental psychology', in S. Meadows (ed.) *Developing Thinking*, London: Methuen.

Troyna, B. and Hatcher, R. (1992) *Racism in Children's Lives: A Study of Mainly-White Primary Schools*, London: Routledge.

Vygotsky, L. (1956) *Selected Psychological Research*, Moscow: Academy of Pedagogic Sciences.

Wood, D. (1998) *How Children Learn and Think*, Oxford: Blackwell.

Chapter 9

Morality and the goals of development*

Erica Burman

Developmentalism is a beguiling creed, to be a developer of backward lands an attractive vocation. We all want to see ourselves as bearers of aid, rectifiers of past injustice. To be sent among a distant nation as a conveyer of progress can only make one feel good . . . It boosts self esteem. It is to regain certainty and purpose, to cast away the ennui and despair of decaying industrial society and to restore bracing faith in the goodness and charity of one's fellow men and women.

(Morris, 1992: 1)

This chapter addresses the treatment of morality in developmental psychology. The debates and criticisms generated in this area can be regarded as encapsulating in a microcosm the limitations of current developmental models. While the moral assumptions permeating models of moral development have attracted some critical attention, their exhibition within this arena should be understood as only one particular instance of what is a general problem. In this chapter the moral status of models of moral development is located within the broader cultural and political landscape within which developmental psychology functions. The remaining questions about whether developmental psychology can outgrow rather than simply process, mature and recycle the conservative and culture-bound presentations of early twentieth-century privileged men are complex. But a prerequisite for this is to understand what these theories are and do.

Piaget's rules on children's games

In *The Moral Judgement of the Child* (1932) Piaget describes his investigations of children's developing appreciation of morality. He conceived of morality as

* This is an edited version of a chapter that appeared in *Deconstructing Developmental Psychology*, London: Routledge, 1994.

systems of rules, and his aim was to understand how we acquire these rules. In line with his paradoxical model of the child both as asocial and as party to insights that civilisation has knocked out of us, Piaget held that most of the moral rules we learn are imposed and enforced on us ready-made by adults. However, he saw in the 'social games' played by children the opportunity to see how these rules are constructed and interpreted by children. By asking children to teach him how to play the game of marbles and asking questions about who had won the game and why, Piaget built up a picture of character-istic ways in which children of different ages both practised and accounted for the rules.

Piaget traced a development in children's play from regularities or rituals that an individual child devises to amuse herself which are full of idio-syncratic habits and symbols, to an imitation of some aspects of what others are doing in terms of rules she has devised but assumes hold generally. At this point, he argued, children may believe themselves to be playing together, but may in fact be playing entirely different games in parallel, without seeing the need for a shared set of rules. This clearly ties in with Piaget's ideas about childhood egocentrism. By about 7–8 years, he claimed, children began to see the game of marbles as a competitive game structured by rules. The success of the game depends on mutual co-operation between players according to col-lectively upheld rules. By 11–12 years (in what he later termed formal oper-ational thinking) Piaget argued that children are interested not only in rules governing the particular game or version of the game they are playing, but in reflecting upon the total set of possible variations that might be called upon in a given case – in other words a hypothetico-deductive approach character-istic of formal reasoning. At this point we should note that, for Piaget, it is the appreciation and engagement with *competition* that is taken as the indicator of sociality.

This work formed the basis for a wide-ranging exploration of children's moral understanding. He explored children's awareness of rules by asking children such questions as 'Can rules be changed?', 'Have rules always been the same as they are today?' and 'How did rules begin?'. At the second stage (which would be called 'preoperational' in his later work), children's imita-tion of rules was based on a perception of rules as sacred and unalterable, despite violating these rules in their own play. Once again childhood ego-centrism is used to account for this paradox. Piaget identified a develop-mental progression from *heteronomy*, where the self is undifferentiated from the (social, moral, physical) context, to *autonomy*, where the individual chooses to engage in particular social contracts. He traced a change in approach towards rules from an initial *unilateral respect* (where rules are obeyed due to adult constraint) to *mutual respect* (where rules are social conventions operating to maintain fairness). He went on to pose stories involving minor misdeeds to children, investigating their ideas about responsibility in terms of moral questions he considered relevant to children, such as stealing and lying. The outcome of his clinical interviews with children was that he claimed, in contrast to older children and adults, young children judged the naughtiness of an action by its results rather than by the agent's intentions, that is, the magnitude of the damage is treated as the index of the scale of the misdeed.

Kohlberg on Piaget

Laurence Kohlberg (1969a, 1969b, 1976), a US developmental psychologist, elaborated on and developed Piaget's work on moral reasoning to put forward a series of six stages and three levels in the development and articulation of moral judgement from childhood to adulthood. He based his work on the classification of the kinds of moral reasoning displayed by individuals of different ages when they were confronted with hypothetical dilemmas. The most celebrated 'dilemma' used to elicit the underlying structure of people's moral reasoning was about a penniless man, Heinz, who urgently needs an expensive medicine to save his wife's life, and which the pharmacist refuses to give or supply on credit. Should he steal the drug? Here there is a conflict between the values of property and life. We should pause to note that, in the transition from Geneva to the US and from the 1930s to the 1960s, a process of methodological and taxonomical rigidity has taken place. The ascription of moral level has become a question of classification according to age or stage: from premoralism, to conformism, to individual principled morality.

A number of claims underlie the framework. Firstly, the stages are said to be universal and fixed. Secondly, the sequence is invariant, with variation only in rate of progression or fixation at a particular stage. And, thirdly, each stage is a structured whole, with characteristics of reasoning associated with a stage related together into a total world-view. All this is reminiscent of Piaget's model of the relations that hold between the organisation of cognitive operations. In terms of evidence used to support this model, there is apparently fairly widespread support for the claim that the stages occur in a fixed order (Colby et al., 1983). There is also cross-sectional support, in that higher stages are reported among older subjects. In addition, some longitudinal studies suggest that over a period of years individuals tend to advance to higher stages (Walker, 1989). Even some cross-cultural work lent support, with Kohlberg (1969b) identifying the same sequence of stages (with the stories slightly adapted), in the US, Britain, Taiwan, Mexico and Turkey, and the stages and sequences confirmed in other societies by Edwards (1981). So it seemed as though the arena of moral development had been pretty well sorted out. Or had it?

Kohlberg's dilemmas

From the 1970s some critical voices emerged which suggested that the sorting process was on a less than equitable basis. It seemed that the ascription of the moral highground was of uncertain validity, of contested value and unfair distribution.

In terms of methodological criticisms, a first problem arises from basing a classification of moral level on verbal reports. Unlike Piaget's early work, Kohlberg's model relies exclusively on what people say about what (other) people should do, based on hypothetical situations. But being more thoughtful, circumspect, taking more factors into consideration does not necessarily mean that people behave more morally. Further, the practice of investigating moral reasoning via hypothetical situations makes the moral problems posed even more detached and distanced. In this context Carol Gilligan's (1982) work on women's reasoning about the real-life dilemma of whether or not to terminate a pregnancy provides a particularly striking contrast.

Secondly, corresponding to the work challenging what is seen as Piaget's rather pessimistic view of children's abilities, there has been some work which seeks to analyse and minimise the linguistic and narrative demands of the task. Stein et al. (1979) reformulated Heinz's dilemma into a story about a lady who had a sick husband and had to steal some cat's whiskers in order to make the only medicine that would save his life. Despite the fairy-tale genre and simplicity of the story, they report young children as having difficulties understanding it. They suggest that the children do not draw the obvious inference that the medicine will save the man's life since they cannot maintain the major goal in mind while trying to pursue the subgoals of securing the whiskers and making the medicine. In order to engage with the dilemma, the task presupposes the ability to understand a complex narrative and to think through alternative courses of action, both of which may be more complicated than the process of making moral judgements alone.

Criticisms addressed to the theory rather than the procedures by which it was arrived at also take a number of forms. In the first place, it is claimed that it addresses only a very restricted notion of morality. While this is not the place to go into alternative (such as behavioural or psychoanalytic) models of morality, the Kohlbergian model of morality as moral reasoning cannot engage with issues of moral commitment, and individual priorities or differences of moral salience of particular issues. Nor does it address the subjective experience of feelings of guilt and shame which, as Kagan (1984) notes, children exhibit from an early age. Once again we see that a cognitive developmental model which prioritises rationality cannot theorise its relation with emotions except insofar as emotions are regarded as subordinate to, or at best by-products of, cognition.

The rigidity of representation of morality also fails to deal with domain specificity, familiarity and, further, the reality of the conflicting moral codes and priorities we are subject to (Turiel, 1983; Song *et al.*, 1987). Moreover, not only is this a model which treats talk about moral behaviour as equivalent to moral activity, it also fails to address how accounting for the morality of one's behaviour tends to follow rather than precede the actions. Hence these accounts measure moral rationalisation rather than reasoning (Hogen, 1975).

Double standards: gender-differentiating rights and responsibilities

One of the most influential criticisms of the model is that the stages do not fit female development. Carol Gilligan (1982) points out that both Piaget and Kohlberg derived their stage norms from studying boys and men. She challenges the capacity of the model to express women's psychological development. She reinterprets boys' and girls' accounts of Heinz's dilemma, where in terms of Kohlbergian criteria the girls would be scored as reasoning at a lower moral stage of development. She points out that the girls' and women's reservations about stealing the drug were based on additional considerations arising from an engagement with the context, such as the effect on the wife if the man was imprisoned for the crime and the worry about who would care for her if she fell ill again.

Although it is unclear whether she is advocating improving or abandoning it, Gilligan therefore throws the model of moral development that Kohlberg proposes into question. In tracing a linear progression from undifferentiation or attachment to autonomy, she argues that it subscribes to a model of morality based on individual rights and freedoms of the kind enshrined in Western legal systems, whereas, she holds, women's moral development is characterised by a much more contextualised morality concerned with conflicting responsibilities and care – that is, concerned with responsibilities and relationships rather than rights and rules. She argues that Kohlberg's model emphasises separation rather than connection by taking the individual rather than the relationship as the primary unit of analysis.

Gilligan ties these different conceptions of morality to the different roles traditionally accorded to men and women. Since women define their identity through relationships of intimacy and care, the moral issues women face are to do with learning to assert their own needs without seeing this as 'selfish'. For both sexes, she argues, the issues that we face are to do with the conflict between integrity (separateness) and care (attachment), but that men and women approach these issues with different moral orientations. For men the emphasis is on 'equality', based on an understanding of fairness, equal respect, balancing the claims of other and self. In contrast, women's morality, she claims, is more oriented to issues of responsibility, with recognition of differences in need that an equal rights approach cannot address – an ethic of compassion and care and not wanting to hurt. Gilligan calls for the necessity for these contrasting moral orientations to be seen as complementary rather than one being systematically downgraded, and ultimately for them to be integrated into a more adequate vision of moral maturity. While there are problems with the idealisation of women's qualities within this account (see Sayers, 1986), the value of this work lies in demonstrating the limited application and far-reaching devaluation of women structured within the cognitive developmental model.

Culture and the goals of development

A further serious difficulty with Kohlberg's model lies in the status of the sixth stage, which represents individual moral conviction as the most advanced morality beyond the respect for democratically arrived at and contractually maintained rules (Stage Five). Firstly, few people are designated as attaining the higher points on the developmental ladder (with Jesus Christ, Mahatma Gandhi, and Martin Luther King named by Kohlberg as among the lucky few – among whom he also includes himself!). This raises questions about the theoretical status of the highest point of development. Secondly, some cultures are recorded as not reaching even beyond the second stage. There are clearly methodological difficulties involved in the study of people from one culture by those of another. These are issues that anthropologists routinely address, although some have been known to rely on psychology with disastrous results (see, e.g., Hallpike, 1979). The suggestion that Kohlberg's stages can be related to the 'complexity' of societies (Edwards, 1981) sets up a hierarchy from 'primitive' to 'complex' which simply reflects a Western cultural bias. It may, however, be more accurate to make a distinction between rural and urban societies, with Stage Five reported much less frequently in the former (Snarey, 1985). But this calls for an analysis that connects cognitive/moral development with culture and context.

However, a further issue comes into play when researchers measure indigenous people's abilities and interests by means of a test devised outside their own culture. Here developmental psychology reproduces and bolsters the dynamic of imperialism by offering tools that produce a picture of inferiority and moral underdevelopment through the ethnocentric and culturally chauvinist assumptions that inform both theory and tool (Joseph et al., 1990). Kohlberg later reformulated some of his claims about Stage Six so that it is now seen as an ideal, rather than a necessary, endpoint of development (Levine et al., 1985). This, however, seems to offer a rather cosmetic change which leaves the methodological, and moral-political, problems intact.

In this we can see played out problems common to all developmental psychological theories that claim to hold generally. The postulation of a starting state and an endstate involves the prescription of the endpoint, the goal, of development. We talk in terms of 'progressing', 'advancing' from one stage to the next. But the norms by which we evaluate that development may be far from universal. In particular, as we have seen, the individual autonomy of conscience of Stage Six fits well with the modern, Western ideology of individualism. But this is not the highest point of moral development for all cultures, many of which value obedience and respect for elders and tradition over personal conviction. Kagan (1984) notes that in Japan the guiding principle of social interaction is to avoid conflict and maintain harmonious relationships. With such a different value system and contrasting view of the relationship between individuals, we could expect that a Kohlbergian Stage Six person would be considered aberrant and amoral in according personal principles more importance than societal expectations.

Further, the model of 'man' prescribed in Kohlberg's (and by implication Piaget's) model derives from particular social interests, based on a liberal model of society seen as functioning by means of social contractual arrangements between people (Simpson, 1974; Sampson, 1989). The rationality which is so highly valued in the cognitive developmental model ties in with a bourgeois conception of the individual which either accepts class divisions or denies their existence (Sullivan, 1977; Buck-Morss, 1975). In its celebration of autonomy, Kohlbergian theory therefore partakes of a liberal view that sees society as composed of independent units who co-operate only when the terms of co-operation are such as to further the ends of each of the parties. This also clearly recalls Piaget's definition of social interaction in game playing through competition. Not only does this lead to an asocial view of the individual, in terms of the ascription of pre-social interests, it also sets up a form of conceptual imperialism in its application to cultures which do not share this underlying model. Sullivan treats this model as a case example of the political and conceptual problems wrought by an inadequate theory of the social: thought is severed from action, form from content, the abstract from the concrete and, ultimately, emotion from intellect.

Developmental psychology and the developing world

Some of the methodological and moral difficulties described above have been reflected in the failure of the project of cross-cultural psychology. On practical grounds researchers were forced to recognise that the cultural assumptions held by research 'subjects' about the nature of the task demanded of them did not always correspond with that intended by the researchers. Cole *et al.* (1971) found that the African Kpelle consistently failed Piagetian classification tasks when asked 'how a wise man' would organise piles of foods and household items together. It was only when in despair the researcher asked how 'a fool would do it' that they exhibited the typical Western classification based on type (sorting similar items together) that had been defined as task success, rather than functional relations that reflected the ways the items were used.

Such examples highlight that the problems are more than mere practical or technical difficulties, and cast doubt on the entire project of developmental psychology. The presentation of a general model which depicts development as unitary irrespective of culture, class, gender and history means that difference can be recognised only in terms of aberrations, deviations – that is, in terms of relative progress on a linear scale. The developmental psychology we know is tied to the culture which produced it. And, while such insights have had some impact within academic psychology, they are maintained in policy and in popular representations of childhood and child development.

The image of the active, natural, innocent child functions within the economy of cultural representations of children in so-called developing countries in ways which castigate poor people for their poverty, lapse into racist assumptions about child neglect and penalise the children of the poor rather than promote their welfare. Claire Cassidy (1989) discusses how, when poverty and ignorance lead to malnutrition in Third World countries, this is sometimes treated by welfare workers as an example of parental neglect. There is a failure to distinguish between culturally normative and deviant forms in evaluating child development in 'other' cultures. In purveying what is advertised as a general, universal model of development, developmental psychology is a vital ingredient in what Jo Boyden (1990) has termed the 'globalization of childhood'. While Western sentimentalised representations of children are rooted in the attempt to deny children's agency (notwithstanding the claims of child-centredness) and prevent social unrest, the key dimensions that have come to structure Western organisation of childhood are being inappropriately imposed in 'developing' countries. The division between public and private has been central to Western industrialisation, but it should be recalled that poor people have less privacy, and that street children may have none at all (although see Glauser (1990) for an analysis of the distinction between children *of* the street and children living *on* the streets). But Western conceptions of children as unknowing, helpless and in need of protection from the public sphere may actually disable and criminalise children who are coping as best they can. All too often, policies and practices developed in the West function more in punitive than protective ways for Third World children – even in literal ways by being dispensed by the police, who in some Third World countries have been responsible for the murder of children in their custody.

Similarly, while the regulation of child labour is clearly important, attempts to abolish this in line with Western practice frequently ignore the extent to which families (and children) are dependent on the incomes children generate, and would therefore need to be compensated in order to let their children attend school. Further, the schooling which is on offer is often of varying quality, and may often take the form of enforced assimilation to a colonial language. The schooling experience may therefore be one which fails rather than enables children. The Western priority accorded to education may therefore be misplaced in the sense that this is unlikely to be organised around principles of personal development or enlightenment.

The undifferentiated, globalised model of childhood not only fails to address the varying cultural value and position of children (Zelizer, 1985), but also ignores gender as a structural issue in development (in both the senses of individual and economic development). Aid agencies are now being forced to recognise that specific priorities need to be set up for girls and women (e.g. Wallace and March, 1991), while the role of gendered meanings in structuring not only entirely different subjectivities and livelihoods, but actual nutrition and survival is gradually emerging through the efforts of women's organisations (Scheper-Hughes, 1989; Batou, 1991).

In general, the concept of childhood on offer is a Western construction that is now being incorporated, as though it were universal, into aid and development policies (Burman, 1994). Associations between the development of the child and the development of the nation or State are familiar. Indeed many aid policy documents present their rationale for promoting child survival and development in terms of the future benefit to the State (e.g. Myers, 1992). But there are other resonances I want to mobilise here. Tim Morris opens his account of his experiences as an aid worker in the Middle East (in the extract I have positioned at the beginning of this chapter) with a critique of the cultural chauvinism, complacency and personal investments set up within aid work. Just as he is exposing the problems inherent in defining goals for societal development, so too do the same problems arise within the determination of the direction and endpoint of individual development. The notion of 'progress', whether of societies or through 'the life span', implies linear movement across history and between cultures. Comparison within these terms is now being recognised as increasingly untenable. In particular, the implication that there is a detached, disinterested set of devices or techniques for this purpose, such as developmental psychology purports to provide, illustrates the extent to which we have come to believe in the abstract disembodied psychological subject, and dismiss all it fails to address as merely either supplementary or inappropriate. [. . .] Developmental psychology therefore functions as a tool of cultural imperialism through the reproduction of Western values and models within post-colonial societies. [. . .]

References

Batou, J. (1991) '100 million women are missing', *International Viewpoint*, 206: 26–8.

Boyden, J. (1990) 'Childhood and the policy makers: a comparative perspective on the globalization of childhood', in A. James and A. Prout (eds) *Constructing and Reconstructing Childhood: contemporary issues in the sociological study of childhood*, Basingstoke, Hants: Falmer.

Buck-Morss, S. (1975) 'Socio-economic bias in Piaget's theory and its implications for cross-cultural studies'. *Human Development*, 18: 35–45.

Burman, E. (1994) 'Poor children: charity appeals and ideologies of childhood', *Changes: International Journal of Psychology and Psychotherapy*, 12, 1: 29–36.

Cassidy, C. (1989) 'Worldview conflict and toddler malnutrition: changeagent dilemmas', in N. Scheper-Hughes (ed.) *Child Survival and Neglect*, Dordrecht: Reidel.

Colby, A., Kohlberg, L., Gibbs, J. and Lieberman, M. (1983) 'A longitudinal study of moral judgement', *Monographs of the Society for Research in Child Development*, 48, (1–2): (no. 200).

Cole, M., Gay, J., Glick, J. and Sharp, D.W. (1971) *The Cultural Context of Learning and Thinking*, New York: Basic Books.

Edwards, C.P. (1981) 'The comparative study of the development of moral judgement and reasoning', in R.H. Munroe, R.L. Munroe and B.B. Whiting (eds) *Handbook of Cross Cultural Human Development*, New York: Garland.

Gilligan, C. (1982) *In a Different Voice: psychological theory and women's development*, Cambridge, Mass.: Harvard University Press.

Glauser, B. (1990) 'Street children: deconstructing a construct', in A. James and A. Prout (eds) *Constructing and Reconstructing Childhood*, London: Falmer.

Hallpike, C. (1979) *The Foundations of Primitive Thought*, Cambridge: Cambridge University Press.

Hogen, R. (1975) 'Moral Development and the structure of personality', in D. DePalma and J. Foley (eds) *Moral Development: current theory and research*, New York: LEA.

Joseph, G., Reddy, V. and Searle-Chatterjee, M. (1990) 'Eurocentrism in the social sciences', *Race and Class*, 31, 4: 1–26.

Kagan, J. (1984) *The Nature of the Child*, New York: Basic Books.

Kohlberg, L. (1969a) 'The child as moral philosopher', in J. Sants (ed.) *Developmental Psychology*, Harmondsworth: Penguin.

Kohlberg, L. (1969b) 'Stage and sequence: the cognitive developmental approach', in D.A. Goslin (ed.) *The Handbook of Socialization Theory and Research*, Chicago: Rand McNally.

Kohlberg, L. (1976) 'Moral stages and moralisation', in T. Lickona (ed.) *Moral Development and Moral Behaviour: theory, research and social issues*, New York: Holt, Rinehart & Winston.

Levine, C., Kohlberg, L. and Hewer, A. (1985) 'The current formulation of Kohlberg's theory and a response to critics', *Human Development*, 28: 94–100.

Morris, T. (1992) *The Despairing Developer: diary of an aid worker in the Middle East*, London: IB Taurus.

Piaget, J. (1932) *The Moral Judgement of the Child*, London: Routledge & Kegan Paul.

Sampson, E. (1989) 'The deconstruction of self', in J. Shotter and K. Gergen (eds) *Texts of Identity*, London: Sage.

Sayers, J. (1986) *Sexual Contradictions: feminism, psychology and psychoanalysis*, London: Tavistock.

Scheper-Hughes, N. (1989) 'Culture, scarcity and maternal thinking: motherlove and child death in Northeast Brazil', in N. Scheper-Hughes (ed.) *Child Survival: anthropological perspectives on the treatment and maltreatment of children*, Dordrecht: Reidel.

Simpson, E. (1974) 'Moral development research: a case of scientific cultural bias', *Human Development*, 17: 81–106.

Snarey. J.R. (1985) 'Cross cultural universality of social-moral development: a critical review of Kohlbergian research', *Psychological Bulletin*, 97: 202–32.

Song, M.J., Smetana, J.G. and Kim, S.Y. (1987) 'Korean children's conceptions of moral and conventional transgressions'. *Developmental Psychology*, 23, 4: 577–82.

Stein, N., Trabasso, T. and Garfin, D. (1979) 'Comprehending and remembering moral dilemmas', in S. Goldman (ed.) *Understanding Discourse: interactions between knowledge and process*, symposium presented to American Psychological Association, September.

Sullivan, E. (1977) 'A study of Kohlberg's structural theory of moral development: a critique of liberal social science ideology', *Human Development*, 20: 352–75.

Turiel, E. (1983) *The Development of Social Knowledge: morality and convention*, Cambridge: Cambridge University Press.

Wallace, T. and March, C. (1991) *Changing Perceptions: writings on gender and development*, Oxford: Oxfam.

Zelizer, V.A. (1985) *Pricing the Priceless Child: the changing social value of children*, New York: Basic Books.

Chapter 10

Moral understanding in socio-cultural context

Lay social theory and a Vygotskian synthesis*

Helen Haste

The problem

There is major debate in developmental psychology. It has been fuelled in part by cross-cultural evidence of different conceptions of morality and self, but also by gender studies. The conflict is between those who search for basic processes inside the head of the individual, and those who search for them in the interaction between persons. Many people see these as irreconcilable positions. In this chapter I argue for a model that bridges this gap.

For the first position in this conflict, the starting point is the evidence for *structural development*, manifested in qualitative changes or 'stages' of reasoning as in the well-known accounts offered by Piaget (1932) and elaborated by Kohlberg (1984). This model of development assumes that the *individual* constructs meaning. 'Development' reflects qualitative reconstruction of meaning in ever more integrated forms. Though few would claim that this reconstruction happens in social isolation, the role of other individuals is mainly seen as a sort of catalytic intervention, providing challenges that, in Piaget's terms generate *disequilibration*. Stagewise development assumes progress moves toward increasing complexity and, by implication, increasingly adequate understanding. The structural pattern of development is presumed to be universal.

In contrast, those who take the second position argue that the Piagetian model is embedded in a highly individualistic conception of development, that ignores the social and cultural context in which the child develops (e.g. Harré and Gillett, 1994; Cole, 1995). Such critics cite the evidence for widely differing models of the self and of morality across, and even within, cultures. Their contrasting position is that the very concepts of the self and morality depend on social processes and are shaped through language and culture. Through discourse with others, the growing child learns what is morally

---

* Specially prepared for this Reader based on a chapter that first appeared in *The Moral Self*, Cambridge, MA: MIT Press, 1993.

salient, and how to invoke values and goals for moral solutions consistent with the expectations of the culture. He or she similarly learns appropriate ways of relating to others and of conceptualizing such relationships.

This situation seems to be a theoretical impasse: cultural variation is frequently cited as a terminal blow to individualistic conceptions of development, and there seems to be no place for stages or qualitative changes in individual reasoning when the primary process of development is seen to be inculcating the growing child into a socially constructed world of meaning.

Vygotsky as synthesis

I want to explore a synthesis. In my view the importance of Vygotsky's approach is that he saw the individual *as an active agent*, making sense and constructing meaning within a social and a cultural environment. Vygotsky provides a resolution to the division between individualistic and social approaches. I need not recapitulate the details of Vygotsky's theory, but I will refer to key ideas. I conceptualize Vygotsky's theory as a triangle because this seems to me to represent his ideas and also the way in which they highlight, as well as potentially resolve, the division (Figure 10.1). This triangle conceptually separates 'social' processes at the level of culture and 'social' processes of interaction and does not see these levels simply as macro and micro levels of the same process.

Vygotsky maintained that the individual 'makes sense' of the world and that individual thought processes and their structure are worth investigating. However, he differed from Piaget in the primary role that he assigned to language in the development of thought. He also made a celebrated, much-quoted and much-researched statement that there is a 'zone of proximal

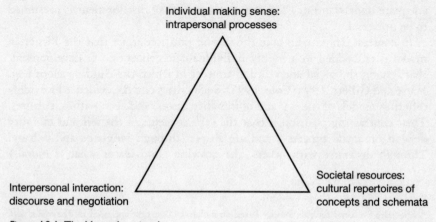

Figure 10.1 The Vygotsky triangle

development', arguing that concepts first come to the attention of the individual through interpersonal action and discussion; only later are they internalized by the individual. Finally and crucially, he argued that knowledge is possible only within a given socio-historical or socio-cultural context.

What I have chosen to term the Vygotsky triangle consists of the individual (who has some agency in 'making sense'), the interpersonal nexus (within which meaning is constructed and negotiated through discourse and performance of shared tasks), and the culture (the socio-historical context that constitutes the repertoire of available frameworks within which both interpersonal discourse and individual cognition are constrained and constructed).

The triangle can be translated (with some oversimplification for clarity) into the debates outlined above, in the following ways:

Traditional cognitive-developmental approaches (deriving from a Piagetian perspective) are firmly at the 'individual' corner of the triangle, treating the 'interpersonal' nexus primarily as a catalytic process. The burgeoning work on the 'Zone of Proximal Development' (ZPD) has captured the imagination of many erstwhile cognitive developmentalists who have felt the limitations of purely individualistic approaches. The power of the concept of ZPD is as a *bridge* between the 'individual' and the 'interpersonal' which recognizes the role of the peer or teacher in introducing the growing individual to new concepts. This is quite consistent with the 'catalytic' model, which maintains that peer interaction facilitates development.

In contrast, much traditional social psychology, particularly work on small groups is located at the interpersonal corner of the triangle. It has focused only on the relationship between the interpersonal and the individual. Recent European social psychology represents a shift towards the third point of the triangle. For example the work of Moscovici on social representations (Farr and Moscovici, 1984) links the cultural and the interpersonal. So also does work within 'discursive psychology' (for example Potter and Wetherell, 1987, Harré and Gillett, 1994). In these approaches, the interpersonal conversation is the *crucible* of social meaning, but the culture is the main resource for frameworks of meaning. An important point of this recent work is that the interaction is *both ways*: the culture does not merely constrain what can be known; it is itself changed through discursive processes, which generate new frameworks for meaning.

Another perspective comes from cultural psychologists (see Stigler *et al.*, 1990; Cole, 1995) who make links between the interpersonal and socio-historical points of the triangle. Their work shows how interpersonal processes act as the mechanism by which the culture is made explicit to the child, rather than only facilitating the child's own construction of meaning. The evidence of major differences in frameworks and schemata illustrates the role of the culture. What the child learns within a particular domain depends on how the culture defines the goal, role and nature of that domain. Studies by Saxe and by Lave, for example, show that ways of conceptualizing even arithmetic can differ strikingly in different cultures (see Wertsch, 1985a, 1985b; Lave, 1990).

The advantage of a Vygotskian approach is that it integrates the three points of the triangle, whereas currently much writing focuses on the relationship and interaction between two of the points while simply ignoring the third point. So, 'hardline' social constructionist discussion that starts from the position that social processes generate meaning has tended to play down the role of individual construction, limiting development to an increasing 'expertise' in expressing the culture's requirements. In contrast, the traditional cognitive developmental perspective that starts from an explanation of the individual's construction of meaning, considers interpersonal processes merely as facilitating the individual's reconstruction of meaning. Furthermore, a key feature of the cognitive development perspective is the search for *universals*: interest in cultural variation has therefore been about commonalities rather than diversities. Finally, although interpersonal interaction (especially the Zone of Proximal Development) has generated a lot of research in developmental psychology, the issue of the historical and cultural context has not penetrated the discipline so extensively. Recognizing socio-historical context is more radical; it involves taking seriously cultural variation in how experience is conceptualized, and not assuming there are universals (Bruner and Haste, 1987).

Lay social theory

I want to present the concept of *lay social theory* as a way of applying a Vygotskian framework to children's moral understanding. As I use the term, 'lay social theory' is a way of giving an account, providing an explanation, telling a story, that makes sense. It has much in common with 'folk models' (D'Andrade, 1987). It implies that our lay social theories will be comprehensible within the culture; that there are shared common-sense assumptions, values and meaning.

Let us consider, for example, a lay social theory about crime. This lay social theory would comprise schemas for what constitutes a crime, the law, a criminal, and so forth. It enables anyone in our culture to understand the implications of statements such as 'Marijuana should be decriminalized' or 'Political prisoners are not criminals'. A lay social theory of crime also contains beliefs about the causes and cures of crime. So, the belief that strong punishment is important in the prevention of crime is both part of a schema about what motivates crime, and a reflection of an underlying theory about psychological processes. A lay social theory implies explanations and prescriptions for behaviour or beliefs and presupposes a series of events or related elements rather than a single focus.

Lay social theories are not just constructed inside people's heads: they are the product of interaction and discourse. They are embedded in cultural practice and meaning. Let us consider a simple example, which is widely used in social psychology – the idea of a 'script' that was developed by Schank and Abelson (1977). The classic version is the *restaurant script*. This embodies a precise sequence of actions and interactions. The individual comes to know these, and their social and cultural meaning, through personal experience and the guidance of experienced diners, such as parents. People usually go to restaurants after some years of eating in the family, and after exposure to secondary descriptions in drama or stories. Actual participation in the action takes the form of an apprenticeship, with continual commentary from the accompanying adult. The child is explicitly directed to take certain actions ('Sit here', 'Put your napkin on your knee') but the child also hears talk that implies various aspects of the script. 'What do you want to eat?' indicates a *choice* which is usually not part of the family meals script. 'The steak is rather expensive, why not have the fish?' also departs from home eating by bringing in the idea of paying for food, and it also communicates the idea of thrift. Comments like: 'The waiter is very slow' or 'Those people over there don't seem the usual type for this restaurant' express norms for waiters' behaviour, and for social categories.

This example shows lay social theory in practice, and how it emerges. We can detect all the elements of the Vygotsky 'triangle' in Figure 10.1 in operation. An individual's lay theory engages with culturally available scenarios or scripts that not only provide rules for action but also explain events and predict outcomes. Although the individual actively tries to make sense of experience, 'making sense' requires accessing the wider repertoire of lay social theories actually available within the culture. The formulation, evaluation, and selection from that repertoire depend upon interpersonal interaction and continuous discourse. Teachers, parents, peers and siblings continually comment on the child's behaviour in ways that make assumptions about what are the appropriate ways of thinking, talking and acting (Much and Shweder, 1978; Shweder and Much, 1987; Dunn, 1987; Haste, 1987a).

In decoding these assumptions, even more perhaps than through direct precept, the child learns what is taken for granted, what is assumed and required. What is said reveals what is taken for granted as tacit, shared knowledge. (Sometimes referred to as 'prolepsis' (See Goncü, 1998; Stone, 1998).

Decoding tacit knowledge is a crucial part of how the growing child discovers what needs to be made sense of. An example of this process can be seen in the following common type of exchange:

A: It's ten o'clock.
B: I've been to the dentist.

B immediately decodes A's statement as accusing B of being late, which was

A's intention. B responds with a factual statement that carries with it the shared understanding that going to the dentist constitutes an acceptable reason for being late.

Thinking of development as a cultural and social process shifts us away from a concentration on individual processes that are 'inside the head'. As I have stated, cognitive developmental models start with the individual and – if they consider social processes at all – perceive the social world, and interaction with others, as moderating or stimulating individual cognitive processes and development. For the cultural-social position, social processes are central. What 'develops' is the individual's skill in managing the moral expectations of one's culture, which are expressed through linguistic and symbolic practices.

Vygotsky's argument that one cannot isolate the individual from historical and social context also contrasts with the assumption made by cognitive developmental models, that psychological processes are universal. The research agenda is to explore cultural practices in action, and to see how the individual, as an intentional being, becomes expert in cultural skills. This means focusing less on the final product inside people's heads, and more on what goes on in social and linguistic processes, like *narrative and discourse*, and how these organize the individual's experience (Vygotsky, 1978; Tappan and Packer, 1991, Cole, 1995).

Work on social interaction (e.g. Dunn, 1987) demonstrates that children are very skilled in negotiating moral and social conflict at an early age, and invoking appropriate justifications. A study of Japanese nursery school children found that most disputes were resolved by compromise and bargaining, in which children were very skilful, and which used moral justifications (such as 'it's his turn') (Killen and Nucci, 1995). Such activities demonstrate the daily involvement of young children in effectively negotiating moral and social justifications that are acceptable in their peer group.

In summary, how a situation is interpreted and what is perceived to be salient reflect familiar cultural scripts. Frames and schemas for 'making sense' emerge through everyday discourse and negotiation of meaning with significant others. This discourse takes place within the wider social context; culturally specific frames delineate what is available and salient for the discourse.

According to this integration of Vygotsky, the process is dialectical. It involves culturally available scenarios, normative expectations, and desired goals, which are accessed by the individual in part through the media (the individual–societal interface) and in part through continuous social interaction (the individual–interpersonal interface).

In my view, we can still retain a conception of developmental stages within a model of discourse and cultural context. I would argue that a child's development does reflect reconstruction processes through stages, which represent increasingly differentiated, qualitatively more complex understanding. But the salient elements of that understanding will depend on what schemas are culturally appropriate. Thus one must postulate stages *within* whatever happens to be the culturally prevailing 'lay theory' of the self, or morality.

Cultural variation and its implications

Let us explore this Vygotskian perspective in relation to concepts of selfhood, and morality.

A rich vein of anthropological material reveals how varied are human conceptions of selfhood (see for instance Geertz, 1975; Rosaldo, 1984; Shweder and Bourne, 1984; Shweder and Much, 1987). Embedded in selfhood are cultural assumptions about roles, relationships, and self-worth that underpin morality. The (male) Western model of the self gives enormous weight to individuals' personal autonomy and freedom, purely because they are persons rather than because of their roles. It focuses on the self as the agent relating to others, rather than on the interconnection of persons. Self-worth is therefore seen in terms of the individual being able to act freely and responsibly *vis-à-vis* others, who are free, separate selves. Performing a 'role' is not enough for this is seen as hiding a public face rather than acting as an individual. In contrast, in societies that locate the self in roles and think of the interrelationship of selves, performing a role can be coterminous with morality and self-worth.

What do we do with evidence of cultural variation? As we have already seen there are usually two ways of approaching the problem. The dilemma is:

1   Do we assume that development is primarily a matter of the individual mind engaging in construction and reconstruction, albeit facilitated by the cultural and social environment, and ultimately arriving at some common understanding that expresses universal requirements of the human condition?
2   Do we assume that not only *what* we know but also *how* we know derives entirely from our cultural heritage? In the latter case culturally specific meaning is granted to that experience and this sets the framework for the child's development. Therefore, the growth of 'understanding' is in fact growth of an increasingly sophisticated appreciation of that meaning system.

The distinction is between universalism and relativism. The first approach implies that there are universals in development; that there are commonalities in conceptions of selfhood and moral codes despite local variations in the expression of values and concepts. The second approach is more relativistic. It implies that each society may generate very different ways of ordering human experience and of inculcating the growing child into the culture, so that concepts, values, and the processes of development cannot translate across boundaries and, indeed, may even be incomprehensible across cultures.

There is, however, a third option, which goes beyond the dichotomy of relativism and universalism: pluralism. Let us consider some examples which illustrate the issues. Shweder's work in India is particularly relevant. He and his colleagues administered Kohlberg's 'Heinz dilemma' (about a man forced to decide whether to steal medicines for his dying wife) to villagers. One of their respondents was a very morally sophisticated reasoner who came to very different conclusions, supported by very different arguments, from that expected within Western culture. This respondent was obviously using a high stage of moral reasoning, but it was impossible to score him on the Kohlberg measures because his arguments were too far away from the Western position (Shweder, 1990).

Cultural psychologists argue that we should not be looking for universal moral stages, but trying to understand moral diversity. A focus on justice may be very far from the primary ethical concerns of some cultures. If researchers apply Kohlberg's dilemma to try to measure 'justice' reasoning, rather than eliciting people's usual moral framework, stage scores may be misleading, but more important, the results would fail to give a true picture of people's moral lives. Members of other cultures, particularly if they are educated in a Western system, may have access to an ethic based on justice and so be able to give responses to moral dilemmas couched in terms of justice, but it may not be a true reflection of their preferred mode of thinking about such issues. From his Indian data, Shweder draws the conclusion that there are serious flaws in both a stage model and a model that makes 'justice' central to morality. In studies with his Indian respondents he found that self-worth was rated as more important than preservation of life for its own sake, and that autonomy meant not individualism but rather the surrender of material possessions and the pursuit of self-understanding (Shweder and Much, 1987; Shweder, Mahapatra and Miller, 1987).

Many studies on moral reasoning demonstrate cultural variation – different lay social and moral theories which reflect different moral priorities and accounts of what makes a 'good person' – and why. In a study that compared United States and South Indian adults, Miller and Bersoff (1995) explored different moral perspectives on family relationships. They found that Americans saw family life as existing primarily to meet the needs of every individual member, and they resolved dilemmas about conflicting needs in these terms. Indian respondents saw the family unit as having intrinsic value over and above the needs of the individual members, so dilemmas were resolved in terms of the family's overall needs, rather than the individual's needs. Americans valued psychological support and enhancing relationships, whereas Indian respondents valued selflessness and serving the well-being of others. Comparing reasoning about the 'Heinz dilemma' in the United States and Japan, Iwasa (1992) found no difference in level of moral stage, but qualitative differences in why human life was valued, which reflected cultural norms. Americans were concerned to prolong the length of life, Japanese to make it purer and cleaner. Hence, the majority of Americans thought Heinz should steal, whereas the majority of Japanese thought he should not. A pluralist perspective would conclude that there are several 'lay moral theories', as it were, of which justice is but one. These examples are taken from cross-cultural studies of conceptions of self and morality. In the next section I consider the plurality of lay social theories, even within a culture.

Morality and self: gender and lay social theory

In this final section I shall take the example of gender to illustrate the ways in which lay social theory operates and the ways in which individuals have access to different kinds of explanations within a culture.

Carol Gilligan (1982/1993) has argued that women focus on different aspects of moral dilemmas from men. Men focus on justice, which is the dominant theme of Kohlberg's method of measurement, whereas women focus on caring and responsibility. Gilligan argued that these different ethics, or 'moral orientations', rest on a deeper issue, how we think about selfhood. An ethic of justice is the natural outcome of thinking of people as *separate* beings, in continual conflict with one another, who make rules and contracts as a way of handling this. An ethic of caring and responsibility follows from conceptualizing selves as being in *connection* with one another.

The simple argument that women 'think differently' about moral issues is open to challenge. Several studies find that sex differences in the use of moral orientations are less important than the kind of dilemmas under consideration and that each sex is competent in each mode, but that there are gender-linked preferences (Johnston, 1988; Pratt *et al.*, 1984; Nunner-Winkler, 1984). These findings support Gilligan's argument that there is more than one moral 'voice', but not her claim that the 'caring' voice is more apparent amongst women. It therefore supports the argument for a diversity of 'lay social theories' of morality.

The importance of Gilligan's findings of different moral and self orientations lie as much in what they reveal about the pluralistic moral orders in Western culture as in how such moral orders map onto gender. I would argue that gender operates as a 'subculture' and facilitates the growing individual's expertise within one system rather than another.

Gilligan and her associates utilize both self and ethical elements in differentiating the two orientations. Our studies at the University of Bath have partially replicated Gilligan's work and extended it somewhat. We did not use Gilligan's coding system but began with our own data and the differences that we found emerging within our own sample (Wingfield and Haste, 1987; Haste and Baddeley, 1991; Haste, 1992). We found interviewees adopting a distinctive 'separate' or 'connected' orientation in areas similar to those noted by Gilligan: friendship, responsibility, promise keeping. They reflect different lay social theories about selfhood, and its interrelation with morality.

We asked our respondents about promise keeping: 'Why is it important to keep a promise?' We coded as 'separate' orientation, seeing promises as contracts between autonomous persons, implying that a contract requires the participants to be trustworthy persons. Trustworthiness is an attribute of the person; people adopting a 'separate' orientation talk of 'being that kind of person'. They emphasize the quality of the *promiser* rather than the *function of the relationship*.

> 'If you say you're going to do something and you don't do it, then it's not going to make people want to trust you, or believe you, or rely on you at all.'

In contrast to seeing trustworthiness as an attribute of the person we defined a 'connected' orientation as a focus on maintaining relationships as the primary goal of conflict resolution. For these respondents, breaking a trust involves letting others down and causing hurt, or betraying a relationship by no longer showing trust. Trust is the defining characteristic of friendship, an attribute of a relationship between persons:

> 'I think [trust] is something that shouldn't be lost. Because there's not really that much that you can give someone, that doesn't cost anything, that doesn't require anything in return, so I think it needs to be there, just to have.'

In other words, the two orientations reflect different aspects of Western cultural norms about the self and about promising, and are embedded in different lay social theories of relationships. These alternative conceptualization of morality and self can be illustrated by comparing the comments made by Adrian and Karen. Adrian was 17 years old. His view of people and of himself, emphasized 'character', discipline and order. This came out in many of his answers. Adrian consistently produced 'separate' responses. Karen, on the other hand, was 15. She adopted a 'connected' orientation and continually invoked the schema of 'hurting'. A key element of Karen's connected orientation is the idea of *listening*, it recurs often in her language. Where Adrian was inclined to invoke rules, Karen invoked perspective-taking and listening. (These cases are considered in greater detail in Haste, 1992.)

One area that differentiated the two orientations especially well was loyalty. We posed a dilemma about two best friends. While one of them was on vacation, the protagonist (the friend who stayed behind) was invited by the other's boyfriend or girlfriend to go to a disco. Should they go? Should they kiss?

Adrian's response was typical of the 'separate' orientation, reflecting a lay social theory about friendship as rights and delegations about 'territory' and 'codes' of loyalty:

'Well at least if he goes, there's always a chance that he can keep an eye on her, and if he's a really good friend, he can refuse her advances. But if she goes on her own there's no telling who she's going to pick up.'

In contrast, respondents having the connected orientation placed themselves in the roles of various members of the triangle, and they used the language of hurting or causing unhappiness. Karen said:

'If Mandy knew, it would be all right, but not if she didn't know. Then I wouldn't do it because she's my best friend, and that's hurting her.'

Our findings are consistent with the distinctions that Gilligan found between the different orientations in responses concerning self and morality, but our data shows that an individual's self–other orientation extends outside those fields of the moral domain defined by interpersonal relations and the management of conflicting personal interests. We found that these lay social theories of 'separation' and 'connection' also emerged in discussion of social order and social systems. This is the 'public' dimension of the infrastructure of moral reasoning. A key element of Kohlberg's theory of moral development is the extent to which individuals are able to take multiple perspectives. As people progress through the stages of moral reasoning, they are able to conceptualize an increasingly 'societal' perspective. This indicates parallels between lay social theories that underpin the 'moral' domain, and those which underpin the understanding of social order.

To investigate this, we presented our respondents with a modified version of Adelson and O'Neil's (1966) story concerning a thousand people who are marooned on an inaccessible island and have to develop a society. In the responses we identified different conceptualizations of the Islanders' problems and resolutions which reflected the distinction between 'separate' and 'connected' orientations. Characteristic of 'separateness' according to our coding was the imposition of rules by a body of experts or people with power to deal with conflicts. An ordered world of rules and roles provides clear expectations, boundaries to territory and behaviour limits. Order is achieved through a top-down organization run by experts accountable to the community. The goal is an ordered system within which people have tacit or explicit contracts and sets of rights and roles. When Adrian was presented with the dilemma, he saw the Islanders as needing order and expertise. The main problems he saw were the distribution of resources and the safety of people who might get lost and injured. His solution was structured leadership that drew on experts with the right background:

'Better off organized together, with one or a group of leaders, people with leadership qualities, skills, knowledge . . . say there'd been a captain, somebody who had authority beforehand.'

In contrast, a 'connected' perspective on the Islanders' problem focused on the development of social mechanisms to facilitate cooperation and resolution of conflicts through negotiation – a bottom-up model of community government. Karen illustrated this by stressing community, communication between the islanders, and the human side of organization. Karen's underlying schema was that society requires the qualities, writ large, that work in individual interaction, such qualities as empathy, concern for others, and the social skills needed to maintain harmony. A community arises out of cooperation and collaboration. There is an implied interdependence and awareness of the needs of others. What needs to be established are mechanisms of contact, cooperation and communication (Haste and Baddeley 1991; Haste, 1992).

These examples happen to come from a boy and a girl, but even though we did find a sex-linked pattern in our small study, we also found some girls who used a separate orientation and some boys (though fewer) who used a connected orientation.

The importance of these examples, all of which come from advanced Western cultures, is that they show remarkably different ways of dealing with issues of real-life and hypothetical situations. Karen and Adrian are talking in very different ways across a wide range of issues. Yet each of them is quite embedded in British culture; and each of their perspectives is entirely comprehensible to other members of the culture. They are drawing on different schemata, and applying different lay social theories with some quite profoundly different assumptions about what works and what motivates people. My analysis of what is going on is that each has found different model congenial, not that each has invented or constructed a model in isolation. Further evidence from these interviews shows that peer groups engage in a considerable amount of discourse in everyday life. What these adolescents are reporting about as their own perspectives and schemata is a common orientation for their group. Elsewhere (Haste, 1991) I explore the relationship between different lay social theories and political understanding. My findings suggest that parents' political beliefs contributed to the available schemas used by adolescents, but it is also clear that the adolescents incorporated these schemas as their *own* lay social theory. Moral development in other words, is a continual dialectic.

Conclusion

In this chapter I have attempted the task of considering the implications of intra- and intercultural differences in conceptions of the self, and the evidence for how this is related to the lay social and moral theories that individuals use in ordinary life. I provided a model derived from the dialectical perspectives of Vygotsky, locating the process of 'making sense' within a social and sociohistorical context while retaining the principle that 'structural' development is manifested in the development of individual thought. I have argued that taking a pluralistic perspective allows us to integrate social and individual processes, rather than, as is often the case in current debate, seeing these as theoretically incompatible. I think that what is now needed is considerable research on interpersonal interaction and discourse and on the relationship between the schemas that young people use in their lay social theories and what is available to them through media and peer culture, including the subculture of gender. Some of this work is already being done.

Cultural evidence, and the principles of the new field of cultural psychology, lead us to ask how individuals reared with different conceptions of the self generate moral systems. The answer we can gain from a more detailed comparison of the 'separate' and 'connected' orientations in Western samples is that different things are seen as salient in the situation, different issues as problematic, according to the individual's basic orientation toward relations with others. The concept of lay social theory, I have here argued, gives us a framework for seeing how the individual applies schemas, scripts and scenarios, to make sense of situations that are defined by the culture, and experienced by the self, as problematic .

But a final question remains: is there a resolution of the divide between cognitive-developmental approaches (which take as given the individual's construction and reconstruction of the self and morality as manifested in stages of increasing cognitive complexity) and social-psychological approaches (which argue that once we accept social interaction as the crucible of understanding and concepts, there is no place for the concept of stages)? I contend that a Vygotskian perspective enables us to see individuals as acting on their experience to reconstruct the self and morality, within a social context that both limits and facilitates development. But to see people in this way, cognitive developmentalists have to become pluralists, rather than universalists.

References

Adelson, J. and O'Neil, R. (1966) The growth of political ideas in adolescence. *Journal of Personality and Social Psychology*, 4: 295–306.

Bruner, J.S. and Haste, H., eds (1987) *Making Sense: The Child's Construction of the World*. London: Methuen.

Cole, M. (1995) *Cultural Psychology*, Cambridge, MA.: Harvard University Press.

D'Andrade, R. (1987) A folk model of the mind. In D.F. Holand and N. Quinn (eds) *Cultural Models in language and thought*. Cambridge: Cambridge University Press.

Dunn, J. (1987) Understanding feelings, the early stages. In J.S. Bruner and H. Haste (eds), *Making Sense: The Child's Construction of the World*. London: Methuen.

Farr, R. and Moscovici, S. (1984) *Social Representations*. Cambridge: Cambridge University Press.

Geertz, C. (1975) On the nature of anthropological understanding. *American Scientist*, 63: 47–53.

Gilligan, C. (1982, 1993) *In a Different Voice*. Cambridge, MA: Harvard University Press.

Gilligan, C. (1986) Remapping the moral domain: New images of self in relationship. In T.C. Heller, M. Sosna, and D.E. Wellberry (eds) *Reconstructing Individualism*. Stanford, CA: Stanford University Press.

Gilligan, C., Ward, J.V. and Taylor, J.M. eds (1988). *Mapping the Moral Domain*. Cambridge, MA: Harvard University Press.

Goncü, A. (1998) Development of intersubjectivity in social pretend play. In M. Woodhead, D. Faulkner and K. Littleton (eds) *Cultural Worlds of Early Childhood*. London: Routledge.

Harré R. and Gillett, G. (1994) *The Discursive Mind*. London: Sage.

Haste, H. (1987a) Growing into rules. In J.S. Bruner and H. Haste (eds), *Making Sense: The Child's Construction of the World*. London: Methuen.

Haste, H. (1987b) Why thinking about feeling is not the same as feeling about feeling, and why post-androgyny is dialectical, not regressive: A response to Philibert and Sayers. *New Ideas in Psychology*, 5: 215–21.

Haste, H. (1990) Moral responsiblity and moral commitment: The integration of affect and cognition. In T.E. Wren (ed.), *The Moral Domain: Essays in the Ongoing Discussion between Philosophy and the Social Sciences*. Cambridge, MA: MIT Press.

Haste, H. (1991) The dissolution of the right in the wake of theory. In G. Breakwell (ed.), *Social Psychology of Political and Economic Cognition*. London: Academic Press.

Haste, H. (1992) Lay social theory. In H. Haste and J. Torney-Purta (eds), *The Development of Political Understanding: A New Perspective*. San Francisco: Jossey-Bass.

Haste, H. (1993) *The Sexual Metaphor*. London: Wheatsheaf Books.

Haste, H., and Baddeley, J. (1991) Moral theory and culture: The case of gender. In W. Kurtines and J. Gewitz, *Handbook of Moral Development and Behaviour*, Vol. 1. Hillsdale, NJ: Erlbaum.

Iwasa, N. (1992) Postconventional reasoning and moral education in Japan. *J. Moral Education*, 21 (1): 3–16.

Killen, M. and Nucci, L. (1995) Morality, autonomy and social conflict. In M. Killen and D. Hart (eds) *Morality in Everyday Life*. New York: Cambridge University Press.

Kohlberg, L. (1984) *The Psychology of Moral Development*. San Francisco: Harper and Row.

Lave, J. (1990) The culture of acquisition and the practice of understanding. In J. W. Stigler, R. Shweder and G. Herdt (eds) *Cultural Psychology: Essays on comparative human development*. Cambridge: Cambridge University Press.

Miller, J.L. and Bersoff, D.F. (1995) Development in the context of everyday family relationships: Culture, interpersonal morality and adaptation. In M. Killen and D. Hart (eds) *Morality in Everyday Life*. New York: Cambridge University Press.

Much, N. and Shweder, R. (1978) Speaking of rules: The analysis of culture in breach. In W. Damon (ed.) *Moral Development*. San Francisco: Jossey-Bass.

Nunner-Winkler, G. (1984) Two moralities? A critical discussion of an ethic of care and responsibility versus an ethic of rights and justice. In W.M. Kurtines and J. Gewirtz (eds) *Morality, Moral Behaviour and Moral Development*. New York: Wiley.

Piaget, J. (1932) *The Moral Judgement of the Child*. London: Routledge and Kegan Paul.

Potter, J. and Wetherell, M. (1987) *Discourse and Social Psychology*. London: Sage.

Pratt, M.W., Golding, G. and Hunter, W.J. (1984) Does morality have a gender? Sex, sex-role and moral judgement relationships across the adult lifespan. *Merrill-Palmer Quarterly*, 30(4): 321–40.

Rosaldo, M. (1984) Towards an anthropology of self and feeling. In R. Shweder and R. LeVine (eds) *Culture Theory: Essays on Mind, Self, and Emotion.* Cambridge: Cambridge University Press.

Schank, R. and Abelson, R. (1977) *Scripts, Plans, Goals and Understanding.* Hillsdale, NJ: Lawrence Erlbaum.

Shweder, R. (1982) Beyond self-constructed knowledge: The study of culture and morality. *Merrill-Palmer Quarterly.* 28: 41–69.

Shweder, R. (1990) Cultural psychology, what is it? In J.W. Stigler, R. Shweder, and G. Herdt (eds) *Cultural Psychology: Essays on Comparative Human Development.* Cambridge: Cambridge University Press.

Shweder, R. and Bourne, E. (1984) Does the concept of the person vary cross-culturally? In R. Shweder and R. LeVine (eds) *Cultural Theory: Essays on Mind, Self and Emotion.* Cambridge: Cambridge University Press.

Shweder, R., Mahapatra, M. and Miller, J.G. (1987) Culture and moral development. In J. Kagan and S. Lamb (eds) *The Emergence of Morality in Young Children.* Chicago: Chicago University Press.

Shweder, R. and Much, N. (1987) Determinants of meaning. Discourse and moral socialization. In W. Kurtines and J. Gerwitz (eds) *Moral Development through Social Interaction.* New York: Wiley.

Stigler, J.W., Shweder, R. and Herdt, G., eds (1990) *Cultural Psychology: Essays on Comparitive Human Development.* Cambridge: Cambridge University Press.

Stone, C.A. (1998) What's wrong with the metaphor or scaffolding? In D. Faulkner, K. Littleton and M. Woodhead (eds) *Learning Relationships in the Classroom.* London: Routledge.

Tappan, M.B. and Packer, M.J. (1991) *Narrative and Storytelling: Implications for Understanding Moral Development* New Directions for Child Development, Editor-in-Chief, W. Damon, No. 54. San Francisco: Jossey-Bass.

Vygotsky, L. (1978) *Mind and Society.* Cambridge, MA: Harvard University Press.

Wertsch, J. (1985a) *Vygotsky and the Social Formation of Mind.* Cambridge, MA: Harvard University Press.

Wertsch, J. (1985b) *Culture, Communication, and Cognition.* Cambridge: Cambridge University Press.

Wingfield, L. and Haste, H. (1987) Connectedness and separateness: Cognitive style or moral orientation? *Journal for Moral Education*, 16: 214–25.

Part IV

Negotiating competence

Chapter 11

Children in action at home and school*

Berry Mayall

Introduction

This chapter is concerned with children's experiences of their daily lives as they are lived in two social settings, the home and the school. The argument of the chapter is that whilst children undoubtedly view themselves and may be viewed as actors in both settings, their ability to negotiate an acceptable daily experience is heavily dependent on the adults' understandings of childhood and of appropriate activities by and for children in the two settings. Broadly, parents and teachers present different sets of understandings of childhood and of programmes of activities for children. The lived experience for children is that life at home is more negotiable than life at school. What children learn and the value they put on their knowledge and that of adults is interrelated with the character of children's interactions with the adults.

The long and continuing tradition whereby adult behaviours towards children are conditioned by the understanding that they are best regarded as beings in process rather than as members of the category people has been linked into adult considerations of how best to educate children. Durkheim drew on psychological theory to enunciate a theoretical formulation which still carries currency today. Influenced by Rousseau's writings in *Emile*, he was clear that childhood, a period of growth, was characterized by both weakness and mobility; childhood is unstable:

> In everything the child is characterized by the very instability of his nature which is the law of growth. The educationalist is presented not with a person fully formed – not a complete work or a finished product – but with a becoming, an incipient being, a person in the process of formation. Everything in child psychology and in educational theory derives from the essential characteristic of this age, which is sometimes

* This is an edited version of a chapter that appeared in *Children's Childhoods Observed and Experienced*, Lewes: Falmer Press, 1994.

manifest in the negative form – as the weakness and imperfection of the young person – and at other times in the positive form as strength and need for movement.

(Durkheim and Buisson, 1911, in Pickering, 1979)

Durkheim ties these psychological insights together with a sociological defin-ition of the functions and goals of education.

Education is the influence exercised by adult generations on those that are not yet ready for social life. Its object is to arouse and develop in the child a certain number of physical, intellectual and moral stages, which are demanded of him by both political society as a whole and the social milieu for which he is specifically destined.

(Durkheim, 'Education and society', 1922, in Giddens, 1972)

This complex of knowledge – psychological and sociological – presented the teacher, and continues to do so, with a clear underpinning for the exercise of authority. In this chapter, I want to suggest how school and teachers are experienced by children in the light of, as it seems to me, the continued force of the analysis developed in the first quarter of this century.

The home, the other main social setting where children spend their days, is conditioned by somewhat different understandings of childhood, of the proper activities of children and of how adults should behave towards and with children. It should be noted, though, that there has been little work on these topics, as regards parental knowledge about and behaviours towards school-age children. The Newsons' data (collected in the late 1960s on 4-year-olds and in the early 1970s on 7-year-olds) are unique here, but are inevitably conditioned by their particular interests – in mothers' views on discipline and training. Indeed these interests, together with the data they consequently collected, allowed them to state that 'The whole process of socialization – the integration of the child into the social world – is the cornerstone of the parental role.' The parents' task in the early years was 'to mediate cultural expectations and beliefs and to ease him out of the total egocentricity of babyhood into modes of behaviour which will be acceptable in a wider world' (Newson and Newson, 1978, p. 441). This vision would probably be judged by many parents as offering only a partial account of how they define what they do and should do. Some more recent work has sug-gested that whilst parents, or to be precise mothers, accept socialization tasks, both on the common-sense understanding that they are integral to parenting, and because the Psy experts (Donzelot, 1980) tell them to do these tasks, they also, and centrally, operate on experiential knowledge acquired by living with their children. This experience teaches them a complementary set of under-standings. Thus mothers indicate that from the earliest days they regard their baby as a person with individual character and wishes. They recognize their child's right and wish to make her own way, to establish her own space and to construct a social life within the family and beyond (Halldén, 1991). It is also obvious to parents who spend their days with small children that they wish to participate in the social and household activities they observe taking place. As Liedloff (1986) describes (though for a society less hedged about with dangers and complexities than ours) parents recognize these wishes and enable children to take part in cooking, cleaning, self-care, social occasions. Her analysis is intended to draw attention to Western parental deficiencies as regards respect for children as social beings; but it seems to me to draw attention to an essential understanding that parents develop in daily life with their children. The understanding that this individual child has rights and wishes, abilities that will be used and built on, and an innately social nature – underlie these parental understandings, based on experience (Mayall and Foster, 1989; Mayall, 1990).

This brief sketch of teacher and parent understandings of children and of appropriate adult behaviours draws attention to the differing social frameworks within which children, according to their own accounts, attempt to live out a reasonably acceptable daily life. Whilst we may be becoming accustomed to recognizing in theory as well as in practice that children can appropriately be viewed as actors, it is also important to recognize the varying limitations on their actions imposed in different social settings.

Are children different?

As the above paragraphs suggest, this chapter uses as a starting point consideration of the interplay of agency and structure, in order to consider where children stand as actors, negotiators and acted-upon. Thus this chapter is concerned with the activities of children in relation to and in interaction with adults and the ways in which and the extent to which they act to modify the social settings where they live their daily lives. As commentators note, it is critical to take account in these transactions of power relationships (for example, Giddens, 1979; Craib, 1993). These relationships can be characterized through the proposition that adults have organizational control over children's activities (Oldman, 1994). In this chapter, I wish to pursue the point that whilst children may be regarded as part of the group people (rather than outside the category people, or subsumed as part of the family or as parental offspring) the critical and distinctive characteristics of the sub-group children's interactions with both other people and with daily settings depend not so much on their absolute powerlessness *vis-à-vis* adults, but on the precise nature of the power-relationship between the children and the adults in any given setting. Thus I want to suggest that the level of their powerlessness varies according to how the adults in specific social settings conceptualize children and childhood. Childhood, it is argued here, is not experienced as one consistent set of relationships; rather its character in time and place is modified by adult understandings in those times and places of what children are, and what adult relationships with children are proper.

In particular, I wish to indicate some characteristics of two settings, the home and the school, in order to highlight how and why children's social positioning with regard to adults differs in the two settings. In carrying out this analysis, I aim to show how an adult outsider's/theoretician's view of children's social positioning can be counter-balanced with that of children themselves, to indicate their own understanding of how their position differs at school as compared to home.

In contemplating people in a social context, one may examine how agency and structure co-exist, interact, engage with each other to perpetuate, deconstruct and re-construct institutional and individual behaviours and norms. It is critical to bear in mind that people's impact on other people and on social conventions or requirements will vary across settings; and that this point is dramatically important as regards children's success in affecting their social environments. Thus the proposition exemplified below that children have ability to influence and modify their social environments itself requires modification: by taking account of the impact of adult constructions of childhood and adult assumptions of authority in any given setting.

> The unfolding of childhood is not time elapsing just for the child: it is time elapsing for its parental figures, and for all other members of society: the socialisation involved is not simply that of the child, but of the parents and others with whom the child is in contact, and whose conduct is influenced by the child just as the latter's is by theirs in the continuity of interaction.
>
> (Giddens, 1979, chapter 3, p. 139)

Giddens' summary suggests that children's experience of and interaction with adults is unitary, of a piece. Yet I think it is not only children themselves but the onlooker who is struck by the relatively high ability children have to influence adults and social conventions at home, compared to their relatively low ability to do so at school. The rigid social norms and goals of the school represent, as Craib (1993) puts it, 'congealed action', and are relatively impervious to individual challenge, in particular to children's challenges.

Study of people in their interactions within social settings raises issues about identification and identity. Thus each person will feel more or less a part of any given social arena, and may have different degrees of identification in relation to different arenas. These points are commonly recognized in considering, for instance, the case of children who spend time in hospital, but they are less seriously considered or recognized as regards their days in school. Though adjustment to school entry is a topic for study, thereafter the character of children's identification with school and of their identity as schoolchildren has been relatively neglected. Still less is known about children's identification with home. What does school mean to children, and do they belong to school? Children's own accounts suggest that not only as individuals, but also as a social group, their sense of belonging has widely different intensity and complexity in relation to the home, as compared to their relation with the school. The interactive dynamics of individuals within social settings will also play an important part in constructing specific identities for people and in shaping what they may and may not do. In their first five years children may be observed to acquire an identity at home, which continues to be developed in succeeding years. But on entering the social world of the school, children have to acquire, work on and develop another identity – that of schoolchild (cf James, 1993). Since the interplay of the child at school with the adults and with the social norms of the school will have a different character from these interplays at home, and since the adults construct the child differently in the two settings, a child may well construct a separate identity for herself as schoolchild. I am suggesting, therefore, that whilst issues of identification and identity concern people in general, including children, children differ from other people in their experience, for adult constructions of them available and brought into play vary radically as between adult social groups; mothers at home and teachers at school provide strikingly different accounts of children and childhood.

These ideas about the variability of people's sense of who they are may be well recognized by adults in thinking about their own lives and those of others. We feel different at home and at the workplace. But these ideas have had less currency and salience as regards children. Indeed they fly in the face of the essential propositions of developmentalism. The supremacy of developmentalists' ideas of children and childhood has allowed us to bask in the comfortable view that children are the same children wherever they are. Their emotional, relational and cognitive competences and incompetences, relate to their age and their stage. In this vision, children can be observed and described as having attained a certain level of development and competence whatever the social context, rather than perceived as people whose competence, confidence, knowledge and interactions vary according to the social context. The goal of much developmental psychology, to find universal truths about 'the child', blinds us to the personhood of children, viewed both as individuals and as groups, and their exposure to the same social forces as anyone else.

Thus far, then, the argument goes, children are similar to adults, in that they similarly are agents in interactive encounters. It is argued, though, that their identity varies widely in response to adults' constructions of them. Where they also differ from adults, crucially, is as regards intergenerational issues. The crucial distinction that makes children children is that they are not adults; as individuals and as a social group, they lack adulthood. This lack can be defined variously as deficiency, disadvantage, and/or oppression. The components may vary according to individual and societal standpoint. What is common to the intergenerational relationships of children to adults, is that children are inferior to adults. This inferiority is demonstrated in many ways: children are not allowed to make decisions affecting them; must defer to adult knowledge and authority; and they have little economic power (Oldman, 1994). More generally, one may say that, in any given society, the relationships between the generations are governed by generational contracts (Alanen and Bardy, 1991), which set out adults' understandings of the division of labour in that society, and the permitted and required activities of children. The inferiority of children is demonstrated, if we need further demonstration, by the fact that they have little negotiating power as regards the intergenerational contract. They must work within it.

However, I am arguing here that within this intergenerational contract, children's identities, knowledge, permitted behaviours, their negotiating power and their interactions vary according to social context. A wide range of factors play into the character of adult–child relations and interactions and serve to determine decisions, and children's independence and choice. These factors and how they are brought into action, weighed and modified will be discussed below. They include: adult understandings of what children can, may and should do; children's confidence in relationships and in their rights to choose and determine their daily lives; and the social norms of the setting. The essential argument proposed here is that the home and the school present children with widely differing social environments as regards the workings of the intergenerational contract and the workings out of tensions between the child as actor, or agent, and the impact of the social structure itself.

Children at home and school: an empirical research study

This chapter draws briefly on some data I collected in a study at an inner-city primary school, which had a reception class for 5- and 6-year-olds and age-grouped years above that. The school was popular with local parents and the teachers themselves rated it highly. I spent two terms in 1991 in the school, two days a week, mainly as a helper in the reception class (5- to 6-year-olds), and in class 5 (9- to 10-year-olds). I collected data as field-notes from observation, through informal and more focused conversations with children (in twos and threes), through whole class discussions and, with the older children, through some writing. I kept running notes on conversations with teachers, and interviewed them more formally. I also talked with and interviewed the headteacher, the secretary, the four helpers/supervisors and some mothers of the reception class and older children.

The study had a specific focus: on the health care of the children, including their own participation in health care, at home and at school, and how they learned about health-related behaviours. However, these topics were approached, not so much through direct questioning or discussion, as through the elicitation of accounts of daily life, from both children and adults. Mothers' accounts of daily life with children, and, as it turned out, children's own accounts, tend to raise issues of the division of labour in care (childcare and health care), including children's part in decision-making. These are framed by discussion about or assumption about some key concepts: independence, consent, negotiation, authority, social norms, social habits. The data collected are therefore useful for considering how children make their way as agents in relation to adults: how far they interact and negotiate, how far the social norms of the setting are fixed or mutable in response to child and adult action and how far the actors – child and adult – work within and in tension with intergenerational relations and contracts.

It should be noted that presented here is an outline of some complex data, which are considered in more detail elsewhere (Mayall, 1993; Mayall, 1994). The aim here is to highlight the main points for discussion.

Children at home

Both the home and the school are commonly regarded as sites of socialization, and the evidence is overwhelming that mothers at home and teachers at school recognize and accept their socialization tasks. However, whilst health, education and welfare professionals and policy-makers unite in giving primacy to the home in the first five years, the ascribed division of labour is much less clear once children start school. Certainly mothers in my study regarded their work as continuing in respect of their 5- and 9-year-olds; and the teachers regarded socialization as a central task through the years of primary schooling. The characteristics of the implementation of socialization in the two settings are very different.

At home socialization takes place in a social context governed by personal relationships within which negotiation is a legitimate and normal activity, which structures knowledge, activity and experience. For the youngest children, these relationships will be the most important in their social worlds. My data suggest that they are for the top juniors too.

Further to these essential points, a range of factors complicates and modifies the socialization agenda. Children teach their mothers to characterize them as people. Both mothers and children value children's independence. Children at 5 assert their confidence as members of the family; and their competence and knowledge in day-to-day health maintenance, within their mothers' protection and provision. Mothers value children's independent activity both as evidence that they are becoming capable, and to relieve the burden on themselves. For mothers have other agendas: paid work, unpaid household and family work, personal relationships and social lives. As has also been noted, mothers value the home as the place where their children can be themselves, can behave in ways that public social worlds may not approve of (Halldén, 1991). There is therefore emerging from both children's and mothers' accounts a definition of 5-year-old children as health-care actors in their own right. In sum, although some of mothers' goals and behaviours may be subsumed under the broad heading socialization, the character of mother–child interactions may perhaps more accurately be defined as mutual social learning and teaching.

Thus, both children and their mothers promote the view that children play an important part as agents in structuring and restructuring the home as a social institution. Children do not just belong to the family; they, to an extent, together with other family members, continuously create the family. They construct and refine relationships and social customs, and negotiate the division of labour within the home, settling conditionally for duties and freedoms, and re-negotiating these over time.

Yet children perceive that the norms of their home and their daily life at home are structured by adult authority, though families will vary according to how far parental directiveness is the driving force and how far children operate on a long lead (du Bois-Reymond et al., 1993). Adult control as a structuring force is something not commonly stressed in mothers' accounts of their daily lives with children. Whilst mothers stress personal relationships, how to enable children to develop well and how to manage children in their best interests (for mothers are continuously under instruction from health staff), children themselves give greater prominence to power issues. At both 5 and 9, children in the Children at Home and School Study, when talking about family life, noted their subordinate position and adult control over their activities, though there was more emphasis at 9 than at 5 that they found it more restrictive and irksome.

For the 5-year-olds, that parents demanded certain behaviours was both recognized and accepted, and the protectiveness and provider-function of mothers was a modifying, softening and enabling factor. Nevertheless, at 5, children understood there were unresolved issues at stake. For instance, if your room is your room, why should you bow to parental demands that it meet their standards of tidiness? For the 9-year-olds, parental authority was more of a constraint, in the face of their growing competence and the development of their own individual patterns of daily life both within and beyond the home. However, the affective relationship provided a context which both made parental authority essentially acceptable and provided the context for negotiation. Furthermore, parental authority did not reach into every corner of their lives; but impinged in respect of some norms, tasks and activities. And, a further positive point; it was evident that children felt they did contribute to the maintenance of the home as an ongoing social environment and experienced their contributions as satisfying.

Both sets of children in my study noted the consensus prevailing between adults and children at home: that children's duties, responsibilities and actions as regards health maintenance were a proper topic for negotiation between adults and children. This was the case as regards both self-maintenance and home maintenance. I am referring to such matters within self-care as dressing appropriately, washing, dental care, consuming a socially approved diet; as well as to the activities that determine the home's character as a healthy place to live: shopping, preparing food, setting tables, clearing up, washing up, social relationships. What children should do and what should be done to them was a matter for interactive negotiation, within the understanding that children were people rather than projects.

In sum, therefore, I am suggesting that children's evidence on the home is that intergenerational authority was mediated by recognition of their status as people with the ability and right to take responsibility for health-related decision-making. The adult goal of socialization was crossed with the adult and child goals of encouraging independence, and of making space for individuals in the home to pursue their own agendas. Consent to do and to be done to was negotiable, and was indeed negotiated within a framework of critical personal relationships.

Children at school

The social institution of the primary school presents children with a different weighting to various agendas. For a start, the school differs from the home in its character as an institution with accepted social goals and norms formalized within and implemented through the regime; or as has been neatly put: standardized modes of behaviour (Radcliffe-Brown, quoted in Giddens, 1979, p. 96). The goals of delivering a curriculum and of socializing the children are realized in, notably, the grouping of children, the organizing of the children's day, and in the monitoring of performance and behaviour. As one observer puts it; activities are bureaucratized (Hartley, 1987). The school as a social institution is a setting where (obviously but) crucially, adult authority is more salient and less challengeable than at home.

Many schoolteachers (including those studied) think of their schools as child-centred, as model environments, as havens of ideals and good practices in an imperfect world. The school's goals, delivery of the curriculum, social norms and practices are founded on knowledge of the 'facts' of child development. This set of understandings amongst schoolteachers is critical as far as children are concerned, because they find they are not taken seriously. If children challenge school norms, teachers find it irrelevant to attend to the points underlying the challenge. Since the school is a model environment, the fault must lie with the children – or their homes – if they dislike it.

Furthermore, it is intrinsic to the developmental view that the socialization of children is an ongoing task throughout childhood, until they reach the goal of mature adulthood. With each year-group, therefore, the teacher's task is to socialize the children, since (according to the teachers I interviewed) she faces poorly socialized children at the start of the school year and ends it having moved them further along the road. This vision compounds with adult knowledge of the school as ideal environment to ensure that children have no legitimated voice. They never reach maturity or independence at school. The independence that teachers say they aim for in children turns out to be conformity with school norms, both academic and social.

These adult understandings and the rigid structures framing and maintaining them leave children little scope for negotiation. Adult knowledge and moral codes are not regarded by the adults at school as negotiable by children. Furthermore, the social patterning of relationships ensures that children are mostly dealt with as a group, and that individual relationships between child and teacher are not thought appropriate. Thus the interactive, negotiated processes whereby for children at home knowledge grounded in valued individual relationships is developed are not available to children at school.

And whilst parents at home have many agendas, and may value leaving the children to manage aspects of their daily lives themselves, as well as welcoming their wish to spend time developing their own activities, teachers have no other interests during the day than those of socializing and teaching the children within the frameworks of their understandings of the good child.

It is also of considerable interest that the emphasis by schools on the psychological dimensions of childhood runs alongside (and perhaps determines) the low-grade recognition of children's physical health as an appropriate concern for the teachers. The low status of the physical care of the children can be seen in, for instance, the fact that schools are not required to include trained health care workers as staff. It is common for the treatment (of illness and accident) to be delegated to low-paid helpers, dinner ladies or supervisors (rather than, say, to a health professional). Indeed, the data suggest, teachers prefer inculcating moral precepts within a health education framework to recognizing children's wish to negotiate a health-maintaining environment at school. At a more general level, it may be observed that in their discourse and their practice, teachers emphasize the relevance of the psychological over the physical in considering children's well-being and behaviour, and tend to relate school academic performance to psychological rather than to physical factors. The school and the education system downplays the whole child in favour of the psychological child.

Within this complex social setting, children find that the competence and self-reliance they have acquired before they start school is devalued once they get there. The ordinary daily self-care they carry out at home, as regards pacing the day with activity and rest, eating, drinking, going to the toilet, is all subjected at school to the demands of the school day, mediated through the teacher. At the age of 5, according to my informants, learning school norms, and establishing an acceptable social life is both challenging and stressful, as well as fun. Being refused permission to go to the toilet, or get a drink, can be distressing. So can sitting in a noisy hall eating food you have had no part in choosing.

By the age of 9, the children indicated that they have learned how to manage self-care within school limits. Whilst they recognize the value of school-based education as a good, they also understand the implications of compulsory all-day schooling as regards health maintenance: some are acutely aware of the health-damaging aspects of school routines, boredom and tedium, noise, stressful social relations with adults and children, from which and from whom they cannot escape.

Children provide a useful corrective commentary on the adult commentator's view that as schoolchildren they act as agents, both since they work themselves, and turn themselves into employable citizens, and since they provide work for others – that is, teachers. Undoubtedly, children's accounts indicate their recognition that they regard themselves as engaged, essentially, in a useful and productive enterprise. But they also indicate their understanding that they are the objects of the school enterprise, persons to whom actions are done; and, further, that they are powerless to reconstruct the school as a social institution to meet their own ideas about what would constitute a child-friendly educational setting. For them, the school is indeed an impervious, congealed construction of social norms.

In sum, from the children's point of view, the intergenerational relationships of the school are founded on adult direction, within laid-down social norms. Compared to life at home, life at school offers little scope for negotiation with the adults in authority, though children do learn to work the system or to skive off; or for independent activity. Children find themselves treated as group members rather than as individuals, and as objects of socialization rather than as participating people.

From the children's point of view, the principal site of health care activity is at home, and during their daily life at school, they are conducting a holding operation, health-wise. Their psychological health (as defined by teachers) takes precedence over their physical. Or to put it another way, the school is less holistic than the home in its understandings of children and its dealings with children.

Discussion

It may be useful, though inevitably it is a crude representation, to summarize schematically the main points made above about children's experience at home and school.

Contextual factors influencing learning and behaviour

Home	School
socialization as negotiation	socialization as prescription
adult authority in context of relationships	adult authority in context of institutional norms
adult construction of child as actor	adult construction of child as project
child construction of self as subject	child construction of self as object

The above schema summarizes the main points made earlier about children's positioning at home and school, and their opportunities for participating in decision-making, in learning and activities.

Common observation and research data on children at home and at school, indicate that children's social positioning is very different in the two settings. Crucially, intergenerational relationships differ not only because the social construction of the child differs as between mothers and teachers, but because the social setting of the home presents a different frame from the school.

For at home children are identified not merely as socialization objects but as participants in and negotiators of their social worlds, and thus as important family members. At school, they are essentially projects for adult work. In complement to these differing understandings of agency, the two settings differ as frameworks for daily life. Whilst both may be coherent social systems, as regards relations and interactions between underlying beliefs and overt behaviours, the social system of the home is less formally defined and operated and more open to negotiation; the school's social system is both more fixed and overt as regards the linkages in place between goals and practices, and less open to negotiation.

Indeed, the two settings have different kinds of cohesion. The home is holistic, in that its functions as socialization setting are coherent: the social norms of the home are constructed and implemented by the adults. Yet because the interests of the participants are individual, varied and are played out in both the home and in arenas beyond the home (at work, at school other social settings, the wider family), adult control has to be flexible to take account through interactive processes of these other and varied agendas. School, on the other hand, is coherent in other senses: it is a closed, complete system, where goals and practices cohere, and where the activities of the teachers (during the school day) are limited to a focus on the teaching and training of the children. It is thus less flexible and open to negotiation. Thus it comes about that we can see the home as place of negotiation within relationships and the school as prescriber within social norms.

This chapter is arguing, therefore, that children's experience in social settings compared to that of adults is the same but different. It is critical to recognize the power of adult constructions of the child to shape childrens experience in different settings. Because adult experiential knowledge about children differs so widely from theoretical psychological understandings – at least as commonly and crudely represented to and by adults in the 'caring' professions, children live along with and interact with two contrasting adult constructions of the child: as person and as project. Whilst parental understandings may have been somewhat affected by the Psy-complex: the intervention and supervision of representatives of the welfare stage (Donzelot, 1980): children are constantly active at home to provide experiential correctives to these outsiders' views. At school, however, teachers are shielded by social conventions and shield themselves from direct interaction with individual children; and thereby from the lessons such interaction would provide. In an earlier study, my colleague and I observed a similar insulation: health visitors who had children of their own did not use their experiential knowledge in their paid work, but, like their childless colleagues, relied on book learning about the management of children (Mayall and Foster, 1989).

It seems to me that these contrasting constructions of children are more extreme than any available as regards adults; and they are crucial for children's experience. For in complement to how they are regarded, children's own construction of identity will vary between settings. Though at school they may adopt an alienated response, that is may resist being downgraded from personhood to projecthood, in order to survive they will have to accept some of the conventions of the game. These can include not only conformity, but calculated measures to work the system, and tactical balancing of the advantages of deviance against those of conformity. At home, it seems that adult constructions of children in general match more closely those of the children – broadly, children are regarded and regard themselves as valued people. However, we need to know much more about children's experiences at home. In particular, for instance, research is needed to investigate the importance of siblings; to study whether they in some circumstances act as a form of childhood group defence against power (cf Dunn, 1984). We also need further investigations of friendships and of activities in children's own domains – where they construct social worlds outside, or alongside, adult-controlled settings (for example, Moore, 1986; Ward, 1994).

The argument proposed here has implications for the kinds of work that are necessary to increase understanding of children's social relations. It is necessary to break down discussion of intergenerational relationships to take account of social context and of adult and child constructions within them. And it is necessary to study the processes whereby these factors operate, and whereby social norms are constructed and implemented. Study of process requires detailed investigation of adult–child interactions within social settings. It is perhaps at this point in debate about these complex issues that the long-established conflict between sociology and psychology can be if not resolved then tackled, through using the strengths of both to carry out these investigations. What is required is work which tracks the construction, modification and development of social norms and behaviours in a range of settings over time; critical factors to be taken into account will be children's and adult contributions, the flexibility of the social setting, the impacts of larger social forces (societal expectations of, for example, the family, the school). Very little work (as far as I know) has been done using this approach, on the home – which in any case is notoriously difficult to study in depth and over time. As regards the school, study of process has been mainly to do with the early adjustment of children to primary school.

In this chapter, I have reported only briefly on a detailed study which attempted to explore the complex interactions outlined. This chapter, and the study on which it is based, are limited mainly to consideration of children as a social group in their daily interactions with adults. The study took some account of age and of gender, but has not to any important extent tackled some important dimensions of difference within categories: children (individual difference as well as ethnicity and class); homes (the character of parental authority, socioeconomic and cultural considerations); schools (strength of authority structures, class size). At this stage in studying children and childhood it has seemed to me important to focus primarily on childhood status and experience at general levels, as a basis for taking account of difference (Qvortrup, 1991).

Nevertheless, I hope this chapter has contributed to the task of breaking away from the idea of 'the child', by at least considering children as construed and in interaction in two settings. The chapter has focused on how characteristics of specific social environments (the home and the school) are critical in determining children's experiences and activities. This has involved as a necessary; enterprise taking account of children's perspectives. and indeed putting them at the centre of the analysis.

References

Craib, I. (1993) *Modern Social Theory: From Parsons to Habermas* (2nd edn), London, Harvester Wheatsheaf.

Donzelot, J. (1980) *The Policing of Families: Welfare Versus the State*. London, Heinemann.

Du Bois-Reymond, M., Buchner, P. and Kruger H.-H. (1993) 'Modern family as everyday negotiation: Continuities and discontinuities in parent–child relationships', *Childhood*, 1, pp. 87–99.

Dunn, J. (1984) *Sisters and Brothers*, London, Fontana.

Giddens, A. (1972) (Ed) *Emile Durkheim: Selected Writings*. Cambridge, Cambridge University Press.

Giddens, A. (1979) *Central Problems in Social Theory: Action, Structure and Contradiction in Social Analysis*. London, Macmillan.

Halldén, G. (1991) 'The child as project and the child as being: Parents' ideas as frames of reference', *Childhood and Society*, 5, 4, pp. 334–56.

Halldén, G. (1994) 'Establishing order: Small girls write about family life', *Gender and Education*, 6, 1. pp. 3–17.

Hartley, D. (1987) 'The time of their lives: Bureaucracy and the nursery school', in Pollard, A. (Ed) *Children and their Primary Schools*, London, Falmer Press.

James, A. (1993) *Childhood Identities: Social Relationships and the Self in Children's Experiences*, Edinburgh, Edinburgh University Press.

Liedloff, J. (1986) *The Continuum Concept*. Harmondsworth, Penguin.

Mayall, B. (1990) 'Childcare and childhood', *Children and Society*, 4, 4, pp. 374–86.

Mayall, B. (1993) 'Keeping healthy at home and school: It's my body so it's my job', *Sociology of Health and Illness*, 15, 4, pp. 464–87.

Mayall, B. (1994) *Negotiating Health: Children at Home and Primary School*. London, Cassell.

Mayall, B. and Foster, M.-C. (1989) *Child Health Care: Living with Children, Working for Children*, Oxford, Heinemann.

Moore, R.C. (1986) *Childhood's Domain: Play and Place in Child Development*, London, Croom Helm.

Newson, J. and Newson, E. (1978) *Seven Years Old in the Home Environment*, Harmondsworth, Penguin.

Oldman, D. (1994) 'Childhood as a mode of production, in Mayall, B. (Ed) *Children's Childhoods Observed and Experienced*, London, Falmer.

Pickering, W.S.F. (Ed) (1979) *Durkheim: Essays on Morals and Education*, London. Routledge and Kegan Paul.

Qvortrup, J. (1991) 'Childhood as a social phenomenon – An introduction to a series of national reports', *Eurosocial Report 36*, Vienna. European Centre.

Ward, C. (1994) 'Opportunities for childhoods in late twentieth century Britain' in Mayall, B. (Ed) *Children's Childhoods Observed and Experienced*, Lewes, Falmer.

Chapter 12

Discourses of adolescence

Young people's independence and
autonomy within families*

Julia Brannen

This chapter is concerned with the significance of young people's transitions
from childhood to adulthood within British society. It starts with a brief
overview of public and official discourse concerning the definition of boundaries between adolescence and adulthood. Next, drawing upon a London-based
study of the parenting and health of young people (Brannen, Dodd, Oakley
and Storey, 1994), it considers different social constructions of adolescence
as defined by parents and their 16-year-old children, the impact of these
constructions upon the ways in which parents and children negotiate their
relationships with one another, and the implications of these patterns of
negotiation for young people's independence and autonomy within their
families of origin.

Public policy discourses of adolescence

The essence of being a young person is not in being but in *becoming*. That is,
adult society values young people primarily because they are adults in the
making (Frankenberg, 1993). Public discourses are much occupied, though
not necessarily very consciously or coherently, with defining the boundaries
between childhood and adulthood, the points at which young people
acquire rights and responsibilities which pertain to adult status. However,
the age of majority varies across different areas of social and economic life.
For example, the voting age for UK young people was reduced in 1969
from 21 to 18 years and recent changes in family law give young people a
greater say in matters which affect them (Roll, 1990). The raising of the
school leaving age from 15 to 16 which occurred in 1972–3 is a counter
example. More recently, changes in the UK Social Security legislation have
abolished young people's right to unemployment benefit in the 16–18 age
group and lowered benefit levels for the single unemployed in the 18–25

---

* This is an edited version of a chapter that appeared in *Children in Families: Research and
Policy*, Lewes: Falmer Press, 1996.

age group. The transition implies no ordered progression of increased rights and responsibilities.

The ambiguities surrounding the age of majority is a reflection of the heterogeneity and unevenness of cultural, social and economic change. Not surprisingly, public discourses concerning young people are themselves often contradictory. On the one hand, young people are constructed as having rights and considerable autonomy through their status as consumers. On the other hand, adolescence is being extended and parental responsibility prolonged as high levels of youth unemployment have led to a severe contraction in the numbers of (mainly working class) young people joining the labour market following the end of compulsory schooling. Norms have been restructured which emphasize training and education for young people despite the continuing decline in job opportunities (Jones and Wallace, 1992). Old discourses of parental responsibility have acquired a renewed emphasis with parents expected to continue being responsible for their young people's material well-being and for their development as citizens. This discourse is legitimated on moral rather than practical grounds. Underpinning public discourses is the construction of young people as threatening the moral and social order but in the context of the retraction of the Welfare State. Yet despite the importance policy makers place on parents as agents of socialization and social control, there is virtually no support for them. This neglect of the parents of young people is reflected in the failure of academic research to consider young people as part of households and families (Jones and Wallace, 1992; Allatt and Yeandle, 1992).

Professional and academic discourses

Whilst professional and academic discourses are part of the public discourse, each constructs young people in particular ways. Until recently sociologists have studied youth as a social category within the wider society in contrast to the way that they have studied children namely within the close confines of family. Generational relations within families have been neglected and young people have been studied within the public domain – in schools, peer groups, lifestyles and private markets. The household domain, which is a key arena in which the transition to adulthood takes place, has been ignored. Young people's transitions to adulthood from their own perspectives have been less evident. The theoretical focus has been the issue of the social control of, rather than the extension of rights and responsibilities to, young people in the transition to adulthood. Moreover, the concentration upon youth within the public arena has led, until recently, to the neglect of young women.

By contrast psychologists have focused directly upon young people's transitions to adulthood from the perspective of young people as individuals and within the context of the private sphere of family life. Through the prism of developmentalism, focusing on biologically based change and its consequences for psychological development, the transition is structured as a scheduled passage characterized by emotional turmoil and a process of identity formation (see Coleman, 1990 and Rutter, Tizard and Whitmore, 1976, for a discussion). Adolescence is normatively portrayed in terms of a process of separation from parents and the development of ambivalent feelings towards them. The assumption that young people should strive for independence and that parents should be facilitative of their attempts is not questioned. Like sociology, the psychological model of adolescence has paid little attention to gender.

Health educators regard young people as a prominent target for their messages although teenagers are one of the healthiest groups in the population, judged by any standards. Health education models assume that biological development in adolescence is accompanied by an increase in personal responsibility for health (see Graham, 1979 for a critique). Drawing (implicitly) upon developmental psychology for a model of adolescence, health education conceptualizes young people as free individuals who in their normative passage to independence make autonomous decisions about health and lifestyles quite independently of their families. Insofar as health educators take account of social relations, they focus on the inculcation of life skills and the consequent enhancement of young people's self-esteem, assertiveness and problem solving (Tones, 1983; Collins, 1984; Nutbeam, Hagland, Farley and Tillgren, 1991). The growth of self-esteem is supposed to equip young people to resist peer group pressures and to conform to messages delivered by schools and other health educationists. With the focus on the individual, the family context is ignored.

Academic and professional discourses and, in some cases, public policy discourses premise their ideas on western cultural values concerning the rights of the individual. This perspective, as Gilligan (1982) has pointed out, is also implicitly gendered – that is it is based on a male model of development. Gilligan argues that a female model of development lies in the continuing importance of attachment of young women to their families and more generally of their responsibilities and obligations to others.

The individual rights discourse is culturally as well as gender blind. It takes little or no account of the fact that cultural values concerning the regulation of young people by parents, kin, and communities and their transitions to adulthood may differ from those presumed by academics and professionals. For example, parents born and brought up in non-western societies may have different expectations concerning the rights of elder versus younger household members. Different norms may operate with respect to the significance of the household as a collectivity as distinct from the notion of the individual household member (see also Song, 1996). Thus adolescence may not necessarily be defined in individualist terms as entailing an increase in young people's rights to autonomy and independence.

Parents and young people's constructions of adolescence

In the Adolescent Health and Parenting Study, the aim was to explore the transfer of responsibility from parent to young person, particularly around health issues. The study included a mix of families of different ethnic/cultural origins and social class groups which enabled us to investigate whether adolescence was constructed differently by different groups of parents and young people. While we did find that adolescence was constructed in a variety of ways by parents, we of course found that these different social constructions did not necessarily translate neatly into different patterns in terms of young people's actions. Young people as social actors develop their own agendas, and are subject to, and act upon, a variety of influences deriving from a number of different contexts. However, ethnic origin was still the factor most likely to discriminate between young people in our study with respect to health and risk-taking behaviours (Brennen, Dodd, Oakley and Storey, 1994).

The following discussion highlights the variety of ways in which parents define adolescence and its consequences in terms of the negotiation of relationships between parents and their 16-year-olds. These data are based upon both mothers' and fathers' accounts and those of the young people concerning their relationships. In the first discourse of adolescence, parents construct their obligations and young people's transition to adulthood from an individual rights perspective; young people are ideally freed from parental interference in their move to *achieving* independent adult status. In the second construction, parents' management of, and young people's active participation in, the transition to adulthood is prescribed according to institutional rather than personal rules. The change in young people's status at this point is an *ascribed* rather than an achieved passage.

The conceptional distinction between parents in terms of their expectations of young people's status transitions translates into different approaches to the regulation, or control, of young people which have consequences for young people's independence and autonomy. Parents' strategies of control are conceptualized as follows: (a) 'institutional' modes of control whereby parents enforce prescribed forms of behaviour with respect to young people's status within the household; (b) 'personal' modes of control in which parents assume that young people control their own destinies, that is they create their own passage through adolescence as autonomous household members with minimal overt interference from parents (Bernstein, 1971, 1975). Personal modes of control rely heavily on strategies of covert parental influence especially through communicative means while institutional modes assume direct rule enforcement if norms are infringed. While in practice there is likely to be a mix of different control modes within households, nonetheless distinctive characterizations can be read from parents' and young people's accounts.

These discourses of adolescence are structured by social class, culture and gender. Ideas and expectations concerning ascribed status changes – notably the prescribed age at which working-class young people were (once) supposed to enter the labour market – are class-related and originate from the time when there were plenty of low-status jobs available for 16-year-olds. Expectations of achieved status changes are also class-related and occur mainly in professional middle-class households. Transitions to adulthood are governed by culture as well as class, with some groups placing greater importance upon continuing attachment of young people to their families and kin and other groups emphasizing the importance of individuals' right to separate from them. Discourses are also differentiated according to the sex of the parent and the young person.

As suggested above, the cases in our study can be grouped conceptually according to a typology composed of two dimensions. One dimension relates to dominant constructions of adolescence within families and households: young people's pathways to adulthood as individualistic, individualized and developmental versus collectivist status changes in the context of generational attachment – hierarchical as well as horizontal. These different constructions imply different modes of control by parents of young people and lead to the negotiation of different types of relationship. The study households can be grouped according to these constructions as determined by parents and according to the outcomes as brought to bear by young people themselves. The two dimensions can be considered in relation to one another and, as the following grid suggests, there are four possible patterns (Figure 12.1). In practice the households distribute themselves between three of the cells: (A) those where the transition to adulthood is an achieved status and in which young people have relatively high autonomy; (B) those in which the transition is ascribed and young people acquired high autonomy; (C) those in which the transition is ascribed and the young people have low autonomy but high responsibility. We found no cases in cell D where the transition is achieved with young people having relatively little autonomy.

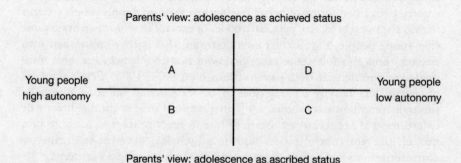

Figure 12.1 A model of parental discourses of adolescence

The transition to adulthood: achieved status and high autonomy

These parents and, to a lesser extent, their young people subscribe to an individual rights model of the transition to adulthood. Young people are ideally expected to free themselves from parental control and interference as they move towards adult status. Expectations shift from the role of the parent as the overt agent of social control to a greater emphasis on *internal* self-control exerted by young people (Bernstein, 1971, 1975). In this group, parents adopt covert control strategies through modes of communication while allowing young people a considerable degree of autonomy. However it is important to note as the cases will suggest in practice mothers are those who engage in communicative strategies with young people.

Concepts of 'child-centredness' and 'person-centredness' apply to some households in this group and, as others have shown (Walkerdine and Lucey, 1989), this approach may also typify early child-rearing practices. The discourse is shaped by professional ideologies but also by popular discourses around the self. Self-development and the successful negotiation of intimate relationships are defined as central goals. Intimate relationships are voluntaristic and commitment is founded on choice. Relationships are constantly renegotiated as couples decide to stay together only as long as they like or love one another and are in receipt of reflexive rewards (Giddens, 1991).

Within this group of households, young people renegotiate, with parental legitimation, their relations with their parents. Thus the young person pushes for independence and the parent creates new conditions which allow this to occur and which at the same time provide a new basis for the relationship. In this process, norms governing relations between parents and young people are renegotiated and rules as such disappear; the goal is for the relationship to develop into an 'adult-like' relationship based on equality, reciprocal liking, trust and understanding. Thus parents endeavour to become friends and confidants to their children: 'It's very open. It's a very trusting relationship . . . It's a friendship.' (Mother talking about her relationship with her daughter.)

In behaving like a friend or confidant, the parent must still exercise some control in order to fulfil the requirement of a 'responsible parent'. This dilemma is solved in terms of the employment of a new kind of communication pattern whereby communication becomes the mechanism of control enabling parents to monitor young people outside face to face relationships. Young people are thus required to inform parents of the activities in which they engage outside the home. This surveillance involves a shift from visible to invisible forms of control (Bernstein, 1975).

Communication also sets up an arena in which bargaining can take place between young people and parents. Thus if young people perceive parental communication as too intrusive, they may develop counter-strategies to fend off parents and to create boundaries around their presumed autonomy. A crucial strategy available to young people is to withhold information about their external activities or to threaten to do so, thereby testing parents and exposing the invisible power upon which the relationship rests.

In this group, parents were concerned not to appear prescriptive and controlling. For parents and 16-year-olds the most contentious issue at this point concerned going out and about or staying in. Thus parents sought information from young people concerning their whereabouts. The grounds whereby parents justified this requirement are various and suggestive of weak rather than strong rule enforcement. For example, in the following example, a UK-born father claims that communication is a matter of 'common politeness' and implies that the 'rule' is applicable to all household members:

> Letting everyone know what the hell is happening which is a rule . . . and having friends in, the rule is 'you tell us'. Again, it's a rule of what-you-call-it – common sense, politeness, manners rather than a rule.

Some parents simply say that they *like* to know, rather than require to know, where their young people are or when they are coming home. This language, too, is suggestive of weak rather than strong rules:

> No hard and fast rules. I just *like* to be told when they are coming in, where they are going and they all know they can ring if they need a lift.
> (Mother)

In this last remark, the mother suggests that the way is also open for the young man to make demands upon his parents for their help and protection – namely the invitation to telephone her for a lift. Knowledge is represented as reciprocal: just as the parent knows the whereabouts of the young person, so too the young person knows about the availability of the parent to help out.

In addition to preference and common politeness, some parents – notably mothers – give a further justification for knowing about their children's whereabouts, namely that knowledge alleviates worry. The extent to which worry emerged as a maternal rather than a paternal issue is remarkable. While we might expect more non-UK-born parents to express worry about their young people because of racism in the society, worry as an 'excuse' articulated more commonly among the UK-born mothers. Thus, a mother said that she worried if her son did not notify her in advance when he stayed out in the evening. Moreover, she presented her tendency to worry as a personal failing rather than a result of real external dangers:

> I always like them to phone up if they're not coming straight home because I have a dinner waiting . . . I would worry if they didn't . . . Worry is one of my downfalls. I do see dangers.

In accordance with her failure to see her own feelings as legitimate, she remarks that it is her son's dinner which is the main reason for his coming home on time.

For mothers worry had markedly less legitimacy than other reasons for trying to restrict young people; worry was seen as a female weakness to which only mothers were 'prone'. The fact that worry is a likely consequence of bearing a life-long responsibility for children from their birth onwards was insufficient justification for exerting control over them. Similarly, no recognition was given to the fact that worry is also a product of the contradiction between norms of parental responsibility and of young people's supposed autonomy.

In controlling young people's comings and goings mothers in this group used the interrogative mode: 'Where are you going? Who are you going with?' rather than the imperative mode – 'You can go out' or 'You can't'. For these parents the *form* of communication was the form of control. The following case concerns a middle-class household in which the mother operates a communicative strategy *vis-à-vis* her oldest daughter, Sandra. The family is comfortably off; it is also white, British and middle class with liberal values. Sandra's father is a middle manager in a public relations company, and her mother is a teacher. Both parents have struggled financially to send Sandra and her siblings to private schools. Sandra is not restricted by her parents and at weekends often frequents clubs in central London returning home in the early hours. She describes her relationship with her mother as both 'close' – in affect terms – and 'open' – meaning that she mostly tells them about her whereabouts. Her mother's portrayal is one of parental licence in response to her daughter's bid for greater freedom:

> We don't clamp down rigidly. We gradually got to that stage without too many major upsets . . . It's letting them do these things they want to . . . I still get worried, but you've got to allow them to do certain things. You just can't say no all the time.

Sandra describes herself as a discloser: 'I can speak to people, the people I'm closest to – friends, my mum, my cousin', while her mother claims, 'She'd certainly talk to me about it. I wouldn't say everything, but she certainly talks to me about most things.'

Both mother and daughter appear to have discussed a number of key issues both in the present and the past. For example, they discussed the start of Sandra's periods, and a number of other matters relating to sex and sex education. Sandra's mother says Sandra talks to her about her boyfriend, though somewhat superficially. According to Sandra, her parents know that she has had sex, though information was relayed through the discovery of her diary. Quite how this happened was not revealed, but Sandra did not make any complaint in the interview about 'prying parents': 'It was through a diary. It was very stupid. It caused quite a lot of tension . . . But they got over it.' Where such a discovery was made by parents who adopt more overt (institutionally based) strategies of control, they would probably have responded much more severely. Certainly young people in those households in which different cultural values operated with respect to young people's independence went to great lengths to keep their 'illicit' activities secret from their parents.

In accordance with the communicative strategy of control adopted by her mother, Sandra is expected to say where she is going, with whom and for how long. As Sandra says, her parents are fairly free and easy about her going out, but, 'My mum likes to know where I am and, er, what time I'll be back . . . They do try to let me be as independent as possible.' In return for being open about her activities, Sandra has a high degree of autonomy. Through the acquisition of information from her daughter, Sandra's mother alleviates her own anxiety about her welfare, and her sense of maternal responsibility is discharged. Thus, though she lacks the power to constrain her daughter, she feels that at least she knows where she is.

These parents drew upon the discourse of 'individual rights', the right of a young person to create his/her own trajectory to adulthood. Thus adulthood constitutes an achievement of the individual young person while parents' role is not to obstruct or contradict the normative notion of the young person's rights. The new status of a young person as an adult is not conferred mechanically in the sense that the young person steps into a new status with clearly defined responsibilities and duties. Rather it is a person-centred passage which the young person is expected to construct for herself and in which she exerts control over herself. These ideas resonate with the sociological concept of individualization which is used to refer to a new social process in which young people as social actors construct their economic and social pathways in terms of jobs and leisure activities.

Transition to adulthood: ascribed status and high autonomy

In these households parents confer autonomy upon young people in response to a scheduled status change which is governed by class norms and the structure of the labour market. The study provides some variability in the extent to which young people stayed on at school or entered the labour market at 16. Until the 1970s entry to the labour market for working-class young people was expected to take place at the end of compulsory schooling; it was not a matter of individual negotiation but was socially scheduled. In contrast to the mainly middle-class, group (a) households, working-class parents in group (b) marked young people's entry into the labour market as a moment in *time* and as an event having practical and symbolic significance by giving them greater individual freedom. In this group parents move from a situation whereby they overtly control young people according to a set of explicit norms which proscribe certain activities and put limits around their freedom to a situation in which when their young people enter the labour market they expect them to become masters and mistresses of their own destinies. These young people assumed adult status as workers; they were not simply treated differently according to age criteria.

Sally Rimmer had recently left school and found a job in an optician's. She was living with her mother, a single parent who had two (low-status) part-time jobs, and her elder sister who was also at work. Both mother and daughter describe having a 'close' relationship, which, they said, was based on 'trust' and 'friendship'. Her mother noted, somewhat hopefully: 'Deep down, she thinks we can sit and talk about anything.' Even before Sally left school, her mother allowed her some freedom but expected to have some say about her daughter's whereabouts. Looking back to this time, she admits to some lack of success in controlling her daughter: 'I think you do worry, but, basically, you've got to put your trust in them to a certain extent. You can only guide them.' Since leaving school, Sally acquired a new boyfriend who was much older than her. However despite being 'close' to her mother, Sally was not forthcoming about her relationship, which annoyed her mother:

> She didn't tell me. He's five years older than her . . . I think she's been out with him a few times before she told me. I was a bit annoyed . . . I said I'd sooner *know* than not know.

Like the mothers who deployed communicative strategies, Sally's mother wanted her daughter to talk to her about her new relationship, but since her daughter's new status as a worker gave her the right to be independent, she found it impossible and unjustifiable to insist on having a say about her daughter's relationships.

Working-class fathers also expected their sons to be significantly more independent at the point when their sons joined the labour market. Unlike the fathers in group (a) who did not describe themselves as ever having been strong disciplinarians, these fathers saw themselves as much less strict when their children left school. A father described a change in his uncompromising attitude to bringing up his son – 'My philosophy is if a kid's done wrong, beat him' – when his son started work. However, these fathers justified this change in attitude in a variety of ways and not always in terms of young people's changed status. Some fathers said they had also vacated the authoritarian role with their youngest children. One of these fathers, whose prowess as a sportsman was failing, said that, at 55, he felt generally 'past it', and that he could no longer compete with his sporty son. Also, he believed that the disciplinarian role he once played with respect to his older children was 'rather out of date'.

Once they've left school, you can only take so much responsibility. Once they are over 18 or they're out earning money, they've got to be responsible for their own actions. They are expected to be semi-adult. When they're kids at school, yes, parents should be responsible. They should expect to know where their kids are.

(Father)

Like other fathers in the study, these UK-born, working-class fathers did not describe themselves as particularly 'close' to their young people who, they said, were closer to their mothers. Few shared interests with their young people. (Sport and going to the pub constituted the main interests shared with sons.) Communication over personal matters was rare whatever the sex of the young person. Insofar as any sons disclosed their feelings (not a manly thing to do), they did so via their mothers who were also the main channels of information between young people and fathers. It is interesting to note that the son who had the best relationship with his father described it in terms of being able to talk and joke, and have an equal relationship. But he also referred to their former hierarchical relationship before he started work and more generally underlined the difficulty men have in displaying affection towards one other:

Yeah, we have [a good relationship]. Like we talk more now. We sort of understand each other. We joke now and that . . . We go bowling [and drinking] and have a good laugh . . . I care for my Dad, as well as Mum, but it's harder for a bloke to say it's – like that . . . It's mainly my Dad's more in charge 'cos he's like . . . He's the man of the house . . . But we're mainly sort of equal now, like since we've all left school.

(Son now at work)

Transition to adulthood: ascribed status and low autonomy but high responsibility

In this group, parents conferred greater responsibility upon young people as they got older – for example, expecting them to take care of others, to contribute to household chores, and to pay due attention to their studies. However, these parents did not grant them or see them as having a right to greater individual autonomy based on ideas of self-development and individual rights. The approach of adulthood signified greater responsibility for *others* notably to household members or the wider kin group (see Song, 1996). New duties were part and parcel of explicit or understood cultural expectations concerning age-appropriate behaviour rather than adolescence as a distinctive phase of the life course. These norms were clearly understood by parents and young people even if the latter did not always abide by them. The idea that parents should no longer attempt to regulate their young people or that young people were exempt from normative regulation by virtue of becoming 16 was significantly absent.

This group of households includes a substantial number of parents born and brought up outside the UK, most in India or via East Africa while a few came from the Middle East. Their expectations of 16-year-olds and their concepts of adolescence differed significantly from those of UK-born parents. For example, psychological notions of adolescence as a time of emotional turmoil were notably absent. Signs of rebelliousness in young people and conflict with parents were construed as abnormal, individual characteristics rather than a necessary part of adolescence. Where parents reported young people as being emotional, they sometimes described it as a pathological response to being 'torn between two cultures'.

These parents, moreover, regarded the notion of young people 'leaving home' as a typical facet of British lifestyles and as undesirable and often highly problematic. They said that their young people 'never leave home', by which they meant that they stayed part of the kin or family group. Several said that the notion of encouraging young people to leave home had directly resulted in the current UK social phenomenon of widespread homelessness among young people. Compared with UK-born parents, the non-UK-born parents were more likely to favour continuing ties of material support and obligation, especially the idea of giving significant financial help to children at the point when they set up house. They were also more likely to favour their children giving them support in old age.

Parents of Asian and Middle Eastern origin clearly did not expect their young people, especially girls, to engage in leisure activities outside the home: to go out at night with friends; to mix with peers; to have opposite-sex relationships (sex was automatically ruled out); to smoke; to take alcohol; or to engage with drugs. These issues were not negotiable. Parents did not define non-engagement in terms of health prevention. Parents aimed to protect their children by keeping them safe at home regarding these activities as emanating from western culture and threatening the moral character of young people. Especially with respect to young women, they put at risk their reputations and hence their marriageability. These parents did not speak the language of personal responsibility nor did they articulate the idea of taking risks in moderation. This is not to say however that young people in these households never engaged in these activities. However, they were significantly less likely to do so compared with young people of UK-born parents. Moreover, those who did engage kept their activities secret from their parents. Young people did not overtly flout institutional norms and thus acted in accordance with norms of 'respect' for parents but might act on quite different beliefs in other social contexts.

Parental expectations of these young people were not necessarily couched simply in terms of prohibition. Positive emphasis was placed upon respect for elders. Young people as they grew older were expected to take on additional responsibilities especially *vis à vis* adults, notably entertaining guests to the house. As well as the addition of responsibilities, young people gained exemption from other duties such as household tasks on the grounds of their status as students. In many of these households, considerable emphasis was placed upon the value of studying and not simply upon education as a means to an end.

Aznive's parents, who came from a country bordering the Persian Gulf and were members of a Christian religion, did not expect their daughter to be independent at 16. Aznive was also the eldest child with a younger brother and sister who were still at school. They live over her father's shop (a chain grocer's) in which mother and daughter work unpaid. In this household the father rather than the mother appeared to set the rules. Aznive described her father as 'very strict' while her father's account makes it clear that he was in practice very concerned about the kind of people with whom his daughter mixes, fearing that, in associating with young men, she might lose her (sexual) 'respectability': 'I'm very strict on that. If I lose my temper, they know it.' Paternal authority appeared to have become especially marked in Aznive's adolescence. Aznive said that she and her father were closer during her childhood: 'We've grown apart just a bit.' Asked how she thought her father felt about her, she responded 'He tends to hide his feelings, and doesn't like to express himself too much. But I know he cares about me.' Caring was thus expressed not through affect but through paternal strictness. In his interview, her father did not put into words what he felt for his daughter, and said he did not know his daughter's view of their relationship. One reason for the father's silence might be that he felt uncomfortable with a female interviewer, though the alternative argument is persuasive – that his failure to articulate care in affect terms means that it cannot be divorced from his paternal role.

According to Aznive, her teenage years brought increased domestic responsibility. She was expected to help her father unpaid in the family business. She shouldered most of the housework, including taking care of her younger siblings during her GCSE examinations, because her mother had to go away to recover from a severe attack of rheumatoid arthritis. Aznive had largely conformed to parental expectations, but also displayed some resistance to the restrictive regime. Thus, despite acknowledging that her upbringing had made her more responsible – in accordance with her parents' view of what her new status should be, she was also making a bid for more autonomy. In her account, she describes the emergence of a 'freer' side to her character, an identity which she conceals within the grumpy demeanour she adopts in the private sphere of her family:

> I went through a stage where I was rude to my parents. I don't know why. I just snapped at them all the time . . . I went through a stage when I wanted to be myself – to have my own space type of thing . . . They say girls mature quicker than boys. I must have had it hard in my early teens

... [Parents] were very strict ... 'cos at home I have quite a lot of responsibilities, and, like, I've taken these responsibilities seriously ... Like when I go out with my parents – 'cos there's a lot of social activities ... I know how to handle myself. I'm a very kind of mature person. But when I'm with my own friends I'm totally different. I can relax and be myself.

Unsurprisingly, Aznive did not discuss sexual matters with her father, and did not expect to: 'With my Dad, I can only tell him certain things that he needs to know.' Nor did they talk about educational decisions at the end of the fifth year. Her mother's recent serious illness was also not discussed. With her mother she described herself as 'more open'. Her father also states that, 'She can talk to her mother.' Asked about discussing boyfriends and sex education, he replied curtly, '[My children] know my opinion very well.'

Relationships in this group are qualitatively different with respect to sons compared with daughters, with sons having more autonomy than daughters but significantly less than sons in other groups. The following case concerns a father and son of Chinese origin. Again, it was the father who set limits upon his son's autonomy. Interestingly, the father but not the mother proffered himself for interview, albeit with some reluctance. Chenglie Wang's father was a mild-mannered man whose son described him as 'easygoing' and 'unselfish' – 'Whatever he does, he does for us, like. When he works so hard he's working for us.' His manner and style belied his rather authoritarian orientation to parenting. Of peasant roots, he grew up in Malaysia and moved continents twice in order to pursue his studies, finally completing his architectural training in the UK. His main aim was that his children should 'do well at school', and he was no less strict with his youngest child, his only son, Chenglie. He restricted his son's activities and vetted his friends, wanting to know 'what type of family ... how they study'.

Chenglie was generally in agreement with his father's educational aspirations, and was aiming to go to university. He accepted and conformed to the house rules:

I wouldn't say there are strict rules. But all the children [his sisters are grown up but live at home] know what they should be doing, what's expected of them. No one says ... It's like a mental compromise between all of us. We all know where we can go and where we can't. [*How do you feel?*] I think it's good. I mean we can know, learn about rules that are always there. [*Like?*] Like you always have to study ... You can't always go out everyday – stay out to a really late time. There are set rules. Everyone knows them.

While Chenglie abided by the rules, describing himself as a 'young adult ... still under the guidance of parents', he was slightly resentful that his parents saw no place for 'fun' in his life. Moreover, as already indicated, he respected his father for his 'provider role'.

Neither party described the relationship as 'close'. Significantly, Chenglie mentioned a connection which belonged to the past rather than the present – the way his father used to help him with his maths homework. He excuses his father now on the grounds that, 'He's so busy', and also makes some interesting comments concerning the different caring styles of his two parents. While Chenglie says that his mother expresses her concern for him by worrying, the fact of fatherhood and his status as the only son are sufficient indication that his father cares for him. However, Chenglie was initially somewhat hesitant in his reply to the question whether his father cared for him:

> I think so . . . My Dad's not a worrier. If you know someone's worrying a lot, then they obviously care for you. If he does, he doesn't show it that much. [*You mean physical affection?*] Not that much . . . But I think he does care, 'cos I'm the only boy in the family and fathers always like to have sons. So if I do well, he's happy.

Worry is seen as a form of weakness here and thereby the antithesis of fatherhood.

Communication between father and son was limited; neither saw it an important issue. Indeed, since Chenglie conformed to the rules, there was little to tell that his parents did not already know. Chenglie described his attitude to disclosure as 'mainly keeping things to myself', while his father's only reference to, and concern about, communication with his son was to do with which subjects he proposed to study. His father assumed that his son was staying on at school. Discussion of sexual matters was taboo, and both Chenglie and his father considered that he was too young to have a girlfriend.

In this household, normative rules governing fatherhood and age relations precluded father and son being close in an affective sense. The son's progress through the education system was their main point of connection. Thus caring was embodied in the shared activity rather than the expression of concern. Since the son largely conformed to the household rules, he had little personal autonomy, and had no need to confide or confess private matters. For the same reason, there was no conflict in the father–son relationship. As another son of Asian origin parents put it: respect demands distance in a relationship:

> [*What do you mean by respect?*] They're older than you. You can't treat them as if they're your age. I can't treat my dad like my best mate, or I'm in trouble. Some things I can say to my friends. I can mess around, joke around. I can't say that to my Dad.

(Sandeep Kumar)

While Chenglie was closer to his mother, there was not a great deal of communication there either. In this respect, Chenglie's remarks about the importance of having a girlfriend (he did not have one) are significant. Asked whether he approved of young men of his age having girlfriends, he commented, 'It's good to have someone to talk to openly.' Paradoxically, the desired goal of openness was undermined by the lack of boundaries between his own world and that of the household.

Conclusion

The discourses which govern young people's transitions to adulthood define not only the amount of independence which young people have but the basis upon which rights and responsibilities are extended to them. I have indicated that the individual rights discourse which is so evident in psychologists' and health educationists' definitions is not necessarily prevalent in all parents' constructions of adolescence and their treatment of their young people. Parental definitions of adolescence, the ways in which parents exert control over young people, the relationships which parents and young people develop with one another and the degree to which young people gain or assume independence are differentiated by social class, culture and gender. Moreover these structural factors interact with one another with different outcomes. The current (1990s) public policy emphasis upon the responsibility of parents and the de-emphasis upon the rights of young people as citizens of the society is likely to impact differently upon different groups within our society. For non-UK-origin parents, especially those from the Indian subcontinent, greater emphasis upon parental responsibility reinforces their own cultural values and practice and may lead to even greater restriction of their young people, especially girls. By contrast, UK-born parents will have to reshape their parenting strategies in ways which may go against their own experience of growing up and contravene their young people's expectations. While we did not focus upon young people's beliefs and actions outside the context of the family, their own accounts testify that at 16 parents' values and modes of control are still salient influences upon them.

References

Allatt, P. and Yeandle, S. (1992) *Youth Unemployment and the Family: Voices of Disordered Times*, London, Routledge.

Bernstein, B. (1971) *Class, Codes and Control, Vol I: Theoretical Studies Towards a Sociology of Language*, London, Routledge and Kegan Paul.

Bernstein, B. (1975) *Class Codes and Control, Vol. 3: Towards a Theory of Educational Transmissions*, London, Routledge and Kegan Paul.

Brannen, J., Dodd, K., Oakley, A. and Storey, P. (1994) *Young People, Health and Family Life*, Buckingham, Open University Press.

Chisholm, L., Buchner, P., Kruger, H. and Brown, P. (Eds) (1990) *Childhood, Youth and Social Change: A Comparable Perspective*, Basingstoke, Falmer Press.

Coleman, J. (1990) *The Nature of Adolescence*, 2nd ed., London, Routledge.

Collins, L. (1984) 'Concepts of health education: A study of four professional groups', *Journal of Institute of Health Education*, 22, 3, pp. 81–8.

Frankenberg, R. (1993) 'Trust, culture, language and time', Consent Conference No. 2, Young People's Psychiatric Treatment and Consent, London, Institute of Education, Social Science Research Unit.

Giddens, A. (1991) *Modernity and Self-identity: Self and Society in the Late Modern Age*, Cambridge, Polity.

Gilligan, C. (1982) *In a Different Voice: Psychological Theory and Women's Development*, Cambridge, MA, Harvard University Press.

Graham, H. (1979) 'Prevention and health; every mother's business: A comment on child health policies in the 1970s', in Harris, C.C. (Ed) *The Sociology of the Family: New Directions for Britain*, Sociological Review Monograph 28, University of Keele.

Griffin, C. (1985) *Typical Girls?*, London, Routledge and Kegan Paul.

Jones, G. and Wallace, C. (1992) *Youth, Family and Citizenship*, Buckingham, Open University Press.

McRobbie, A. (1991) 'The politics of feminist research: Between talk, test and action', in McRobbie, A. (Ed) *Feminism and Youth Culture: From Jackie to Just Seventeen*, London, Macmillan.

Nutbeam, D., Hagland, B., Farley, P. and Tillgren, P. (1991) *Youth Health Promotions*, London, Forbes Publications.

Roll, J. (1990) *Young People: Growing up in the Welfare State*, Occasional Paper No. 10, London, Family Policy Studies Centre.

Rutter, M., Tizard, J. and Whitmore, K. (1976) *Educational Health and Behaviour*, London, Longman.

Song, M. (1996) 'Helping out: children's labour participation in Chinese Take-Away businesses in Britain' in Brannen, J. and O'Brien, M. (Eds) *Children and Families: Research and Policy*, London, Falmer Press.

Tones, B.K. (1983) 'Education and health promotion: New directions', *Journal of the Institute of Health Education*, 21, pp. 121–31.

Walkerdine, V. and Lucey, H. (1989) *Democracy in the Kitchen: Regulating Mothers and Socialising Daughters*, London, Virago.

Chapter 13

Researching children's social competence

Methods and models*

Allison James

This chapter takes as its theme the idea that the methods used in childhood research reflect a set of implicit models of 'the child' and that, in order to carry out informed and ethically sound research with children, we should be attentive to the nature of this relationship. It is not, however, my intention here to prescribe particular methods for studying children, nor to detail their application, for in my view studying children does not, of itself, necessitate the development of new or exotic techniques. Children are in this sense nothing special. But the way we as researchers approach childhood study does need some thinking about in order to lay bare the implicit ideas about children, childhood and children's social lives which we, as researchers, bring to our studies.

The stimulus for this chapter comes from my previous experiences of research with children in which, since the mid-1970s, I have been attempting, along with others in the sociology and social anthropology of childhood, to develop approaches which see children as social actors, as people with their own perspectives on the social world which may or may not reflect those of the adults with whom they engage (James and Prout, 1990). It is a view of children which arises, in part, from a growing realisation of the socially constructed character of childhood itself. Drawing on historical and cross-cultural material a social constructionist perspective argues that the universalistic and dominant discourses of childhood offered by developmental psychology have to be questioned, for expectations about the abilities and competencies of 'the child' can be shown to vary considerably, both cross-culturally and over time (James, Jenks and Prout, 1998). And, as 'childhood' cannot therefore any longer be regarded as an unvarying experience for all children, biological development must be seen as contextualising, rather than unequivocally determining, children's experiences.

The intriguing possibility addressed here is that we, as researchers, may also

---

* Specially prepared for this Reader based on a paper presented at the Children and Social Competence Conference, University of Surrey, 1995.

be contributing to the socially constructed character of childhood. Along with other adults involved with children – teachers, youth workers, child-health professionals, parents – do we, through the kinds of accounts we offer of children's lives and the kinds of experiences which we subject children to also thereby contribute a great deal to the implicit shaping of those child lives? If the answer to this questions is 'yes' then it behoves us to explore in some detail, and with a critical awareness, the possible implications and outcomes for children themselves of our particular views of the way the world works and of children's place and position in that world. In brief, we need become more reflexive about our research, recognising that our accounts of childhood are intimately marked by the particularities of our own stances towards children.

A strategy for researching research strategies

In examining the varied research strategies which have been used to study children and childhood across the social sciences it is possible to identify different clusters of orientations towards 'the child'. These methodological framings are, in turn, often associated with the use of particular kinds of research techniques. Ways of seeing 'the child' shape the ways in which we study children, informing the methods and techniques chosen, designating research populations and subjects – children themselves or their adult care-takers – and framing the interpretation of the resultant data. In this sense my project has echoes of that embarked upon by Bradley for developmental psychology. Bradley argues that

> scientific discussions of infancy make more sense as illustrations of what the world means to particular scientists than as products of a selfless attempt to describe what the world means to babies and their minders.
>
> (1989: 3)

And it confirms Stainton-Rogers's (1992) suggestion that there are, indeed, a set of stories to be told about childhood. My own concern is that, as social researchers, we do not unheedingly repeat these stories in our work *with* children, without consideration of their consequences *for* children. As Jenks (1982) has argued, theories of 'the child' and 'childhood' are all too easily naturalised in the social world. Having come so far as to have made the socially constructed character of childhood now indisputable, within and increasingly outside the academy (Save the Children Fund, 1995; Action Aid, 1995), it behoves us, as social researchers, to become watchful of our own part in that construction (see James and Prout, 1990: 29–31).

Jenks's (1982) twin categorisation of the elements to be distilled from approaches to the study of childhood provide my starting point for a four-fold analytic device with which I shall pursue my methodological exploration. These elements are as follows:

First, a belief that the child instances difference and particularity, and secondly, following from the former, a desire to account for the integration of that difference into a more broadly conceived sense of order and rationality that comprises adult society.

(1982: 10)

For Jenks (1982: 10) the social status of child is constituted through a necessary but contingent relationship of difference with that of 'adult' so that, as he argues, the idea and position of the child in society can only be understood in relation to that of the adult: they define each other through the differences they represent. What a child is, how children are thought about and their positions in society can only be known through contrasting it with what adults are thought to be and the positions they occupy in the social world. In sum, the idea of 'adult' or 'child' only come to make sense in the contrastive relationship they have with one another.

Drawing on this framing I suggest that envisioned in the different research strategies used by social scientists to study children are at least four ways of 'seeing' children (see Figure 13.1). Each of these combines notions of social competence and children's difference with those of children's status to effect four ideal types of 'the child'.

1   *The developing child:* children's status as research subjects is understood to be different from that of adults, and children are seen to have different social competencies.
2   *The tribal child:* children's status as research subjects is understood to be different from that of adults, but children are seen to have comparable social competencies.
3   *The adult child:* children's status as research subjects is comparable with that of adults, and children are seen to have comparable social competencies.
4   *The social child:* children's status as research subjects is comparable with that of adults, but children have different social competencies.

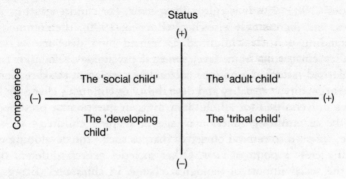

Figure 13.1 Images of 'the child' in childhood research

As heuristic devices these models of 'the child' should not, however, be regarded as inviolate or exhaustive. As frames for research strategies – ways of approaching the study of childhood – they may merge, overlap or alternate. In my own work, for example, I have at different times found my methodological persuasions hovering between the social and the adult child (James, 1993); at other times the practical and conceptual problems thrown up by my research have forced me to write in defence of the tribal child as I confronted, somewhat unwillingly, insistent, nagging evidence of the developing child (James, 1979: 1983). In this sense none of these offers a 'correct' model of childhood from which to embark on research. They are simply analytic devices, which have some utility in allowing us to reflect on the import of our methodological practices, as can be seen, for example, in the further elaboration of these models in James, Jenks and Prout (1998).

The developing child

The model of 'the developing child' continues to inform much contemporary childhood research, guiding research design and techniques. Preeminently associated with developmental psychology this approach is founded on the belief that children possess different social competencies and that these are of different, less mature status to adults. Moreover, within a natural science model, the methods of developmental psychology define a researcher–child relationship in which children are objects of study, to be observed, tested and experimented upon, where their behaviour, feelings and beliefs are interpreted as evidence of relative competence against those standards prescribed for adults. The idea of 'the developing child' persists, not least, I suspect, because of the immutability of the child's body. Common sense tells us that children grow from small to large people and, on the way, acquire the characteristics of an adult body and mind. On the other hand, Clifford Geertz reminds us, common sense is 'what the mind filled with presuppositions concludes' (1983: 29). It is culturally specific. For children within Western societies, and increasingly elsewhere (Boyden, 1990), the commonsensical understanding of their 'childhood' is framed by a discourse of scientific rationality emanating from developmental psychology. Through this, one particularised rationalisation, one cultural perception of the direction, quality, intentionality, normality and desirability of children's changing biology becomes universalised for all children. But, in questioning presuppositions about the determining function of age in shaping children's social competence, we need to remind ourselves that, as such, 'the developing child' is after all merely a point of view. Other societies express different opinions about the social import of biological change in childhood (Briggs, 1986; Reynolds, 1989).

Unfortunately, in many studies of childhood the cultural relativity of children's social maturation is dispensed with. Intentionally, or otherwise, 'the developing child' masquerades as a scientific and universalistic methodology, an ideal type unproblematically informing research design and techniques. Largely derived from the work of Jean Piaget, it embraces unquestioningly the ideas of developmental stages, roughly equating these with the passing of time in a child's life. Thus research informed by this methodological frame takes place largely as age-based studies of childhood, 'years-lived-through' being seen as the one variable which can be held unproblematically constant and consequently left untheorised.

Other examples of this kind of work would be cohort and longitudinal studies of childhood change. Sliced through at a particular age, the child population is surveyed, assumed to be united by the commonality of biological growth and psychological development, and thus diversified only by class, region, gender and ethnicity (Newson and Newson, 1976). Quantitative methods predominate in this approach, supplemented sometimes by more qualitative interviews with parents, and occasionally their children, to gain commentary on and some evaluation of patterns and rates of childhood change.

I have no quibble with this. There are, indeed, likely to be many similarities between the life experiences of 6- or 7-year-old children, experiences which contrast markedly with those of 10-year-olds, precisely because childhood in Western societies is managed for children in terms of age-related stages. Age, as a social construct, works to prescribe and proscribe children's day-to-day activities in schools, in families, in the health service, in the media. Research by Qvortrup (1994), for example, explores the ways in which childhood as a social phenomenon is inscribed in the structural arrangements of any society. Yielding a distinctive discursive space, he shows that the form which childhood takes differs between societies, just as, one imagines, do children's experiences of that space.

And I would go so far as to argue that most of us work with a research design which uncritically incorporates some aspects of the age-related methodological frame which derives from the model of 'the developing child'. What is worrying, though, is that so natural a part of childhood does it seem to be, we think little of it. But, if as Davies (1982) notes, for children 'age is a highly significant characteristic of persons', it might behove us to consider more carefully the extent to which, as researchers, we leave this aspect of our research strategies largely untheorised (1982: 39)

For example, although the ages of children are often given in a study, there is rarely much information about why that particular age group was chosen. Was it especially pertinent to the topic – as is quite clear in studies of school transition (Measor and Woods, 1984; Prout, 1989) – or was it a more arbitrary decision which demonstrates an unconscious assimilation of the model of 'the developing child'? How often do we choose an age group simply because we feel that the children will be 'old enough' to engage effectively with the researcher's project, rather than because at *that* age in *that* society children are sharing a particular social, rather than simply developmental, experience. Rarely do we detail the ages of adult research subjects unless, as in the study of elderly people, it is pertinent to the research topic. In reflecting on our methodology, we should pause, then, to consider why age should be deemed so important when researching children and how far and in what ways we wish our research strategy to incorporate this aspect of 'the developing child'. If we do, then we need to make this explicit.

A similar concern applies in comparative projects. To what extent is it implicitly assumed that differences between one age group and another is an unmediated function of developmental change; simply, a matter of being older? Could it not be read, additionally, or alternatively, as a sign of the children's growing social competence with the age-based cultural contexts which they frequent – the school, the youthclub, the dancing class (James, 1993)? That is to say, might it be a function of their being *there*, rather than simply being? That, in other cultural contexts, examples abound of a considerable disparity between age and physical and social competence (Briggs, 1986; Nieuwenhuys, 1993) should, I suggest, make us think more carefully about the implications of working unreflexively with particular age groups of children or making comparisons between them.

A further and related consideration is that, in industrialised societies, schools are the places in which children are most often studied. They house a ready-made and easily accessible population with whom a range of techniques can be deftly employed: ethnographic work, questionnaires, surveys and interviews. But, aside from studies which specifically set out to explore children's experiences of school – studies of the learning process or life at school (see, for example: Hammersley and Woods, 1984; Pollard, 1985; Whyte, 1983; Davies, 1982; Walkerdine, 1985a, 1985b; Delamont, 1980; Askew and Ross, 1988) – how often do we reflect on the ways in which the school as a research site naturalises the model of the developing child within our studies? As an age-based institution which is hierarchically organised into age classes and shot through with particular power relations, might it not shape the form and style of the research process? To what extent are we led to design our research with the age-stratification of the school in mind and what implications might this have for our research? Would findings about sexuality, gender, ethnicity, friendship, bullying, play and work, for example, look different if they had been gathered outside the context of the school or other child-specific, age-based institutions such as youth clubs or day-care centres?

What little evidence we do have suggests that this might, indeed, be the case. James (1993), for example, notes that the often-remarked gender divisions in the friendships and play of young children may be a function of the school system itself and that, at home or in the street, children may socialise much more in mixed-sex groupings. In one of the few studies to explore children's lives at home and at school Mayall (1994) indicates that data gained from children at school may need to be modified to take account of children's experiences at home where different power relations pertain. Thus socially competent children may be precisely those who are skilled negotiators of these differences of place (James and Prout, 1995). An appropriate methodology would be one which could enable us to track children through these shifting contexts, allowing us to consider the relationship between the social construction of age and children's social and cultural competencies.

Another indication of the subtle, but insidious, underpinning of childhood discourse by the idea of 'the developing child' is the questioning of young children's linguistic competency, something observed long ago by the radical psychiatrist R.D. Laing. In the introduction to his book *Conversations with Children*, first published in 1978, he notes how reaction to his verbatim reporting of children's conversations was greeted with incredulity. Did he invent the dialogue he includes? Did he shape its flow, amend its style? In effect, his interlocutors ask, is it possible that children can say such things? Can they be as naive and, at the same time, as seemingly competent as their conversations suggest and what should we adults make of their talk with us and between themselves? Some seventeen years later this questioning has resurfaced as social scientists begin to take on a more child-centred perspective in their work, and as lawyers in the United States and Western Europe grapple with the testimonies of child witnesses. Questions are being asked about what children can say and what status children's words can have.

The unquestioning embrace of the model of 'the developing child' through the cultural glossing of biological and psychological change was, of course, common to the traditional socialisation research of the 1960s and, as MacKay (1973) notes, it greatly devalued children's competency. Children were less than adult, their actions and utterances signs of undeveloped social skills rather than evidence of a different kind of competence. But, despite being the subject of extensive sociological critique from within a social constructionist programme (Jenks, 1982; James and Prout, 1990), as I have suggested, the legacy of this perspective continues to shadow our research with children. We need not heed it but must recognise it when we see it.

The tribal child

The second methodological approach informing childhood research strategies is that which I call 'the tribal child'. This acknowledges children's different social status in a celebration of the relative autonomy of the cultural world of children. In part a response to the overwhelming dominance of the model of 'the developing child' in which children's incompetence is assumed, research within this tradition begins from an understanding of the child as socially competent. Characteristic of some of the work carried out during the 1970s

(Hebdige, 1979), features of 'the tribal child' continue to inform present research strategies and methods, especially in studies of playground games and youth subcultures.

Ethnographic approaches, now central in childhood research, were first adopted by those working with the model of 'the tribal child' as the most powerful way of asserting the integrity of a child's perspective on the social world, in the face of dominant developmental approaches. In challenging presuppositions about childhood as a process of 'becoming', their project was akin to the anthropologist endeavouring to describe another people's world-view. They wanted to make visible the existence of a separate children's culture with belief systems and social practices foreign to an adult's eye. However, just as many anthropological monographs mistakenly work hard at 'othering' other cultures in an effort to highlight their differences (Fabian, 1983), so too has ethnographic work among children often 'othered' the world of the child. It has done so by making central those children's activities which reflect differences from, rather than similarities with, the adult world, leading to the creation of a wide gulf between the social worlds of adults and children which has been far from inconsequential.

First, following the lead given by the Opies (1969, 1977) and later by Hardman (1973; 1974) in the late 1970s many researchers, including myself, working with a model of 'the tribal child' argued strongly for recognition of an autonomous community of children, relatively independent from the world of adults, in which children established their own rules and agendas. Such a child-centred approach required child-centred cultural contexts, so that the family and household became displaced as a research site by the school or the club. Traditionally the place for socialisation research, the family was conceived as an unsuitable site within which to develop this radically changed perspective on children's competency (James and Prout, 1995).

Only for those working with children in non-industrialised societies did the family remain a research site (Nieuwenhuys, 1994). Such children clearly had a childhood already different enough from a Western childhood through their involvement in family labour and other economic activities that there was no necessity to 'other' them in the conceptual work of exploring a child's perspective. More prosaically, in cultures where the discursive space of child-hood is less marked, and child-centred institutions such as schools are not routinely available, then the family or household must inevitably remain as the key site for researching children.

This rupturing of children's and adults' social worlds yielded other changes in childhood research. Just as anthropologists find perhaps the greatest differences between cultures to lie in expressive systems of belief such as religion, ritual and symbolism, so ethnographers of childhood saw in children's language and games eloquent arenas for revealing children's difference as a new kind of social competence. The net result is a large and still expanding body of ethnographic work on children's games and verbal lore in which children's competency and skill with the different cultural rules of a separate world of childhood is visibly endorsed.

What we do not have, however, are many accounts of the more mundane everydayness of being in a family or the day-to-day experiences of becoming adult. In the rush to establish firm boundaries to the child's world, links with the world of adults were perhaps inevitably underplayed (Munday, 1979). The fact that children do grow up, that they eventually leave the child's world, was something which, though not forgotten, it was tempting to suppress.

Though problematic, this implicit forgetting did, however, have some benefits. Unlike the model of 'the developing child' which down-played children's abilities in relation to those of adults, the tribalising of children allowed children's competency to be framed by a cultural relativism. Children were no longer simply to be judged as non-adult by reference to idealised standards of adult rationality. They were not to be labelled as '*pre*-operational' or '*pre*-moral', or *pre*-anything else. Children were just different. This perspective cast a new light on the question of children's linguistic competencies: what children meant was what they said and the ethnographer's job became simply one of translation and then interpretation. Nor was it a problem that these meanings might not be congruent with those of the adult world. Any ambiguity was welcomed as an illustration of the child's perspective on the world, a competently different point of view. (James, 1979).

This new focus on children's language is admirably demonstrated by Davies (1982). She shows how, much to their teacher's astonishment, the children she interviewed were able to demonstrate a far greater degree of 'linguistic competence in terms of vocabulary, style and analytic muscle' in conversation with her than they showed daily in classroom activities (1982: l63). This she ascribes to her non-directive participatory role among the children which stemmed from her desire to see children as 'people with a perspective of their own and strategies of their own for dealing with the social world that they perceive; as people who have, in fact, a culture of their own' (1982: 1).

Another positive outcome of the model of 'the tribal child' has been the questioning of children's social immaturity which had been a prominent feature of traditional socialisation research and was perpetuated through the use of specific research tools. Sociometric techniques used to research children's friendships are a case in point. Employing these, researchers had long agonised about the instability and fickleness of children's social relationships when compared to those of adults (Putallaz and Gottman, 1981). But, when framed by the model of 'the tribal child', these same tools and techniques yielded a more positive outcome. Researchers studying the resulting network diagrams could begin to account for the changing pattern of children's friendships over time through exploring the meanings which children themselves attribute to friendship. In this way those transitory, unstable friendships were seen as reflecting the particularities of children's social experience, rather than as worrying indicators of some developmental lack (James, 1993). Bigelow and La Gaipa noted in 1981 that 'little is known as yet about what children expect from their friends, how these expectations change over time and the impact of such social cognition on friendship choice' (1981: 15). Working ethnographically with the model of 'the tribal child' has allowed us to begin to fill in that gap.

But, although making substantial contributions to childhood research, the model of 'the tribal child' has not produced a reflexive methodological critique about the radical partitioning of the worlds of adults and children. Thus, although ethnographers keenly describe the process of doing research with children, their accounts do not, for example, adequately address the issues of how far 'cultures of childhood' are something ascribed by adults to children and how far they are part of children's own conceptions of who they are – part of their own identity which, as a consequence, may shape children's relationships with adult researchers.

Mandell (1991), for instance, describes her status *vis-à-vis* her child subjects as one of being 'least adult' and details how she accomplished this. Rejecting the research role of detached observer, Mandel opts for complete involvement and refuses the position of an authoritative adult in the children's world. She climbs into the sandpit and joins them on the swings, arguing that such participatory activities distance her adult self for the children. My question is not whether being 'least adult' is possible. Clearly it may be. Nor whether it works. It may well do. But how far is it desirable? Might we not learn more or at least different things about children and their social world by adopting, as Fine (1988) suggests, the more middle ground of semi-participant or friend?

Let me elaborate. If, as Fine (1988) argues, it is not possible for adults to 'pass unnoticed' in the company of children as age, size and authority always intervene, something which Mandel also reluctantly notes, then might it not be worth reflecting on the significance of those differences? In what circumstances do they assume importance and when are they irrelevant? In ethnographic work with children we need to ask about when we are forced to back-track to our adult selves – perhaps it is when, as adults, we observe one child bullying another or when we forsee a danger that the child does not. In such instances we need to reflect upon what this reveals about the social construction of childhood and children's own understanding of their status as children. Such benefits would add to that noted already by Fine: that 'there is methodological value in maintaining the differences between sociologists and children – a feature of interaction that permits the researcher to behave in certain "non-kid" ways – such as asking ignorant questions' (1988: 17). If as Geertz (1983) argues anthropologists do not have to turn native in order to argue from the natives' point of view, then it is clear that childhood researchers need not pretend to be children.

These criticisms are not intended to signal the retreat from ethnography. Far from it. As an anthropologist this method is my bread and butter. Rather, it is to suggest that if we admit the inevitability of the differences between children and ourselves, acknowledging that, however friendly we are or however small, we can only ever have a semi-participatory role in children's lives, then we might develop tools and techniques specifically for work with children on those occasions when our adultness prohibits our full participation (see below). Noting which differences make a difference between us and when they do (Bateson, 1973) may be as, if not more, informative than attempting to tribalise ourselves in our efforts to work consistently with a model of 'the tribal child'.

The adult child

The heuristic value of adopting a reflexive stance towards research roles with children can be seen in my third categorical child: 'the adult child'. Researchers working with this methodological framework do not see themselves as unobtrusive participants in a separate child's world. Instead, children are envisaged as competent participants in a shared, but adult-centred, world and it is through this mutual understanding that the research relationship develops. Less emphasis is given to the children's social lives with other children, attention being focused instead on children's perspectives on and comprehension of an adult world in which they are required to participate. That two strands of research predominate in the work of those using this model of the child – serious illness and work – is not surprising. In industrialised societies both these are conceptually aspects of adults', rather than children's, lives. Death and labour have no natural place in the ideology of a safe, happy and protected childhood (Holt, 1974; Ennew, 1986). To research these areas, then, is to study children engaging with adult affairs – albeit that they may be surrounded by cultural beliefs and practices (informed by the model of the developing child) that deny the possibility that they might be competent social actors.

Bluebond-Langner's (1978) fieldwork with terminally ill children was a direct consequence of her encountering children who were professional patients. By 9 years old they had been hospitalised 'as many as fifty times . . . [and] . . . had learned a great deal about how the hospital operated, how to manipulate various people and the meanings of various kinds of staff behaviour and expressions' (1978: 238). Her book describes these children dealing competently with an adult world, from whose decisions they were continually excluded while, nonetheless, being subject to its regulation and treatment regimes.

In this context Bluebond-Langner's role as researcher varied, both in time and between children. Not fitting the available conventional adult categories of nurse, doctor or parent she became a kind of friend with whom they could talk and, at times, someone over whom the children could exert control. For her, these were not children inhabiting another world in which she, as an adult, learned to participate. They were people facing difficult choices, with particular needs and desires and thus her questioning was directed by the children and subject to their permission. Participating only when asked, she withdrew on request. In her account, then, there is little sense of the researcher attempting to pass as a child; her relationship with the children was as between equals.

In research on children's consent to surgery, which explores the question of children's rights and decision-making, Alderson is explicit that a model of 'the adult child' frames her research strategy. She observes that any difference between researching children and adults

> lies mainly in the interviewer if she protectively forces children into an adult–child relationship, instead of treating them as mature, competent people. Some children are shy or hesitant, like some adults, but we also met confident, fluent 8-year-olds. Adults tend to make more connections, and to reply in more detail at greater length than very young children. This difference is a matter of degree rather than of kind, and is perhaps less due to immaturity than to children's inexperience. When they are experienced they give mature replies.
>
> (1993: 71)

Like those who would tribalise the child great emphasis is placed upon giving voice to children's own perspectives; but here it is not a vision of a world apart, another culture heard from. Rather the reverse: in these accounts children are observing and analysing the actions of their adult care-takers. Where possible verbatim reportage of children's own opinions about their treatment and doctors', nurses' and parents' actions is provided for children are seen as competent commentators on their illness experiences. To these, Bluebond-Langner and Alderson add their own analytic interpretation, explaining and extending the children's accounts.

Bearison (1991), however, warns against such practice. He contends that 'the adult child' should alone provide the analysis. We need look no further:

> simply listen to the children speaking in their own voices about issues and events that are important to them. There is a great deal to be learned and appropriated from their narratives. They teach us the value of listening to children on their own terms without judging them so that their internal voices will become louder in our time.
>
> (1991: 26)

While his bold presentation of children's narratives is reminiscent of recent experimental ethnographic writing within social anthropology, such an extreme modelling of 'the adult child' does little, in the end, to enhance our understanding of children's lives. Bearison offers us few clues as to how we might approach the narratives he presents so that the children we hear lose, rather than gain, any individuality or personhood. Unlike in Alderson's or Bluebond-Langner's work we do not know which of the 75 children he interviewed is speaking to us. Are they the words of a 3- or a 9-year-old child, an Afro-American, a Hispanic boy or a Caucasian girl? We simply do not know. And yet, if these were adult narratives, it is precisely such details that, as sociologists and anthropologists, we would insist on. By omitting these, in his desire to clearly articulate children's own views on having cancer, Bearison's version of 'the adult child' therefore ironically replicates the universalising tendencies of the model of 'the developing child' to which it (and he) is so fundamentally opposed.

This elision of childhood diversity in the struggle to reclaim children's competency and status is a central tension in the model of 'the adult child'. Even in the most sophisticated renderings age and gender – key differentials of childhood – may be played down as sociological markers of differences between children in the struggle to demonstrate children's practical competence when confronting the starkness of ill-health and disease or the adult world of work. Drawing on her fieldwork in a Norwegian fishing community Solberg (1994), for example, argues strongly that age should be ignored if we wish to see children's perspective on work. In the fishing community children bait fishing lines alongside adults and each baiter is expected to complete the task, irrespective of their status. Child labour, often exoticised and problematised in the literature (Fyfe, 1989) is in this account presented as a normal dimension of these children's lives. Children are competent members of the baiting team.

And yet it is clear that in industrialised societies, and increasingly in those of the South, conceptions of age, and to a lesser extent gender, *do* set certain boundaries to concepts of childhood which work to both prescribe and limit children's activities through delineating specific arenas of action for 'the child'. The child patient does not have the same status and capacities in the eyes of the medical consultant making decisions about the best course of treatment. Nor does the Bangladeshi child worker in the eyes of the Western consumer advocating a ban on child labour. Where these lines are drawn tells us about the differences between the social statuses of child and adult; how they are negotiated tells us about children's abilities as social actors. An appropriate research methodology would be one which would allow us to explore the duality of this structuring of children's lives.

The social child

'The social child' finds its position in the final quadrant of approaches to the study of children. This model, like that of 'the adult child' envisages children as research subjects comparable with adults, but understands children to possess different competencies. I suggest this model permits researchers to engage more effectively with the diversity of childhood in terms of age, gender, cultural context, etc. but, at the same time, ensures that they are accorded status and rights within the research process (Morrow and Richards, 1996; Alderson, 1995).

The model of 'the social child' is neither new nor innovative. It is but a bricolage, drawing lessons from previous approaches, but in its synthesis sets out to overcome some of their limitations by acknowledging that 'childhood' is, for individual children, simply a stage in the life course. Thus, although significant parallels can be drawn between the study of women and that of children (Alanen, 1992) this approach stresses the uniqueness of children: unlike women, they turn into their own opposites. They eventually mature. In endeavouring to encapsulate these different dimensions of childhood, 'the social child' approaches children as social actors, engaged in everyday activities in particular cultural contexts within a discursive space marked out differentially as 'childhood'. This is the good news. The bad news is that this task has yet to be fully accomplished in the methodologies available to current research. In this sense, 'the social child' is still at the planning stage.

However, there are glimpses of its potential, a potential realisable, I suggest, through reflection on the methods we use to study children. Whilst ethnographic research and qualitative interviewing are to my mind the pre-eminent research strategies for studying children's lives, children's limited social experience, combined with their unequal structural position in society, may mean that we need to refine these methods and techniques. Observation, participation and interviewing all entail implicit assumptions about children's competency as we have seen: tools of the trade they might be, but they are far from value free.

Moreover, acknowledging that children have different abilities, but are none the less competent and confident in them, allows us to consider the methodological import of Hebdige's (1979) observation that those who lack power in society may find other forms and means of self-expression beyond the purely verbal. For children the body is clearly an important resource of non-verbal communication, something already recognised in the intensive study of children's games and use of space. But children use other mediums of communication – drawings and stories, for example – which have been less well documented as a resource (cf. Steedman, 1982; Steedman, Urwin and Walkerdine, 1985). If, as I shall suggest, we dispense with arguments about the necessary relationship between age and accomplishment, sociological approaches to children's art or written work opens up a number of method-ological possibilities which can directly explore the duality of children's social experience.

For example, through their schooling, at least in industrialised societies, children are accustomed to paint and draw and are actively encouraged to express themselves on paper. Having been taught these skills, they use them daily and, unlike most adults, are accomplished practitioners. It behoves us then to make use of these different abilities rather than asking children to participate unpractised in interviews or unasked submit them to our observational and surveilling gaze. Talking with children about the meanings they themselves attribute to their paintings or asking them to write a story as I have also done allows children to engage more productively with our research questions using the talents which they, as children, possess (Wilkinson, 1988: 81–90; Ennew, 1994: 67–9; Morrow, 1995).

One example, drawn from my own research, will have to suffice. In a class of 4- and 5-year-old children a group of boys and girls were painting pictures of their families. Robbie drew a picture of his mother, his sister and himself. He was challenged by Tom with the question: where's your dad? and, before Robbie could reply, Tom said: I expect he's dead. As if this were a matter of fact rather than speculation, Tom resumed his own painting, while Robbie compared his picture with those of the other children. A while later he screwed up his painting and embarked on another. This time there were four figures. By way of explanation to Tom, Robbie said: this is when we lived in London, Daddy was there. The questioning routines of an interview, unfamiliar to children, would surely have yielded far less information about notions of belonging and social difference than did this brief interchange over a painting.

To pay closer attention to method in endeavouring to engage with the children's childhood is to recognise that much of children's social experience is highly structured by the adult world – 'free play' in schools in industrialised cultures can only take place, for example, at times and in places previously designated for that freedom. This means that children's social relationships with adults (however friendly and well-meaning) often take place as mediated relationships centred on tasks. In these adults assume the directive role: the teacher, the youth club leader, the swimming instructor, the gym teacher and so on. To be friends with children, the role adopted by many researchers, is from the children's point of view, though welcome, also a potentially uncertain and disruptive action. It leaves many questions unanswered. Who is this woman? What does she want and why does she want it from us? What book is she writing and why can't our names be in it? Perhaps rightly suspicious or cautious, it was clear in my own recent project, for example, that not all the children wished to join me in my researches, while for others *my* interests were definitely not theirs. It was fun to chat about food and football but not about friendship. However, when engaged in a mutual project – such as keeping a chart or diary, writing a story, making a tape-recording – the children were working in a style which was not only familiar to them but one over which they had control.

Familiarity came from the temporary restoration of an adult–child relationship with them, combined with their experience of pedagogic project work in school. It was something they knew how to do and, knowing how to do to it, didn't need to. Not only did these tasks provide additional data on friendship patterns but, doing them together with the children, drew me further into their circle, allowing me to observe more closely the changing and intricate pattern of their relationships with one another.

Thus, for example my use of sociometric techniques with one class of 9-year-old children revealed more about the process of making friends than it did about the specifics of particular friendships. Set the task of inscribing the names of friends and best friends in a friendship booklet, one group of girls let it be known whose names they had chosen to write down. Those who had been included hurriedly added names to their own lists, whilst those who had been omitted crossly scribbled out the namers' names. New pieces of paper were requested, rubbers urgently looked for, and hands carefully placed to cover the listed names. Some asked each other directly 'Did you put me down?', 'Who did you write down?' Answers, knowingly withheld, made the emotional tension run high until one girl devised a solution. She wrote down an acronym based on the letters of all her friends: A.C.L.H.E.N.S. In this manner the whole group of girls metaphorically became one girl, a best friend to all.

As another example, I take Kane's ongoing work into children's decision-making during the experience of fostering (Kane, forthcoming). Kane uses participatory techniques based on those devised with adults as part of Participatory Rural Appraisal, a technique that challenges other images of 'development', in the field of Development Studies (Chambers, 1995). 'Decision-making pocket charts' allow children to reflect on the kinds of decisions which they make and which other people make for them, while the 'pots and beans' task allowed children to think about and evaluate the review process to which, as children in care, they were often subject. Thus while data is produced for the researcher the children also gain a new awareness of their own interests and needs.

These, then, are just some examples of the potentiality for new or additional methods for studying children which the model of 'the social child' offers. In its insistence on recognising children as people with abilities and capabilities different from, rather than simply less than, adults it may persuade us to be more adventurous in our methodology, to find ways in which we can engage children in our research so that our research *on* childhood can be effected through research *with* children. Then we may, I think, be more competent in researching children's competence.

References

Action Aid (1995) *Listening to the Smaller Voices: Children in an Environment of Change.*

Alanen, L. (1992) *Modern Childhood: Exploring the 'Child question' in sociology*, Research Report 50, University of Jyvaskyla.

Alderson, P. (1995) *Listening to Children: Children, Ethics and Social Research*, London, Barnardo's.

Bearison, D.J. (1991) *'They Never Want to Tell You': Children Talk about Cancer*, Harvard University Press.

Alderson, P. (1993) *Children's Consent to Surgery*, Buckingham: Open University Press

Alderson, P. (1995) *Listening to Children*, London, Barnado's.

Askew, S. and Ross, C. (1988) *Boys Don't Cry*, Milton Keynes: Open University Press.

Bateson, G. (1973) *Steps to an Ecology of Mind*, London: Paladin.

Bigelow, B.J. and La Gaipa, J.J. (1980) 'The development of friendship values and choice', in H.C. Foot, A.J. Chapman and J.R. Smith (eds) *Friendship and Social Relations in Children*, London: John Wiley.

Bluebond-Langner, M. (1978) *The Private Worlds of Dying Children*, Princeton: Princeton University Press.

Boyden, J. (1990) 'Childhood and the policy makers: a comparative perspective on the globalisation of childhood', in A. James and A. Prout (eds), *Constructing and Reconstructing Childhood*, Basingstoke: Falmer Press.

Bradley, B. (1986) *Visions of Infancy*, Cambridge: Polity Press

Briggs, J. (1986) 'Expecting the unexpected: Canadian Inuit training for an experimental life-style' (paper given to the 4th International Conference on Hunting and Gathering Societies, LSE London).

Chambers, R. (1995) 'Paradigm shifts and the practice of participatory research and development', in T. Nelson and S. Wright (eds), *Power and Participatory Development*, London, Intermediate Technology Publications.

Davies, B. (1982) *Life in the Classroom and Playground*, London: Routledge & Kegan Paul.

Delamont, S. (1980) *Sex Roles and the School*, London: Methuen.

Ennew, J. (1986) *The Sexual Exploitation of Children*, Cambridge: Polity Press.

Ennew, J. (1994) *Street and Working Children: A Guide to Planning*, London: Save the Children Fund.

Fabian, J. (1983) *Time and the Other: How Anthropology Makes its Object*, New York: Columbia University Press.

Fine, G. (1988) *Knowing Children: Participant Observation with Minors*, London: Sage.

Fyfe, A. (1989) *Child Labour*, Cambridge: Polity Press.

Geertz, C. (1983) 'From the native's point of view', in C. Geertz, *Local Knowledge*, New York: Basic Books.

Hammersley, M. and Woods, P. (eds) (1984) *Life in School*, Milton Keynes: Open University Press.

Hardman, C. (1973) 'Can there be an anthropology of children?', *Journal of the Anthropological Society of Oxford* 4, 1: 85–99.

Hardman, C. (1974) 'Fact and fantasy in the playground', *New Society,* 26 September.

Hastrup, K. (1987) 'Fieldwork among friends: ethnographic exchange within the Northern civilisation', in A. Jackson (ed.) *Anthropology at Home*, London: Tavistock.

Hebdige, D. (1979) *Subculture: The Meaning of Style*, London: Methuen.

Holt, J. (1974) *Escape from Childhood*, Harmondsworth: Penguin.

James, A. (1979) 'Confections, concoctions and conceptions', *Journal of the Anthropological Society of Oxford* 10, 2: 83–95.

James, A.(1986) 'Learning to belong: the boundaries of adolescence', in A.P. Cohen (ed.) *Symbolising Boundaries*, Manchester: Manchester University Press.

James, A. and Prout, A. (eds) (1990) *Constructing and Reconstructing Childhood*, Basingstoke: Falmer Press.

James, A. and Prout, A. (1995) 'Hierarchy, boundary and agency: toward a theoretical perspective on childhood', in A. Ambert (ed.) *Sociological Studies of Childhood*, 7, London: JRAI Press.

James, A., Jenks, C. and Prout, A. (1998) *Theorising Childhood,* Cambridge: Polity Press.

Jenks, C. (ed.) (1982) *The Sociology of Chihdhood*, London: Batsford Academic.

Kane. C. (forthcoming) 'The development of participatory techniques: facilitating children's views about decisions which affect them', in Christensen, P. and James, A. (eds), *Conducting Research with Children,* London: Falmer Press.

Laing, R.D. (1978) *Conversations with Children*, Harmondsworth: Penquin.

MacKay, R. (1973) 'Conceptions of children and models of socialisation', in H.P. Dreitzel (ed.), *Childhood and Socialisation*, London: Macmillan.

Mayall, B. (1994) *Negotiating Health: Schoolchildren at Home and at School*, London: Cassell.

Mandell, N. (1991) 'The least-adult role in studying children', in F. Waksler (ed.), *Studying the Social Worlds of Children*, London: Falmer Press.

Measor, L. and Woods, P. (1984) *Changing Schools: Pupil Perspectives on Transfer to a Comprehensive School*, Milton Keynes: Open University Press.

Morrow, V. (1995) 'Invisible children? Toward a reconceptualisation of childhood dependency and responsibility', in A. Ambert (ed.), *Sociological Studies of Childhood*, 7, London: JRAI Press.

Morrow, V. and Richards, M. (1996) 'The ethics of social research with children: an overview', *Children and Society* 10: (90–105).

Munday, E. (1979) 'When is a child a "child"? Alternative systems and classification', *Journal of the Anthropological Society of Oxford* 10, 3: 161–72.

Newson, J. and Newson, E. (1976) *Seven Years Old in the Home Environment*, London: George Allen and Unwin.

Nieuwenhuys, O. (1994) *Children's Life Worlds: Gender, Welfare and Labour in the Developing World*, London: Routledge.

Opie, I. and P. (1969) *Children's Games in Street and Playground*, Oxford: Oxford University Press.

Opies, I. and P. (1977) *The Lore and Language of School Children*, London: Paladin.

Pollard, A. (1985) *The Social World of the Primary School*, London: Holt, Rhinehart & Winston.

Prout, A. (1989) 'Sickness as a dominant symbol in life-course transitions: an illustrated theoretical framework', *Sociology of Health and Illness* 4,11: 336–59.

Putallaz, M. and Gottman, J.M. (1981) 'Social skills and group acceptance', in S.R. Asher and J.M. Gottman (eds), *The Development of Children's Friendships*, Cambridge: Cambridge University Press.

Qvortrup, J. (ed.) (1994) *Childhood Matters: Social Theory, Practice and Policy*, Aldershot: Avebury.

Reynolds, P. (1989) *Children at Crossroads: Cognition and Society in South Africa*, Clarement, SA: David Phillip.

Save the Children Fund (1995) *Towards a Children's Agenda.*

Solberg, A . (1994) *Negotiating Childhood: Empirical Investigations and Textual Representations*, Oslo: NIBR.

Stainton-Rogers, R. and Stainton-Rogers, W. (1993) *Stories of Childhood: Shifting agendas of child concern*, London: Harvester Wheatsheaf.

Steedman, C. (1982) *The Tidy House*, London: Virago.

Steedman, C., Urwin, C. and Walkerdine, V. (eds) (1985) *Language, Gender and Childhood*, London: Routledge.

Walkerdine, V. (1985) 'On the regulation of speaking and silence', in C. Steedman, C. Urwin and V. Walkerdine (eds), *Language, Gender and Childhood*, London: Routledge.

Walkerdine, V. (1985) 'Child development and gender: the making of teachers and learners in the classroom', *Early Education: history, policy and practice*, Bulmershe Research Publications 4.

Whyte, J. (1983) *Beyond the Wendy House*, London: Longman.

Wilkinson, S.R. (1988) *The Child's World of Illness*, Cambridge: Cambridge University Press.

Chapter 14

Child development: old themes, new directions*

Sheila Greene

Developmentalists have a ready metaphor to hand to describe the history of their own discipline. Thus one might be tempted to pinpoint the date when developmental psychology was born, to view developmental psychology at the turn of the century as being in its infancy and to ask whether or not it has now, after travelling on through its childhood and youth, arrived at its maturity or whether it is still suffering from the *sturm und drang* of adolescence. I have resisted this temptation. Using the metaphor of steady, progressive development through predictable stages may always have been glib, but from the standpoint of the 1990s to write in this way would be to invite embarrassment. We have reached a different vantage point in terms of our general understanding of science and in particular of our understanding of the history of child psychology.

It could be argued, and indeed has been argued most persuasively by Kessen (1986), that for most of this century developmental psychologists shared the Western conviction that the march of science and civilization was leading us onwards and upwards. As a discipline, developmental psychology may well have been more prone than other branches of psychology to this belief in progress, since it is intrinsic to the concept of development itself. In reality, some of the more hopeful recent developments are rediscoveries of insights which were lost or are variations on very old themes.

The notion of science as a linear, unified enterprise advancing towards the truth or truths which could be expressed in universal laws or quantified in theorems was challenged fundamentally by Kuhn's book *The Structure of Scientific Revolutions* (1962) which argued that the history of science could be seen as the struggle for ascendancy between competing scientific paradigms. Kuhn was but one of many theorists who attacked fondly held nineteenth- and early twentieth-century beliefs in absolutist notions such as progress and universal truth. The cherished idols of the modern era have been subject to the sceptical

---

* This is an edited version of a chapter that appeared in *A Century of Psychology*, London: Routledge, 1997.

analysis of those writers who have been influenced by the postmodern shift in consciousness.

Inevitably this postmodern sensibility has become evident in the work of developmental psychologists. Its influence can be detected in a number of changes in contemporary preoccupations and practice. A self-critical stance has been brought to histories of the discipline (e.g. Bronfenbrenner, Kessel, Kessen and White, 1986; Bradley, 1989). There is a new willingness to unpick the previous self-congratulatory discourse, to deconstruct and reinterpret. In this process a tangled story has emerged, or rather numerous tangled stories have emerged. Just as literary history, when re-examined through a feminist lens, permits the rediscovery of buried women writers, the new histories of developmental psychology have disinterred psychologists whose place in the history of the discipline deserves re-appraisal. Accordingly, the work of early writers like Baldwin and Dewey has been reread and re-evaluated (Cairns, 1992; Cahan, 1992). What is of particular interest now is that the work of these rediscovered writers, given its quality and undoubted resonance for psychologists of our time, was relatively neglected in its own time and certainly did not become part of the received history of the discipline. Despite the fact that this century has seen very distinctive phases in terms of the dominant perspectives on child development in Europe and North America, some underlying assumptions about the nature of development and the nature of childhood have been constant, as have underlying assumptions about the appropriate methodology for the discipline. The mood of scepticism and doubt which is emblematic of our time – though not necessarily common to all – has led in recent years to a radical re-examination of the foundational assumptions of the discipline.

What is development?

One mark of the new critical reflectiveness is the attack on 'developmentalism', which could be defined as the imposition of an unwarranted uniformity of structure and directionality onto the changes associated with the ageing process. For most of this century the notion of unidirectional and natural progression lurked at the heart of the word 'development' and at the heart of developmental psychology.

Morss (1990) traces the naturalistic assumptions behind the traditional developmental paradigm back to the Romantic notions of social progress and human perfectibility which emerged in the nineteenth century. Theories about evolution proliferated at this time and the views which were taken up by influential figures like Herbert Spencer and G. Stanley Hall were in many ways pre-Darwinian. Early developmentalists were certainly more concerned with notions to do with recapitulation and evolutionary hierarchies than with natural selection. As Morss notes,

Perhaps the most fundamental assumption concerning an overall picture of individual development is that of *progress*. Derived from, or at least legitimated by biological sources, the notion that the individual gets better and better as time passes has been central to most developmental thinking.

(Morss, 1990: 173)

The most obvious consequence of this commitment to ontogenetic progression can be seen in the proliferation of stage theories of development; Freud, Piaget, Erikson and Kohlberg being examples of the most well-known stage theories in relation to child development. They all see development as moving towards what Labouvie-Vief and Chandler (1978) have called an idealistic end-point, different in each case. Erikson (1950) encapsulates the biological thinking and the prescriptiveness behind these stage theories when he says, 'the healthy child, if halfway properly guided, merely obeys and on the whole can be trusted to obey inner laws of development' (p. 61).

To the extent to which psychologists adhere to an unexamined and outdated form of biological thinking there is undoubtedly a place for the critique offered by radical critics like Broughton (1987), Morss (1990, 1996), Burman (1994) and Bradley (1989). However, they are not alone in their dissatisfaction with the conceptualizations of development which have dominated this century to date and there are definite signs of change. Some contemporary definitions of developmental psychology do not emphasize progression alone, they also emphasize regression. For example, Magnusson states 'Development of living organisms refers to progressive or regressive changes in size, shape and function during the lifetime' (Magnusson, 1995: 20) and Baltes similarly refers to development as characterized by gains and losses (Baltes, 1989). There is much more awareness in contemporary thinking of the erratic and variable nature of psychological change and the extent to which change is a product of exchanges with the external environment rather than a matter of the unfolding of inherent potential. This realization begs the question whether the terms development or developmental are appropriate defining terms for this discipline since the emerging usage of these terms in psychology does not correspond to any dictionary definition.

Despite the fact that adherence to a nineteenth-century form of biological thinking can be seen to have produced a developmental psychology which was unduly prescriptive and universalistic, it is essential that the study of child development comes to terms with the nature of the biological contribution to psychological development and change. In relation to child psychology it is inescapably the case that many psychological changes are prompted by, or associated with, changes brought about by the growth and maturation of the body. Flavell (1970) goes further and claims that 'it is the underlying presence of a biological growth process that lends to childhood changes their inevitability, magnitude, directionality, within-species uniformity and irreversibility' (p. 248).

No one would wish to deny the importance of physical maturation to childhood. However, what is questionable is the commitment on the part of child psychologists this century to the view that psychological change has the same characteristics and dynamic as physical change. Thus, just as the development of dentition occurs in a predictable, universal sequence in all healthy children, so, it has been assumed, does cognition, or attachment, or the self-concept, or moral reasoning. What such a perspective leaves out of account is the fact that, although many of the psychological phenomena of interest are subject to change, the nature of that change may not be identical to or even comparable with genetically prompted physiological changes. Some psychological 'developments' result from a process which can only be understood by reference to the active, constructive role of the person or the meaning-infused interactions of that person with others. Psychological phenomena are to a greater extent socially and historically contingent and many of the important changes that occur in childhood are – to contradict Flavell – not inevitable, unidirectional and uniform.

As doors were opened to awareness of the complex nature of biological influences, the central role of social and cultural influences, the active role of the person in shaping her or his own development, it became clear that human psychological change across time defies neat characterizations and that the old meaning of development has proven inadequate. The restricted developmental paradigm has operated like a straitjacket in this century and it is time for it to be discarded.

In recent decades, the study of child development has been strongly influenced by advances in another discipline, so close as to be at times indistinguishable from it: that is life-span developmental psychology. Of course life-span psychology can be seen to subsume child psychology but for a long time developmental psychology was confined to the study of children and adolescents. Examining psychological development from the life-span perspective casts a very different light on childhood. Much of the challenge to long-lived assumptions about development in childhood arrived with the extension of theory and research into adulthood. Thus the tendency to see childhood as a world apart psychologically has diminished and the inadequacies of reductive accounts of psychological development become strikingly evident when they are applied to adults, to ourselves. Issues to do with continuity and discontinuity, constancy and change are highlighted by a life-span perspective in which recognition of the relative open-endedness and unpredictability of developmental processes has become unavoidable. The life-span developmental approach has helped to highlight the multiple mechanisms involved in the process of developmental change and to indicate the way in which childhood experiences may or may not be carried forward into adulthood (Baltes, 1987; Rutter, 1989).

At this point in time most developmental researchers would see themselves as only just beginning to understand the causes of development. The starting point for early developmentalists was to decide on *where* to look for the explanation – the biology of the organism or the environment.

Nature and nurture

Most child development textbooks start off with a history of the struggle between the empiricists – neatly epitomized by Locke and his *tabula rasa* – and the nativists, championed by Rousseau and his 'noble savage'. The resolution of the conflict, which was seen to continue in child development with the opposing views of the behaviourists like Watson and the maturationists like Gesell, was the civilized compromise of interactionism. Anastasi's paper 'Heredity, environment and the question. How?' (Anastasi, 1958) marked a new way forward and supposedly put an end to the question, 'How much?'. As we have seen in recent years, with publications such as *The Bell Curve*, this question has still not gone away (Hernstein and Murray 1994). In their rational moments the vast majority of child psychologists would reject extreme environmentalism and extreme hereditarian views. However, when it comes to the crunch most developmental psychologists seem to lean in one direction or the other and the old dichotomy can be seen in the emphasis on either genetic determinants or environmental/social determinants. The persistence of this split could be seen recently in the dispute that took place in the pages of *Child Development* between Scarr and Baumrind (Scarr, 1992; Baumrind, 1993). Baumrind took exception to Scarr's view that 'genotypes drive experiences' and argued that 'the details of socialization patterns are crucial to an understanding of normal and deviant development'. Although the vocabulary and the data are different the essentials of the old debate remain.

In relation to the origins of individual differences, the way forward might be seen in the work of those behavioural geneticists, such as Plomin, who do not diminish the role of environment but assert quite convincingly that the data which provide evidence of the strength of hereditary influence on individual development 'provide the best available evidence for the importance of environmental influence' (Plomin, 1989: 105). On the other side, environmentalists find it increasingly difficult to disregard findings on the contribution of genetic factors to individual differences in ability or temperament or on the role of biological preparedness in determining the character of children's activities and experiences. Bronfenbrenner, for example, has taken the biological into fuller account in recent modifications of his ecological systems theory (Bronfenbrenner and Ceci, 1994). Plomin considers that, 'modern theory and research in both nature and nurture are converging on the interface between them' (Plomin 1994: 20). New concepts, such as niche-picking, active, passive and evocative genotype-environment effects and proximal processes, are emerging as researchers struggle more assiduously to answer the question, '*How?*' by identifying the mechanisms involved in the interplay between genes and environment (Scarr and McCartney, 1983; Bronfenbrenner and Ceci, 1994). But not all developmentalists would see this approach as representing the way forward. Gottlieb, for example, thinks it is time to abandon entirely the nature–nurture dichotomy since it is an unfortunate hangover from 'a pre-formation like pre deterministic view of human development that has persisted to the present day . . . one that holds that traits are caused by genes in a straightforward unidirectional, manner' (Gottlieb, 1992: 8). Instead Gottlieb calls for a recognition of the 'non-linear, emergent, co-actional nature of individual development' (Gottlieb, 1992: 171).

At a species level, the importance of biologically based propensities and competencies cannot be denied, although the resurgence of interest amongst developmentalists in evolutionary theory as a grand explanatory framework (e.g. Belsky, 1995) is surprising, given its inability to account for complex psychological phenomena and its reliance on circular reasoning (see, for example, Lerner and von Eye, 1992).

What develops?

For most of this century, the focus of interest in relation to the psychological development of the child has been very restricted. Even the so-called 'grand theories' which have dominated child psychology in this century can be seen as focusing on an aspect of children and their psychology rather than the full picture. Thus we have 'the child as conditionable organism' of the behaviourists, 'the instinctual child' of Freud, 'the child as logical thinker' of Piaget. More recently we have the child as information processor and the social child.

There are interesting signs of attempts to break down the long-standing barriers between the realms of cognition, emotion and social development, which can be seen, for example, in recent work on social cognition (e.g. work on the theory of mind and person perception) and on the social-regulatory function of emotions (e.g. work on emotional self-regulation and social referencing). A consequence of the adoption of the supposed natural science method by mainstream child psychology has been the fragmentation of 'the child'. As Magnusson (1995) notes we have concentrated on variables rather than persons. In recent years there has been a welcome renewal of discussion of the need for an holistic model of development and models have been offered by a number of theorists such as Magnusson himself (1995) and Bronfenbrenner (1995).

Adopting a particular perspective on what it is that develops can all too readily lead to a very narrow vision. There are undoubtedly many examples of this kind of narrowed perspective and its consequences from the early days of the discipline onwards, but I will take just one example from the study of infancy.

According to Piaget the development of the concept of object permanence is an essential step on the road to rationality. Piaget observed that if a toy is hidden underneath a cloth in front of the infant's eyes the infant will fail to search for the toy. Others have replicated his observations. Piaget claims that the infant has not yet understood that objects are permanent and that they cannot disappear in this manner. The achievement of object permanence occurs with the development of the child's capacity to represent the world mentally, thus freeing her or him from the here-and-now intelligence which is the hallmark of the sensori-motor period. Although critics of Piaget abound, his interpretation of his observations and the conclusions he drew about the crucial importance of the child's arrival at an understanding of the permanence of objects have been uncontested.

In a recent article, Greenberg (1996) points out that an alternative light can be cast on the child's understanding of the existence of objects. He says, 'Piaget and his intellectual heirs have forgotten that the "permanent" object is in principle and a priori impermanent and incapable of existing forever' (p. 118). Greenberg takes, as an example of Piaget's bias, the pre-operational child's failure to understand the conservation of matter. He re-examines one of Piaget' s examples to do with the children's responses to the dissolving of a sugar cube. Piaget states,

> the conservation of matter does not seem necessary to the child three to six years old in cases of changes of state or even changes of form. Sugar melting in water is believed to be returning to the void . . . Just as the baby begins by believing that objects return to the void when they are no longer perceived and emerge from it when they re-enter the perceptual field, so also the six year old child still thinks that a substance which dissolves completely is annihilated.
>
> (Piaget, 1954: 417–418)

As Greenberg points out, children are correct in thinking that the cube has been destroyed *qua* cube, although they have failed to understand that the matter which constituted the cube is still present in a different form.

Piaget's dismissive approach to the child's understanding of the impermanence of objects, arguably as important to their understanding of the world as an understanding of the possibility of conservation or of the relative permanence of some objects, is seen as a consequence of his emphasis on scientific, logico-mathematical thought. Rationality is thus equated with thinking of objects as permanent, invulnerable and infinite and irrationality with the failure to treat objects as though they had these properties. In fact, the infant must develop a rational understanding of the extent to which objects, including people, can be impermanent. Greenberg's article can be seen as representative of the current, deconstructive approach. It is notable that decades of criticism of Piaget have left untouched Piaget's assumptions about the nature of human rationality and its origins since these particular assumptions were cherished, one assumes, as much by his critics as by Piaget himself. Greenberg can also be seen as representative of the current interest in breaking down barriers between theoretical accounts of the child's cognitive, social and emotional experiences. His dissatisfaction with the received interpretation originated in his interest in 'that other form of reason that concerns itself with those impermanent objects of desire that are the focus of love and hate, hunger and revulsion, attachment and loss' (p. 130). It would seem that very often in the history of child development, the focus of theorists and researchers has been narrowed by an unduly restrictive, received wisdom about what aspects of the child are fit to be studied and what questions are permissible to be asked.

Who is the child?

Putting the child back together again is not enough, we also have to recognize the richness and plurality that exists in the lives of children, the sources of their heterogeneous experiences and the resultant constraints on the production of universalistic accounts of developmental processes.

The object of knowledge for mainstream child psychologists of the twentieth century has been 'the child'. This objectification of children has been the inevitable consequence of the emulation of the natural sciences and the associated quest for universal laws. Clearly there has had to be some recognition of individual differences, but the need to describe 'the development of the child', and the underlying assumption that much of what develops represents an unfolding of natural propensities, leads to a process which has been labelled the normalization of child development (Walkerdine, 1984). In the history of child development, normalization can be seen to go hand in hand with the biological view of development. The discipline has created norms against which all children's (and parents') behaviour has been judged. Normalization constrains all children since it determines people's expectations of them and their own expectations of themselves. Children who do not conform to the natural developmental path are liable to be seen as deviant. In a circular process, children from the culture, class, or gender that is excluded from the definition of what is developmentally the norm are fated to be categorized as deviant, and therefore problematic.

In the latter part of this century, the civil rights movement and other social changes have led to a greater awareness of the extent of exclusion and of the role of science in perpetuating a middle-class, Western and male-centred view of the universe. The picture of ideal or 'normal' development promoted by child psychologists was also permeated with these kinds of bias, although the delusion that science was a value-free enterprise kept people from a recognition of their own embeddedness in ideology.

Since, for most of this century, mainstream child psychology conceptualized the child in much the same way as a chemist conceptualizes an interesting compound, it made absolute sense for the psychologist to take the child into a laboratory for closer inspection and testing. To use Kessen's term, the child was seen as 'isolable' (Kessen, 1979). Bronfenbrenner' s accusation that much of mainstream developmental psychology could be summarized as 'the science of the strange behaviour of children in strange situations with strange adults for the briefest possible periods of time' (Bronfenbrenner, 1979: 19) heralded a welcome awakening of concern for the ecological validity of child development research. The recognition of the problem of lack of ecological validity was part of a movement within developmental psychology to reconceptualize the nature and significance of the child's social context. This reconceptualization has had a perceptible impact on the focus of research, with an increased interest on the part of psychologists in observing children in their home, play or school settings and in understanding how they negotiate and understand their social world. With the recognition of context and a renewed appreciation of the importance of culture comes a recognition of the plurality of children's experiences and an acknowledgement of the narrow cultural focus of much of the child development work carried out this century.

The questioning of traditional assumptions underpinning norms and pre-scribed sequences has led to an increased recognition and understanding of the heterogeneity that exists in children's lives and experiences. It is only comparatively recently that developmental psychologists have taken on board a view of culture as intrinsic to the child's psychology and not just an add-on which could be pared away to reveal the true child underneath. Contemporary child development is thus more about children in their cultures than about the child in isolation.

A further basic dichotomy which has been played out in this century is between the view of the child as passively responding to the forces operating upon him or her versus the view of the child as an active agent in his or her own development. This is a struggle which has reached a resolution. The view of the child as active would appear now to be dominant – which is not to say that the child's behaviours and experiences are not constrained, since inevit-ably they are – but that children play an active role in shaping their own environments and in making sense of them.

Reinstating meaning

It could be argued that, in child psychology, as in other branches of psych-ology, a great deal has been lost by the neglect of the role of personal meaning in human life. Again, one can see evidence of a forgetting of earlier insights. For example Dewey (1899) saw psychology as centrally involved with under-standing issues concerned with meaning and issues concerned with values. He said, 'Psychology, after all, simply states the mechanisms through which conscious value and meaning are introduced into human experience' (Dewey, 1899:150).

Piaget had a great interest in the child's understanding of the world but he saw that world primarily in physical terms. Vygotsky has reminded psychologists of the extent to which the child's understanding of the world, whether it be the world of objects or of people, is socially mediated. As Bruner points out in his recent book, *Acts of Meaning*, 'the child does not enter the life of his or her group as a private and autistic sport of primary processes, but rather as a participant in a larger public process in which public meanings are negotiated' (p. 13). The larger public process is culture which is permeated with meaning.

Bruner (1990) argues that 'psychology stop trying to be "meaning free" in its system of explanation. The very people and cultures that are its subject are governed by shared meanings and values' (Bruner, 1990: 20). He is not alone in his appeal. It is somewhat reassuring to hear a similar view being expressed most forcibly by Sperry, one of the major figures in neuropsychology and a winner of the Nobel Prize, who sees a sea-change not only in psychology, but in science, on the horizon. He sees a time approaching when 'The former stark, strictly physical, value-empty, and mindless cosmos previously upheld by science becomes infused with cognitive and subjective values and rich emergent macrophenomena of all kinds' (Sperry, 1995: 506).

The child's perspective

In line with their out-dated natural science model of their relationship to their subject matter, for too long psychologists have seen as objects the people who were the focus of their observations or experiments – although in a strange inversion of meaning they have referred to them as 'subjects'. In child development, as in other areas of psychology, there is a new appreciation of the necessity to take 'the subject's' perspective into account. There are increasing numbers of studies which involve the observation and recording of meaningful chunks of children's behaviour and in which children's own, naturally occurring activities and narratives are given pride of place. There are many examples. One is Furth and Kane's recording and analysis of the spontaneous pretend play of three 4 to 5 year-old girls who are planning and enacting a 'royal ball' (Furth and Kane, 1992) and another is Dunn's account of the social interactions of young children in their home settings in which she 'observed the children within the drama and excitement of family life' (Dunn, 1988: vii).

Qualitative methodologies, which had been part of the psychologist's armamentarium earlier this century, but had been all but forgotten in the misguided insistence on quantification and nothing else, have been rediscovered and elaborated. An example of the insights to be gained from the application of qualitative methods can be found in the research of Gilligan and her colleagues with adolescent girls. In *Meeting at the Crossroads*, Brown and Gilligan (1992) describe the development of a method of recording, listening to and attempting to understand girls' voices. They were concerned to find an approach which would let the girls speak to them in their own words. They call their method the 'Listener's Guide' and through it they have obtained new insights into the girls' experiences as they travel from late childhood into adolescence. It is interesting to recall that Bühler as far back as 1927 collected and analysed information from the diaries of teenage girls but that this kind of qualitative work fell into disfavour in mainstream developmental psychology for the following half century (Bühler, 1927, cited by Cairns, 1983).

Bruner (1990) and others have called for an approach to children's psychology which is interpretative and hermeneutic. Such an approach, which recognizes the importance of meaning in human psychology and of the need to addresss the existence of subjectivities and inter-subjectivities, may permit a scholarly understanding which is more consonant with the dynamic of children's lives as they are experienced and constructed. An interpretative approach does not mean the abandonment of objectivity, it simply takes account of and respects the role of meaning and subjectivity. It can complement other approaches and methodologies, it does not necessarily supplant them. To use Kagan's terminology, there is a need for both the objective and the subjective frames in developmental psychology (Kagan, 1984). The discipline is impoverished if it fails to find a way for them to co-exist.

Applying the science

Despite early concerns on the part of some child psychologists about 'the perils of popularization' histories of the discipline show that the work of developmental psychologists has never stayed in the laboratory, nor was it insulated from the political concerns and ideological commitments of the time, despite its pretensions to being value-free. As Schlossman (1985) points out, from a very early stage the pressure to apply new theories and supposedly 'pure' research was strong and some psychologists were themselves strong advocates of the view that the redemption of society lay in the proper management of children and that psychology had a major role to play in that process. Schlossman refers to the 'gospel of child development' in the United States, and similarly the Newsons in the United Kingdom refer to 'the cult of child development' (Schlossman, 1985: 65; Newson and Newson, 1974).

Through their interventions in advising parents and teachers and policy makers psychologists have had an impact on the upbringing, education and management of generations of children and also played their part in shaping society's notions about the nature of the child, thus playing a central role in 'the social construction of childhood'.

Child psychology has been involved in a circular process by which it is both directing and directed by the prevalent political and historical circumstances. The way in which child psychology can lend itself to prop up the status quo, or the status which is politically desired, is well illustrated by Riley's analysis of the role of child psychology in the glorification of mother-hood in post-World War 2 Britain (Riley, 1983). At the end of the war, state-funded nurseries, previously needed to enable mothers to join the workforce and support the war effort, were closed overnight and mothers secluded in their homes. Thus the jobs were left to the returning soldiers, and mothers were free to concentrate on producing and raising the next, well-adjusted, generation who, Bowlby's early work assured them, required their constant presence and devotion.

Advice to parents, or, more often than not, to mothers, on child-rearing provides a salutary reminder of the faddishness of child psychology and the problems involved in applying developmental research. Advice to mothers from experts has had a much longer history than that of the formal discipline of child development but the early experts were also in the habit of leaning on access to specialized knowledge or 'science' for the justification of their views.

Hardyment (1983) starts her history of three centuries of advice on child-care by quoting the words of a British physician:

> It is with great Pleasure I see the preservation of Children become the Care of Men of Sense. In my opinion this Business has been too long fatally left to the management of Women, who cannot be supposed to have a proper knowledge to fit them for the Task.
>
> (William Cadogan [1748], cited by Hardyment, 1983: 10)

Nearly two hundred years later the view of 'Men of Sense' was still that mothers are not capable of rearing children properly and that science will provide the answers. Although Watson (1928: 16) considered that 'the world would be considerably better off if we were to stop having children for twenty years (except for experimental purposes) and were then to start again with enough facts to do the job with some degree of skill and accuracy', he swallowed his principles and gave mothers the benefit of his advice and his science.

In magazine articles and in his best-selling book *Psychological Care of Infant and Child* Watson promoted a new and scientific approach to child-rearing based on behaviourism (Watson, 1928). Watson's pronouncements on child-rearing, in which parents were admonished for hugging and kissing their children and in which the main aim seemed to be to produce little self-contained automatons who bothered their parents as little as possible, seem bizarre and unacceptable from our vantage point today.

The influence of Freud, Bowlby and Piaget on child-rearing manuals can also be traced. Hardyment (1984) gives an example of the Freudian, Buxbaum, author of *Your Child Makes Sense, A Guidebook for Parents*, who advised parents that 'from birth onwards children feel the pressures of urgent bodily needs and powerful instinctive urges (such as hunger, sex and aggression) which clamour for satisfaction' (Buxbaum, 1951: vii).

Toilet training created particular difficulties in the household devoted to rearing children according to the Freudian way. According to Fraiberg (1959: 93), the child who produces a bowel movement 'comes to regard this act in the same way that an older child regards a loved person' and to flush it down the toilet was 'a strange way to accept an offering of such value'.

The favoured theories changed in due course. By the 1960s and 1970s the influence of Piaget is more apparent. Leach, the psychologist author of the very popular childcare manual *Baby and Child* (1977), shows her Piagetian leanings when she tells her readers,

> If you provide the space, equipment and time for your child's play, she will see to the development of her thinking for herself. She is the scientist and inventor: your job is merely to provide the laboratories, the facilities and a research assistant – you – when she needs one.
>
> (Leach, 1977: 351)

Twenty years later, this view of the young child as independent scientist does not chime with the currently fashionable Vygotskian emphasis on socially supported learning.

In the last few decades, child developmentalists, fed on cognitive developmental and attachment theories, tell the modern mother that she should always be alert to her child's needs, ready to interact, to provide the right kind of stimulation combined with plenty of warmth and sensitivity. She is expected to be well-informed and actively involved. As Urwin points out, the current emphasis on the need for quality maternal involvement has led to 'the idea that the normal mother can function as a tutor or pedagogue' and that children need lots of 'one-to-one attention' (Urwin, 1985: 182). This expectation creates a burden of obligation which, Urwin' s study suggests, many mothers feel guilty about since they invariably fail to give sensitive, loving stimulation and attention at all times. It is not hard to imagine the feelings of harassed mothers as they read 'housework can seem like pleasant play all over the house if you are prepared to take the baby with you and bounce her on the bed you are making, play peep-bo around the furniture and give her a duster to wave' (Leach, 1977: 270).

A review of the numerous ways in which the findings of developmental psychology have been applied is well beyond the scope of this short chapter. Some of the hailed contributions of the discipline to the welfare of children can be seen, with hindsight, to have been less than helpful. For example the IQ test has often been used oppressively as a way of labelling and excluding rather than a way of understanding and assisting children. Binet himself opposed the view of intelligence as a fixed attribute and said 'We must protest and react against this brutal pessimism. With practice, enthusiasm and especially with method one can succeed in increasing one's attention, memory and judgement and in becoming literally more intelligent than one was before' (Binet, 1909:126). He would probably have been horrified at what happened to his invention. There are plenty of cautionary tales but there is also considerable evidence of success.

Some developmental psychologists today argue that the need for careful analysis, well-informed advice and tried-and-tested interventions has never been greater. From different sides of the Atlantic, leading developmentalists have expressed their concerns about the circumstances in which young people are growing up. Rutter comments on 'the substantial body of literature indicating that . . . there has been a considerable rise in the level of psychosocial disturbances in young people over the last half century' (Rutter *et al.*, 1995: 62). Bronfenbrenner also sounds a pessimistic note, warning of 'a progressive decline in American society of conditions that research increasingly indicates may be critical for developing and sustaining human competence throughout the life course (Bronfenbrenner, 1995: 643).

It is clearly necessary to be cautious about such pronouncements and the criteria for judging whether things are getting better or worse must be subject to the closest scrutiny. Even if there is little change, there are far too many children who are leading lives which are less happy and less fulfilled than they could be. As Erikson said in 1950, 'human childhood provides the most fundamental basis for human exploitation'. At best this exploitation consists of children being used as the repository of the desires and expectations of their parents and their society. At worst, children are neglected and abused or trapped in distressing situations not of their own making. Many children are caught up in the wars and conflicts created by the adults around them and there are, sadly, few signs of change in that direction. Psychologists have a role to play in understanding and helping all of these children. As Scarr noted in 1979,

> Unlike some academic fields of psychology where swings away from application have been pronounced, child psychology has not strayed too far into abstraction. There have always been real children whose welfare could be served by new knowledge and new applications.
>
> (Scarr, 1979: 810)

It is clear that if the psychologist is to act in the service of children he or she does so from a particular value base and that it is incumbent on us to at least make our values clear, open to challenge and revision. Sarason calls for applied psychologists to be 'advocates of social change' rather than 'willing agents of social policy' (Sarason, 1981: 176). Whatever the standpoint one takes, intervening in the lives of children is a political act and should be recognised as such.

Alternative visions of the future

Predicting the future is always a risky occupation. If I had to make a prediction about the major theoretical thrust in the immediate future I would say that it would be in the elaboration of the social and cultural perspective on child development and in the exploration of the child's own phenomenal and subjective world. Lerner and Dixon note the beginning of this shift, commenting that 'the growing interest in contextualism during the 1970s and 1980s was associated with the recession of the other major models to the backburner of theoretical and empirical activity' (Dixon and Lerner, 1992). As Morss (1996) points out, the reincorporation of the social into the developmental perspective on the child takes a number of different forms, ranging from the examination of the child *plus* his or her social influences to radical social constructivism to the Marxist critical psychology of development espoused by Morss himself. Once again it must be recognized that an appreciation of the extent to which the child's psychology is socially constructed is not new. One hundred years ago James Mark Baldwin said 'The development of the child's personality could not go on at all without the modification of his sense of himself by suggestions from others. So he himself, at every stage, is really in part someone else, even in his own thought of himself' (Baldwin, 1897: 30). Implicit in this way of thinking is a systemic view of development which should be capable of successfully incorporating the biological, the social and the personal as inextricably enmeshed, reciprocally influential elements.

Other people's predictions will be quite different. I was interested to see in the recent text book by the British psychologists Butterworth and Harris (1994) that, in a section called 'Developmental psychology in the twenty-first century', their first prediction is 'an ever closer link between developmental psychology and developmental biology . . . Advances in evolutionary theory, in genetics and in the biology of the developing nervous system are beginning to give evidence that converges with the behavioural and cognitive measures typical of developmental psychology.' Their second prediction concerns closer links between developmental psychology and new theoretical models in biology such as 'selectionism' or 'neural Darwinism' (Butterworth and Harris, 1994: 229). This would not be the future as I see it or, perhaps more to the point, as I would like to see it, since it places an emphasis on biological explanations to the detriment of the other sources of explanation. But these eminent British psychologists are probably correct. The future will be built on many different, sometimes compatible and sometimes incompatible visions.

In his examination of the future of developmental psychology, Kessen concludes 'whatever style of reasoning we adopt, the evidence of past decades, from different cultures and from different groups in the United States, supports a strong case against the Grand Simplicities of theory or of method' (Kessen, 1990: 29). His view applies equally to Europe. Whatever the future holds it will not be neat and simple. If it is, we can be sure that we have gone seriously awry. Our examination of the past should tell us that in human psychology the simple formulation is usually an inadequate formulation. The time of Grand Theories in psychology, those which hinge on just a few core concepts, has gone, notwithstanding the claims of evolutionary psychology. Child development has had more than its share of these grand theories, and despite their importance in the history of the discipline, each has toppled in its turn. But the need for Grand Thinkers has not gone. It would seem from the data-driven and, at best, micro-theoretical nature of much of the research in child development – the kind of work which can be methodologically meticulous but terminally uninteresting – that large-scale theorizing is to be avoided. Thankfully, there are many developmentalists who, despite impeccable credentials as empiricists, are also interested in the big issues. I have in mind people like Bronfenbrenner, Rutter, Baltes, Kagan and Bruner. These writers synthesize and systematize and generate fresh hypotheses. To a greater or lesser extent, they are also willing to stand back and ask what it all means and whether it could be done any better. People with the capacity to act and think in this way are always going to be essential in a discipline like developmental psychology, where a self-critical stance may help to guard against answers which may not only be wrong, but also dangerous.

Conclusion

In this century we have explored a multiplicity of methodologies and tried out a multiplicity of theories. The history of the discipline is the history of the assembly and dismantling of theoretical frameworks. The overturning of old ways of viewing the child and the search for the best way to conceptualize his or her development continues but the interest in examining the basic assumptions of the discipline is currently particularly intense as befits this era of scepticism and deconstruction.

As we approach the closing years of the century, there are many recent signs of an increased willingness to confront the complexities involved in understanding children's development and also of willingness to construct conceptual frameworks and methods which will enable the study of these complexities. It is to be hoped that we can use this changed consciousness and the experience accumulated over the past decades to advance to an understanding of children which does better justice to their complex, changing and multiple ways of being in and with their worlds.

References

Anastasi, A. (1958) 'Heredity. environment and the question "How?"', *Psychological Review* 65: 197–208.

Baldwin, J.M. (1897) *Social and Ethical Interpretation in Mental Development: A Study in Social Psychology*, New York: Macmillan.

Baltes, P.B. (1987) 'Theoretical propositions of life-span developmental psychology: On the dynamics between growth and decline', *Developmental Psychology* 23: 611–626.

Baumrind, D. (1993) 'The average expectable environment is not enough: A response to Scarr', *Child Development* 64 1299–1317.

Belsky, J. (1995) 'Expanding the ecology of human development: An evolutionary perspective', in P. Moen, G. H. Elder and K. Luscher (eds) *Examining Lives in Context: Perspectives on the Ecology of Human Development*, Washington, DC: American Psychological Association.

Binet, A. (1909) *Les idées modernes sur les enfants*, Paris: Ernest Flammarion.

Bradley, B. S. (1989) *Visions of Infancy: A Critical Introduction to Child Psychology*, Cambridge: Polity Press.

Bronfenbrenner, U. (1979) *The Ecology of Human Development: Experiments by Nature and Design*, Cambridge, MA: Harvard University Press.

Bronfenbrenner, U.(1995) 'Developmental ecology through space and time: A future perspective', in P. Moen, G.H. Elder and K. Luscher (eds) *Examining Lives in Context: Perspectives on the Ecology of Human Development*, Washington DC: American Psychological Association.

Bronfenbrenner, U., Kessel, F., Kessen, W. and White, S. (1986) 'Toward a critical social history of developmental psychology: A propaedeutic discussion', *American Psychologist* 41: 1218–1230.

Bronfenbrenner, U. and Ceci, S.J. (1994) 'Nature–nurture reconceptualized in developmental perspective: A bioecological model', *Psychological Review* 101: 568–586.

Broughton, J. (1987) *Critical Theories of Psychological Development*, London: Plenum Press.

Brown, L.M. and Gilligan, C. (1992) *Meeting at the Crossroads: Women's Psychology and Girls' Development*, Cambridge, MA: Harvard University Press.

Bruner, J. (1990) *Acts of Meaning*, Cambridge, MA: Harvard University Press.

Bühler, C. (1927) 'Die ersten sozialen Verhaltungsweisen der Kindes', in C. Bühler, H. Hetzer and B. Tudor-Hart (eds) *Soziologische und psychologische Studien über das erste Lebensjahr*, Jena: Fischer.

Burman, E. (1994) *Deconstructing Developmental Psychology*, London: Routledge.

Butterworth, G. and Harris, P.L. (1994) *Principles of Developmental Psychology*, Hove: Lawrence Erlbaum.

Buxbaum, E. (1951) *Your Child Makes Sense: A Guidebook for Parents*, London: Allen and Unwin.

Cadogan, W. (1748) *Essay on the Nursing and Management of Children*, London: John Knapton.

Cahan, E.D. (1992) 'John Dewey and human development', *Developmental Psychology* 28: 205–214.

Cairns, R.B. (1983) 'The emergence of developmental psychology', in P.H. Mussen (ed.) *Handbook of Child Psychology. Volume 1: History, Theory and Methods*, New York: John Wiley and Sons.

Cairns, R.B. (1992) 'The making of a developmental science: The contributions and intellectual heritage of James Mark Baldwin', *Developmental Psychology* 28: 17–24.

Dewey, J. (1899) 'Psychology and social practice', in J.A. Boydston (ed.) *The Middle Works of John Dewey*, Carbondale, Ill: Southern Illinois University Press.

Dixon, R.A. and Lerner, R.M. (1992) 'History of systems in developmental psychology', in M.H. Bornstein and M.E. Lamb (eds) *Developmental Psychology: An Advanced Textbook*, Hove: Lawrence Erlbaum.

Dunn, J. (1988) *The Beginnings of Social Understanding*, Oxford: Blackwell.

Erikson, E. (1950) *Childhood and Society*, New York: W.W. Norton.

Flavell, J.H. (1970) 'Cognitive changes in adulthood', in L.R. Goulet and P. Baltes (eds) *Life-span Developmental Psychology: Research and Theory*, London: Academic Press.

Fraiberg, S. (1959) *The Magic Years: Understanding and Handling the Problems of Early Childhood*, New York: Scribner.

Furth, H.G. and Kane, S.R. (1992) 'Children constructing society: A new perspective on children at play', in H. McGurk (ed.) *Childhood Social Development: Contemporary Perspectives*, Hove: Lawrence Erlbaum.

Gottlieb, G. (1992) *Individual Development and Evolution: The Genesis of Novel Behaviour*, Oxford: Oxford University Press

Greenberg, D.E. (1996) 'The object permanence fallacy', *Human Development* 39: 117–131.

Hardyment, C. (1983) *Dream Babies: Three Centuries of Good Advice on Child Care*, New York: Harper and Row.

Hernstein, R.J. and Murray, C.M. (1994) *The Bell Curve: Intelligence. Class and Structure in American Life*, New York: Free Press.

Kagan, J. (1984) *The Nature of the Child*, New York: Basic Books.

Kessen, W. (1979) 'The American child and other cultural inventions', *American Psychologist* 34: 815–820.

Kessen, W. (1990) *The Rise and Fall of Development*, Worcester, MA: Clark University Press.

Kuhn, T.S. (1962) *The Structure of Scientific Revolutions*, London: University of Chicago Press.

Labouvie-Vief, G. and Chandler, M. (1978) 'Cognitive development and life-span developmental theories: Idealistic versus contextual perspectives', in P. Baltes (ed.) *Life-span Development and Behaviour. Vol.1*, New York: Academic Press.

Leach, P. (1977) *Baby and Child*, London: Michael Joseph.

Lerner, R. M. and von Eye, A. (1992) Sociobiology and human development: Arguments and evidence, *Human Development* 35: 12–33.

Magnusson, D. (1995) 'Individual development: A holistic integrated model', in P. Moen, G.H. Elder and K. Luscher (eds) *Examining Lives in Context: Perspectives on the Ecology of Human Development*, Washington, DC: American Psychological Association.

Morss, J.R. (1990) *The Biologising of Childhood: Developmental Psychology and the Darwinian Myth*, Hove: Lawrence Erlbaum.

Morss, J.R. (1996) *Growing Critical: Alternatives to Developmental Psychology*, London: Routledge.

Newson J. and Newson, E. (1974) 'Cultural aspects of childrearing in the English speaking world', in M. Richards (ed.) *The Integration of the Child into a Social World*, London: Cambridge University Press.

Piaget, J. (1954) *The Construction of Reality in the Child*, New York: Ballantine Books.

Plomin, R. (1989) 'Environment and genes: Determinants of behaviour', *American Psychologist* 44: 105–111.

Plomin, R. (1994) *Genes and Experience: The Interplay Between Nature and Nurture*, London: Sage Publications.

Riley, D. (1983) *War in the Nursery: Theories of the Child and Mother*, London: Virago.

Rutter, M. (1989) 'Pathways from childhood to adult life', *Journal of Child Psychology and Psychiatry* 30: 23–51.

Rutter, M., Champion, L., Quinton, D., Maughan, B. and Pickles, A. (1995) 'Understanding individual differences in environmental-risk exposure', in P. Moen, G.H. Elder and K. Lusher (eds) *Examining Lives in Context: Perspectives on the Ecology of Human Development*, Washington, DC: APA.

Sarason, S.B. (1981) *Psychology Misdirected*, New York: The Free Press.

Scarr, S. (1979) 'Psychology and children: current research and practice', *American Psychologist* 34: 809–811.

Scarr, S. (1992) 'Developmental theories for the 1990s: Development and individual differences', *Child Development* 63: 631–649.

Scarr, S. and McCartney, K. (1983) 'How people make their own environments: A theory of genotype-environment effects', *Child Development* 54: 424–435.

Schlossman, S. (1985) 'Perils of popularisation: The founding of *Parents' Magazine*', in A.B. Smuts and J.W. Hagen (eds) *History and Research in Child Development*, Monographs of the Society for Research in Child Development 50: 65–77.

Sperry, R.S. (1995) 'The future of psychology', *American Psychologist* 50: 505–506.

Urwin, C. (1985) 'Constructing motherhood: The persuasion of normal development', in C. Steedman, C. Urwin, and V. Walkerdine (eds) *Language, Gender and Childhood*, London: Routledge and Kegan Paul.

Walkerdine, V. (1984) 'Developmental psychology and the child-centred pedagogy', in J. Henriques, W. Holiway, C. Urwin, C. Venn and V. Walkerdine (eds) *Changing the Subject: Psychology, Social Regulation and Subjectivity*, London: Methuen.

Watson, J. B. (1928) *Psychological Care of Infant and Child*, New York: Norton.

Index